THE
GARDENER'S
PALETTE

THE
GARDENER'S
PALETTE

THE
GARDENER'S
PALETTE

JOHN DALE
&
KEVIN GUNNELL

HARMONY BOOKS
New York

34058

Published in the United States by Harmony Books,
a division of Crown Publishers, Inc.,
201 East 50th Street, New York, New York 10022.
Member of the Crown Publishing Group.

Conceived and produced by Breslich & Foss, London.

HARMONY and colophon are trademarks of
Crown Publishers, Inc.

Manufactured in Hong Kong

A LOC number for this book is available from the Library of Congress.

ISBN 0-517-58853-6

10 9 8 7 6 5 4 3 2 1

First Edition

ACKNOWLEDGMENTS

Photographs supplied by
Harry Smith Horticultural Photographic Collection
except pp. 34, 35 (top right), 65, 76 (lower right),
91 (top left) John Dale

CONTENTS

ABOVE: Clear yellow narcissi set the light, fresh tone of a spring planting, partnered with other spring classics – iris, anemones and tulips.

LEFT: Large island beds create a striking focal point with a scheme of brilliant colours shading from one hue into another.

true blues, hot pinks and the densest reds and purples. These are lightened by a myriad cooler and more subtle tints and shades, from gentle mauve to acid yellow-green. Shapes and textures range from the delicacy of gypsophila, with its tiny white flowers clustered in loose clouds, to the elegantly folded individual blooms of sweet peas (*Lathyrus*) and roses, to the stately spiked inflorescences of delphiniums, gladioli and verbascum.

Many of the summer-flowering plants go on blooming through late summer and into autumn, particularly if regularly cut or deadheaded – a bonus for flower arrangers who can in this way increase the display season indoors and out. But autumn brings special favourites such as michaelmas daisy (*Aster novi-belgii*) in its range of beautiful pinks, purples and blues, and some of the finest chrysanthemums in rich autumnal tones of bronze, gold and copper.

Different approaches can be taken to seasonal planning. You can accommodate a period of total dormancy in winter and allow the garden to dwindle to a bare framework, focusing your attention on planning and preparing for the next season's display. Alternatively, you can devise a scheme that incorporates the options for late autumn and winter colour. Since this means including shrubs and perhaps conifers that form permanent features of the planting, you will need to select perennials and summer bedding plants that integrate well with the appearance of these features during the growing season.

Winter colour

Choices are limited if you covet winter flowers, although if you can offer a mild local climate or sheltered location you may be able to appreciate the pale beauty of camellias or hellebores. Hamamelis species and cultivars produce spiky yellow flowers on bare branches in late winter to early spring – these shrubs or small trees also provide good autumn foliage colour. Mahonias are early-flowering shrubs with glossy evergreen leaves, *M. aquifolium* also having interesting variable leaf colours in winter. For bright colour, the alternative to flowers is berry clusters that persist from autumn through winter, as in pernettya and pyracantha.

The most reliable sources of winter colour are evergreen foliages, but this does not mean unrelieved masses of green. Cream and yellow leaf variegations are provided by evergreen forms of eleagnus,

ABOVE: **A popular choice for winter colour, the red-barked dogwood, *Cornus alba*, displays its bright, bare stems after leaf fall. The massing of the slender stems provides a dense colour effect.**

RIGHT: **Tall michaelmas daisies (*Aster novi-belgii*) are a reliable source of late-season colour, here forming a background to the graceful blue umbels of *Agapanthus* and offset by the silvery foliage of *Artemisia*. Grey-leaved plants are an excellent foil for most flower colours, specially effective with the blue-mauve-pink colour range.**

euonymus, griselinia, hedera and ilex; *Pittosporum tenuifolium* 'Silver Queen' has silvery leaves on fine black twigs; foliage colour in cultivars of the conifers chamaecyparis and cupressus ranges from yellow through silvery-blue to dense dark green.

Some deciduous shrubs provide an unusual display of coloured stems after leaf fall. The best known is *Cornus alba*, the red-barked dogwood, with strong red stems; other cornus cultivars contribute crimson, red-purple or yellow stems. *Rubus cockburnianus* has a strange, ghostly presence in its arching white winter stems. Ideally, you need space to make a group planting of these shrubs, and a dark background to show up the stem colour.

Scale and texture

The colour effects of flowers are modified by other aspects of their presentation. The great variety of flower and leaf sizes, shapes and habits of growth in flowering plants influence the ways we perceive their individual colours. Small flowers on single stems sprinkled over a mass of foliage do not match the colour intensity of large inflorescences or dense flower clusters. Plants that carry their flowers above the leaves create a different effect from those in which flowers are integrated with the foliage along the stems. Height and viewpoint are also significant – tall flower spikes naturally draw attention even when partnered by equally vivid, spreading flower masses; a carpet of low-

growing flowers that appears solidly coloured from a distance breaks into a pattern of hues and tones when viewed at closer quarters.

This natural variety provides the essential element of contrast that gives a flower planting depth, enhancing effects of light and shade within the colour relationships. Most plantings need this kind of counterpoint. Continuous pools or blocks of strong colour can be heavy and oppressive, whereas the intervention of green foliages seen within and around the flower colours provides the restful element that gardeners appreciate. However, a planting in which all the flowers are small scale and scattered over mounds of leaves can lose the colour impact.

Flower shapes can help to underpin the coherence of a colour scheme. Similar shapes give a kind of harmony to strongly contrasting colours, creating a balance of weight and density; on the other hand a planting of similar colours benefits from the sculptural interest of varied flower shapes. Size also counts; certain colours are naturally dominant and eye catching – typically the most brilliant of the yellows, oranges and reds – and if these are also the largest flowers or flower heads, they may far outweigh accompanying hues. You can draw attention to particularly spectacular shapes and colours by setting them among attractive foliages, removed from competition with other flowers, or by accenting them among broader masses of gentler hues and tones – using, for example, pale yellow, white and creamy tints to surround bright golden yellow or orange.

Large flower heads can also make interesting background shapes, standing out in relief against a wall or hedge, or framing a shady view through trees; or they can form clearly defined focal points in a mixed planting or in island beds. Small-flowered plants make good edging, where they can be appreciated at close quarters. Some are excellent candidates for creating a naturalized effect, planted among grass or in lightly shaded ground beneath trees, where they create a light spangling of intermittent colour.

A combination of rounded flower heads and tall spikes gives variation to the contour and textural interest of this planting of contrasting flower colours.

USING COLOUR

The essential feature of your flower garden is that you should enjoy it, so personal preference is an important element in your choice of plants. Even if you choose to employ a restricted colour palette, there are many different ways in which you can interpret it, incorporating variations of plant height and form, flower size and shape, and the relationships of flower and foliage colours. There are no rules of colour in terms of right or wrong combinations, but there are certain effects that are more or less predictable. So it is a matter of deciding whether you wish to organize the colours in terms of garden design and seasonal range, or simply choose favourite plants, give them a reasonable layout that accommodates their heights and habits, and trust to the inherent harmonies of natural hues and tones.

If you prefer a thematic colour arrangement, there are a few guidelines given below that can help you to pick the colour range and work out how to distribute the colours around the garden. These guidelines involve the interactions of colours and the characteristics that relate to other aspects of design, such as space and form, and the more abstract properties of mood and atmosphere.

The colour wheel
The formal arrangement of the colour wheel is a useful guide to mixing and matching colours. It makes it easy to identify the relationships of pure hues and colour values – the light and dark tones of the hues. The primary colours, yellow, red and blue, are equally spaced around the circle. Midway between each pair of primaries is the secondary colour formed by mixing the pair – orange (red and yellow), purple (red and blue), green (blue and yellow). Between the primaries and secondaries are further colour mixes – yellow-green, yellow-orange, orange-red, red-purple, and so on.

Each secondary colour falls directly opposite a primary, and these opposite pairings are known as complementary colours – yellow and purple, red and green, blue and orange. Complementaries form the strongest colour contrasts, while colours that are adjacent on the wheel are naturally harmonious.

This version of the colour wheel shows pure hues in the outer band; pale tones, or tints (colours mixed with white) in the second band; mid-tones (colours mixed with grey) in the third band; and dark tones, or shades (colours mixed with black) in the central segments. These tonal values are another means of enhancing the harmony or contrast of a colour combination. Complementary contrast is less striking when the colour pairings have lighter or darker values – pale pink with light green, for instance – but a colour harmony can be given greater contrast by selecting different tonal values, such as a light, brilliant blue with deep blue-purple.

Colour themes and combinations
A monochromatic arrangement, using hues, tints and shades of a single colour, can be particularly effective for a small or enclosed garden, or for individual island beds or borders in a large garden. It is not at all monotonous – you can work with a full range of tones, for instance, from palest pink through clear, true reds to deep maroon and wine red; or you can exploit subtle colour variations, as in a range from clear cobalt and sky blue to blues warmly tinged with lavender or purple.

If you want to introduce a note of distinctive contrast, pure white provides harmony with any colour range and can be used to lighten the colour masses. White can also be used on its own. A themed white garden is a popular idea that creates an unusual and dramatic effect; another monochromatic scheme deserving attention is the green garden, particularly helpful for difficult conditions such as damp ground or permanent partial shade.

Colour mixing depends on principles of harmony and contrast. Harmonies derive from using related colours and linked colour series. Yellow and orange, being similar in hue and tone, are natural partners; add red to this combination and the orange acts as an intermediary hue between red and yellow. Similar linkages are made through the adjacent colours in the spectrum of yellow, green and blue, and from blue through blue-purples, violet and mauve towards red. Remember that you can also apply this principle through pale tones – pink, mauve, lavender – and

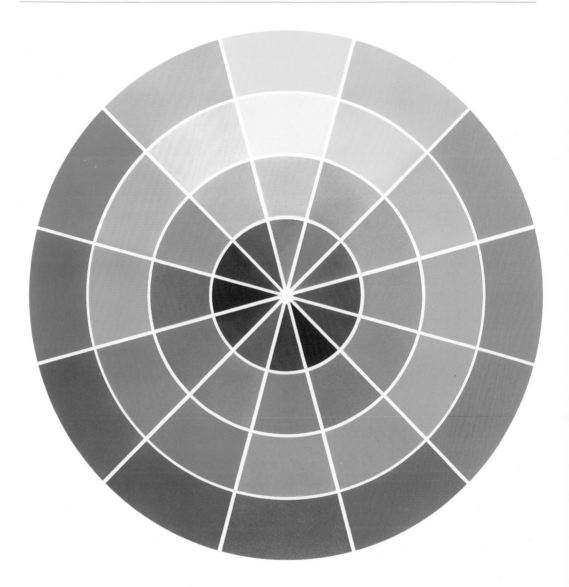

dark colours – deep purples and blues.

Strong contrasts come from juxtaposing colours that are quite unlike each other – classic pairings for contrast are orange and blue, yellow and purple, red and green. Some people find that their high intensity of contrast makes too garish an effect, but it can be softened by selecting hues and tones that subtly adjust the colour relationships. Bright red is very vividly offset by an acid, limey green, but there is more gentleness in the combination of a warm pinkish-red with a rich, dark green; with reds and purples, it is particularly important to consider the modifying effect of the foliage colour. The rather hectic effect of pure blue mixed with bright orange has a calmer interpretation in the pairing of blue and yellow – the contrast is maintained because orange and yellow are closely related, but the effect is softer.

Likewise, yellow and purple together can be too strident, but a more restrained mixture of creamy yellow with lavender-blue and mauve can be quite charming.

Colour in design

Colours are also described as having a 'temperature', relating to colour associations. Blues and greens are the colours of sky and water, therefore cooling and serene, as compared to active, hot colours such as red and orange, the colours of fire, and strong sunshine yellows. Yellows and purples are more variable in temperature, depending upon whether a yellow is influenced towards green or orange, a purple towards blue or red. Warm colours are also considered to be naturally advancing, striking the eye with more impact and rapidity than cool tones. Cool colours tend to recede; distant

colours appear bluish, so we associate blue with distance. A gradation from warm to cool colour is often recommended as a way of enhancing the apparent spaciousness of a garden.

These characteristics of colour affect our perceptions of space in different ways. A preponderance of bright, warm colours or strong contrasts tends to 'flatten' form and space, as the eye is constantly stimulated by the active impression of the colours. In a monochromatic or a broadly mixed colour scheme, the natural variations of colour create pockets of light

Yellow, orange and red are hot, eye-catching colours. The dense pompon shapes of *Tagetes* and *Zinnia* show off the brilliance of the hues.

and shade with intermittent focal points that enhance the three-dimensional effect. Shape and mass are also important in the overall effect of your design. Masses of colour evenly distributed make it less easy to define an underlying structure; strong individual flower shapes and emphatic changes of height create a more sculptured effect.

PLANNING THE PLANTING

When you come to select flowers from the plant directory, make a simple checklist that enables you to analyse suitable combinations with regard to both design of the planting and cultivation requirements. As well as the colour, note the type of plant – annual, biennial or perennial – and its flowering time so you can plan the transitions of the flower display through the growing season. Record the heights of individual species or cultivars – these can vary widely even between closely related plants. To ensure that all of the plants will enjoy the given conditions, briefly note the preferred soil type and aspect (sun or shade).

The majority of flowering plants listed in the directory are quite tolerant of a range of soil types, and many accept partial shade, so finding appropriate bedfellows should not be too difficult. If you begin making your list on the basis of the flowers that you find most attractive, you may have to eliminate a few that you would like to grow because they are not suited to the conditions you can offer. There is more difficulty in devising a planting plan for a problem situation – continual shade or boggy ground, for instance. In such a case, your choices are relatively restricted, as you can immediately see from the cultivation advice given under each plant heading. You can increase the range of colour by including plants with interesting coloured foliages, including shrubs and some perennial species, which may thrive better in poor conditions than plants grown mainly for their bright flowers.

While you are establishing a long-term planting, which includes perennials and shrubs likely to spread widely over a period of years, you may have gaps in your scheme that need temporary filling. For this you can choose from a wide range of annual and biennial plants (and some perennials treated as annuals), raised from seed or bought as bedding plants in strips or trays.

There are various ways you can arrange the plants together, so it is useful to sketch out possible planting plans on paper. In a traditional border, plants range in height from tallest at the back to low-growing at the front, and this is a good rule of thumb for any bed that is backed by a wall, hedge or fence. However, you can vary the effect according to whether you place the tallest plants at centre back or at either end, for instance; and if your view of the border from the house is oblique, you may decide to grade the plant heights so that the tallest are furthest away. The height gradations need not be strictly regimented – you may prefer an undulating, irregular contour to a solidly banked effect of massed flowers and leaves.

Massed plantings cut into sections by paths between the beds can be informally planted, as the constantly changing view means that the different plants can be appreciated in turn. In island beds cut into lawns, paving or gravelled surfaces, you can place the largest plants at the centre and have varying heights roughly graded downward from them in a radial pattern, so there is a symmetry to the all-round view; or you can again establish a planting that is best seen from one view, perhaps facing the house windows or patio.

With the colour combinations, too, there are different choices. You can arrange colour masses as pools, blocks or stripes, and intersperse plants that have single-stemmed flowers with those that form dense flower clusters. If you are planning a monochromatic scheme, the sculptural qualities of leaves and flowers become more important, as texture is a more prominent element when the colour range is restricted.

Colour selection
The following suggestions show how an initial colour idea can be developed in different ways. Beginning with yellow, a quintessential spring colour, you have the generous daisy-like flowers of doronicum; the abundant range of yellow narcissi, with varied petal and trumpet shapes; the fresh, informal *Trollius europaeus*, a garden flower related to the common buttercup; and the delicate spikes of the bell-like flowers of tellima, which stand above soft, bright leaves that form evergreen ground cover.

You can take the yellow theme throughout the growing season with daisy-like forms such as anthemis, coreopsis, helenium, heliopsis or inula, the spectacular tall spikes of verbascum, or the soft, vivid flower plumes of solidago. Rudbeckia and anthemis flower

RIGHT: A vivid splash of colour is not wholly dependent on the flower selection. Plain and variegated golden foliages are used here to give mass to a yellow-themed planting, and will outlast the fading of the blooms.

BELOW: Blue and yellow make a classic scheme for garden colour, creating contrast without any jarring colour notes. Here, the yellows range into cream and the blues into mauve, giving variations of tone and hue.

through into autumn, when you can add the warm golds and bronzes from the colour range of chrysanthemums to your scheme.

Alternatively, choose some of the stronger yellows and grade them into a 'hot' summer scheme that includes brilliant orange and intense red. This can start in spring with tall tulips and fiery-coloured wallflowers (*Cheiranthus*), moving into summer with bright red geums on slender stems, ragged monarda flowers in scarlet, or feathery astilbes of intense hues. Monarda flowers from summer into autumn, as does gaillardia,

certain cultivars of which combine yellow, orange and red in the same flower. Other possible additions for late summer and autumn are crocosmia sprays in orange and flame red, chrysanthemum korean hybrids, and tall-stemmed, fragile poppies (*Papaver*).

Shrubs that contribute to a warm colour scheme include *Acer palmatum* 'Dissectum Garnet', richly coloured throughout the growing season, and the dark red-purple cotinus for deep background tone.

A completely different effect comes from integrating spring and early summer

yellows with white and blue – such as
anemone and iberis in spring, delphinium,
campanula, gypsophila and myosotis in
summer – then allowing the blue theme to
take over and grade into blue-purples for
autumn, perhaps incorporating salvia,
michaelmas daisies (*Aster novi-belgii*) and
lythrum into the planting scheme.
This has a much cooler and more subtle
effect than the yellow-orange-red scheme,
and more distinctive variations in seasonal
character.

Colour in shade

Few flowering plants enjoy deep or
continual shade, but quite a number will
tolerate partial shade or dappled light, as
under trees. Pale hues and tones are
naturally most effective for lighting the
shadows – tellima and trollius (yellow);
bergenia and physostegia (pink); myosotis
and platycodon (blue); convallaria (white);
anemones, tulips and primulas (mixed
colours). Various hosta cultivars
contribute not only pale lilac or purple
flowers, but white, cream or yellow leaf
variegations, and these are plants that
actually prefer a shady site. Useful
flowering shrubs for partially shaded
ground include hydrangea, philadelphus
and vinca.

A white garden

This romantic idea is increasing in
popularity, following the model of a few
famous examples. The white garden is
refreshing and can be pleasantly formal in
design, giving a sophisticated effect.
The section on white flowers in the plant
directory includes a range of flower shapes
and heights, but remember that many of
the plants specially recommended for
chromatic qualities are also available in
white-flowering forms, including stately
lilies and gladioli. You can incorporate
roses and white-flowered shrubs, some
highly fragrant. Another classic element of
the white garden is grey- or silver-leaved
foliages, as in artemisia and senecio.

Pastel tints

The coolness and delicacy of the white
garden can be carried through into

**Hydrangeas and hostas contribute colour
and a strong sculptural presence to a
wooded area of a large garden where the
planting is part of the time in shade.**

coloured schemes if you choose flowers in pale tints – cream, pink, mauve, and the gentler yellows and blues – perhaps interspersed with some white for freshness and neutral contrast. For a permanent planting, there are some beautiful shrubs that will provide light-coloured flowers from late spring through summer – lilac (*Syringa*), deutzia and weigela among the early-flowering types, fragrant philadelphus in midsummer, and escallonia for later flowering. These provide a range of creamy white, mauve and pink flowers, which could be supplemented with roses in light, clear colours, such as salmon pink, lemon yellow and blue-mauve.

The pastel shades also go well with grey foliages, a relaxing combination. Garden pinks and carnations (*Dianthus*) provide the discreet complementary contrast of pale pink flowers, in a range of tints from shell pink to salmon, with mid-toned grey-green leaves and stems. With selected

The white garden must include green foliages, and this overall theme is creatively interpreted using silver-leaved plants and pale green flowers.

cultivars, you will have flowers from midsummer into early autumn. For late colour in a garden themed in pink, you can include the elegant nerine, an autumn-flowering bulbous plant, which produces its finely cut, lily-shaped flowers in clusters on tall stems.

A green garden
Green is more often regarded as the natural background to flower colours, than as a colour in its own right. However, it includes many subtle variations, from almost-yellow hues through true greens to grey-green and blue-green. Euphorbias, ferns and grasses provide interesting textural qualities, as do evergreen shrubs as widely varied in their visual effects as eucalyptus, fatsia and hedera. One

advantage of a green garden is that, if you choose long-lasting and tolerant plants, it becomes a low-maintenance area, although adequate supplies of moisture are important, as the foliages need to retain lush, fresh-looking colour.

The multi-coloured garden

If you favour a very mixed planting of variable colours, you can plan the planting with some attention to heights, spreads and flowering seasons and let the colours mingle more or less randomly as the plants grow together; or you can design a more organized planting in which there are definite colour links travelling through the arrangement of the bed. If you are incorporating annual or biennial plants typically sold as seed strains of mixed colours, it may be advisable to create some solid patches of colour, using shrubs or perennials, that offset adjacent areas of multi-coloured blooms. You also need to consider the overall effect of flower shape

A light-toned scheme of related tints and hues creates a delightful mix in this autumn border, inventively arranged but conveying a gentle character.

and size – whether the plants provide an impression of massed colour in dense flower heads, or points of colour and light with individual flowers or delicate flower sprays dispersed among the foliages.

The cottage-garden style of planting works well as many of the plants traditionally incorported come in hues that naturally integrate across a wide range – white, cream, pink, blue, mauve, purple, the gentler yellows and the deeper rosy reds. Among the lasting favourites are columbines (*Aquilegia*), poppies (*Papaver*) and love-in-a-mist (*Nigella*); candytuft (*Iberis*), stocks (*Matthiola*) and fragrant tobacco plant (*Nicotiana*), which contributes an unusual pale yellow-green among its range of flower colours; pinks, carnations and sweet Williams (*Dianthus*);

and the impressive spires of lupins, delphiniums and foxgloves (*Digitalis*). The cottage garden is planted as a loose, infomal arrangement, accommodating varied heights and allowing lower-growing plants to tumble into one another.

Mobile colour

Annual and biennial plants, and a number of perennials and small shrubs, typically grow very well in containers provided they are adequately watered and, if necessary, fed. Container gardening increases your planting space, essential in many town gardens where there is little open ground, and enables you to bring colour right up to the house in areas where you have paving or gravel rather than grass and soil. It also provides for variations in the seasonal display; you can remove or disguise plants that are past their best and bring to the fore those that are coming into bloom or changing foliage colour. You can also use containers as a supplement to planting in beds, either to make spot-colour links between plantings or to nurture young plants and cuttings that will provide replacement stocks.

Making changes

While a carefully made garden plan gives you the best chance of a long-lasting and attractively integrated flower display, there are some variable factors that may

mean you will wish to make changes once you see how the planting works out over two or three growing seasons. To begin with, if you are incorporating a number of perennial plants or shrubs, these need time to reach their full heights and spreads; if you plant them at the recommended distances, you will initially have some gaps that need to be filled with annuals and bedding plants until the larger plants reach full growth. The plants that you put in annually, whether grown by you or bought as bedding strips, can be varied to try out different colour combinations or shapes and patterns in the overall planting. Alternatively, if you want to achieve an impression of an integrated planting as quickly as possible, you can narrow the planting distances and be prepared to refine the arrangement within a few years, by discarding some of the mature plants.

Another element of cultivation that means your plan may not work out quite as you envisaged is the response of the plants to the growing conditions that you can provide. Many common garden plants are extremely tolerant of varying soil types and moisture levels – you can institute individual watering routines where necessary – but they also have preferences and may perform particularly well or poorly in a given situation. This can affect the eventual height and spread, and the capacity to produce an abundant display of flowers. If a plant fails to thrive, check the cultivation requirements to see whether there is anything you can do to improve soil conditions; it may also be suffering from too much or too little sun. If relocation or a different approach to cultivation does not produce better results, there may be nothing for it but to choose a substitute.

ABOVE: A simple but striking colour feature is formed by the generous blooms of *Ranunculus* massed in a terra-cotta planter.

LEFT: The apparent randomness of the cottage garden is a great part of its charm, though it can be carefully planned to achieve such an effect. Close planting gives coherence to emphatic variations of height and form.

CULTIVATION AND PROPAGATION

The range of plants given in the colour directory includes annuals and biennials, herbaceous perennials, shrubs and trees. Cultivation requirements for species and named cultivars are fully described in each entry, including soil type, preferred aspect and seasonal care.

The recommended method and time of year for propagation is also given in the plant entry, together with any special instructions for the individual species. Annuals and biennials are easily propagated from seed which, as these are short-lived plants, is an efficient and inexpensive way of acquiring stock. Some perennials can also be grown from seed, but those that are slow-growing or do not come true from seed are propagated from existing stock by any of several methods (see below).

Growing from seed
Seeds can be sown directly into the ground in nursery beds or in the flowering positions. Alternatively, seedlings can be started in seed trays, pricked out and grown on until they are sturdy enough to be transferred to their permanent sites. To prepare open ground for sowing, dig it over and allow the soil to settle; rake and tread the ground to firm it, then rake over the top layer again to break down and loosen the soil particles.

The depth at which the seeds are sown is important to successful germination. The seed packet provides clear instructions on sowing times and the depth of soil coverage. Try to sow as

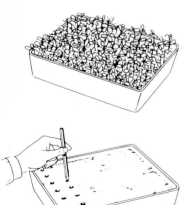

As seedlings develop they must be pricked out to give space for further growth. Prepare a fresh seed tray and make holes in the growing mixture at regularly spaced intervals. Select the strongest seedlings and transfer them to the new container.

evenly as possible – if the seeds are very tiny, it may be helpful to disperse them in some fine, dry sand before sowing.

Prick out the seedlings as soon as they are large enough to handle, to give them space to develop, discarding any that are weak or leggy. Keep them moist, but not too wet. Seedlings started in trays indoors can be hardened off gradually by allowing them increasing periods outdoors during the daytime until the weather is warm enough for the young plants to be planted out.

Root division
Many herbaceous perennials are propagated by division of the roots, the type of root growth determining the method. Plants that develop a mass of fine roots can be divided by lifting the rootball and gently easing it apart, using your hands or a spade. If the roots are fleshy and difficult to separate, as with hostas and astilbes, remove as much soil as possible by knocking or washing it off, then cut the roots into sections carrying developing buds and replant them separately.

Rhizomes are stems that grow horizontally at or below ground level, from which the plant's root system develops. Rhizomatous rootstocks are divided by cutting through with a sharp knife to separate a healthy section bearing roots and buds. Tuberous roots which, like rhizomes, are thick and fleshy, are also cut into sections.

Some plants that develop elongated, heavy roots can be propagated by root cuttings – pieces are cut off and potted up in a suitable growing medium, and each piece generates a new plant.

Cuttings
Stem cuttings from soft-stemmed plants simply consist of a length of stem cut below a leaf node. The lower leaves are stripped away and the end of the stem is inserted in potting mixture. For woody-stemmed plants, heel cuttings are used; the method is similar but where the stem is cut it must be eased away with a small spur of bark attached.

Basal cuttings are small shoots taken from the base of the plant as new growth occurs in spring.

ROOT DIVISION

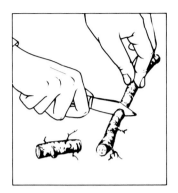

Root cuttings
Many herbaceous perennials are thick-rooted plants that may be propagated during the dormant season. Take short sections of root and cut at an angle on the lower end.

Fill a plant pot with growing mixture and insert the sections of root with the angled end downward. Cover with sharp sand to a level with the pot rim, water and place under a cold frame or cloche.

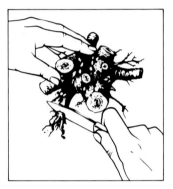

Peony rhizomes
Divide these rhizomes at the end of the growing season. Use a sharp knife to sever sections that carry both roots and buds. Treat the cut areas with fungicide before replanting.

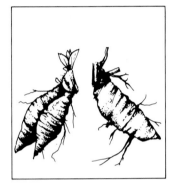

Dahlia tubers
Divide a dahlia tuber after the period of winter storage. Cut through the centre with a sharp knife, making two equal, sturdy sections that can be replanted separately.

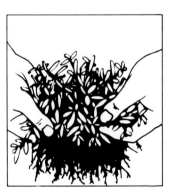

Root clumps
To divide a perennial with a clump of matted roots, lift the rootball and shake off excess soil, then gently ease the clump apart between your hands.

Iris rhizomes
Select a healthy section bearing foliage, roots and a dormant bud. Sever it cleanly and trim the leaves into a short fan. Replant the section with the rhizome stem partially exposed.

CUTTINGS

Heel cuttings
For woody-stemmed plants, detach a section of stem with a small spur of bark at the bottom. Strip the lower leaves and set it in a pot of growing mixture. Cuttings of soft-stemmed plants do not need a heel.

Basal cuttings
Clear the soil at the base of the plant. Select a young shoot and sever it with a small section of blanched stem, then pot it up in growing mixture. Root basal cuttings in spring for autumn flowering.

Layering

In this propagation method new roots are generated from a section of stem still attached to the parent plant. Gradually the layered portion becomes viable as a separate plant and can be severed from the parent. Layering is applied to shrubs with fairly flexible stems. A nick is made in the underside of the stem and that portion is pegged down in the soil and covered. Over time, roots develop and the original stem can be cut back.

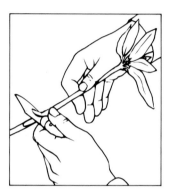

To propagate an established shrub by layering, select a strong stem with a healthy growing tip and trim away some of the leaves. Cut a small nick in the underside of the stem.

Make a hollow in the soil below the plant and bend the nicked section of the stem into the depression. Use a strong wire or wooden peg to anchor the stem in place.

Cover the stem with soil and stake the leafy tip in an upright position. Leave the buried stem to develop roots – this may take a whole season. Check it is securely rooted before detaching the new plant from its parent.

Offsets

Plants that grow from bulbs increase by producing small bulblets. These can be separated from the parent and grown on individually, but it is typically two to three years before they produce flowers.

Care of perennials

The usual time for planting herbaceous perennials is during the dormant season, between late autumn and early spring. Ideally, the ground should be dug over quite deeply before planting and some well-rotted compost or farmyard manure incorporated to improve the soil texture and make it moisture-retentive.

Division of established plants may take place in early spring, as new growth begins, or in autumn as the plant begins to die down. However, there are variations with this and other methods of vegetative propagation for perennials, so follow the specific advice on method and time of year as given under each plant entry.

Tall-growing plants may need staking as they get close to achieving full height. Regular removal of faded flowers encourages extended flowering. At the end of the growing season, when the stems of herbaceous perennials die back after the first exposure to frosts, cut them back to avoid top growth falling and rotting on the soil around the base of the plant, where it provides a haven for pests and diseases.

Planting shrubs and trees

Shrubs and trees are supplied as bare-rooted or container-grown plants. If bare-rooted, they should be planted during the dormant season; container-grown subjects can be planted at almost any time. Avoid planting either type when the soil is either very dry, waterlogged, or frosted hard.

Dig a hole large enough to accommodate the entire root mass. Add some organic matter such as peat or garden compost to the planting hole and surrounding soil. If you are staking the plant, set the stake firmly in the planting hole before you place the tree or shrub in position. If the plant is bare-rooted, spread the roots gently and, as you refill the hole, shake or rock the plant gently to get the soil well worked in among the roots. When the replaced soil is nearly level with the surrounding earth, tread it gently to firm the plant in position.

Water a tree or shrub well after planting, and make sure it has plenty of moisture throughout the growing season – it may need watering weekly in summer if there is little rain. Insufficient watering in the first year is a common cause of failure in young shrubs and trees.

Cut Flowers and Foliages

All the plants listed in the directory provide excellent material for flower arrangements, either freshly cut or preserved. Each entry includes advice on using the plant materials in arrangements, and on how to condition and preserve them.

The basic colour schemes that you might use in arranging are the same as those for garden planting – monochromatic themes, related colours, contrasts of hue or tone, or broad colour mixtures. Indoors, they are seen against a very different background and under different lights, including artificial light, so there are subtle changes in the colour relationships. In the garden, for example, a beautifully harmonious combination of deep reds and purples works well when spread over a wide area and offset by surrounding greens; in a flower arrangement the colour intensity is enhanced by close focus and there are fewer modifying factors. You

may need to adjust the tonal variation, introducing cooler or lighter accents, or bring in extra leaf sprays that give a natural background to the flower shapes.

The colour impression of a flower arrangement depends not only upon the individual hues in the flower selection, but also on the overall mass and shape of the arrangement and the way individual blooms contribute to the design. The delicate white flower clusters of gypsophila create a halo of light, whereas a few white roses or carnations centred in an arrangement make a brilliant, opaque focus. A mass of strong colour, such as red, orange or blue, can be overpowering, the colour density disguising details of form and contour. You can either arrange

The harmony of this arrangement comes from choosing flower shapes and colours that create visual links throughout, but also give an impression of variety.

boldly shaped and coloured flowers in a way that leaves their contours clear-cut against a plain background, or create a distinctive contrast with whatever surrounding flowers and foliages you select.

As with garden planting, there is a large element of personal preference. When you are growing flowers to be used in arrangements, remember to incorporate their attributes as cut flowers in your guidelines for selection – as well as colour and flowering season, you need to take account of shape, size, stem length and growth habit (upright or trailing stems, for instance). This information is highlighted in the graphic boxes featured under the heading of each plant entry.

The container is an important feature of design in flower arrangement. Here the simple shapes and lively motifs of the containers echo the fresh, colourful informality of the flower posies.

Conditioning cut flowers

To display cut flowers and leaves at their best, it is important first to gather them at the right time. Sunlight diminishes the plant's moisture levels and plant materials cut in daytime after exposure to the sun will be likely to wilt quite quickly. Cutting is best done in the morning or evening

when leaves and petals have had time to absorb moisture from the soil and the atmosphere. Carry a bucket of water with you and place the cut stems in it immediately – stems that drip sap when cut, such as narcissi and euphorbia, can be briefly pushed into the soil to stop the sap flowing before you put them into water.

Strip off any foliage from the stems that would be below water level in the arrangement, otherwise it decays and pollutes the water. With woody stems, remove about 2in (5cm) of bark from the cut end and crush them lightly to open the fibres. To seal euphorbia stems (which must be handled carefully as their sap is caustic and can cause severe irritation to skin or eyes) hold the stem end in a naked flame for up to 10 seconds.

Stand the flowers in buckets of water, in a cool, draught-free place, for at least six hours. They can be left overnight or longer, as plant materials will not over-condition. Any that begin to droop during conditioning can be revived by dipping the stem ends in boiling water for about 10 seconds, then returning them to the bucket.

Tulips are a special case, as the stems tend to bend while conditioning. To keep them upright, wrap them together in a sheet of newspaper and tie it loosely before putting them into the water bucket.

Young foliage sprays wilt easily, so they should be treated first by dipping the stem ends in 1in (2.5cm) of boiling water, then floating the sprays in cool water for up to two hours (this treatment should not be applied to soft, felted or hairy leaves). Individual mature leaves, such as those of hosta, bergenia and hydrangea, also benefit from a short period of being completely submerged. Following this, they are conditioned standing upright in water, as for flowers.

To maintain cut materials in good condition after arrangement, check the water level daily and top up as necessary – make sure if you have used florist's foam that it does not dry out. Mist-spraying is also good for maintaining an arrangement – again, a daily spray of clean water keeps flowers and leaves fresh. Do not site an arrangement of fresh flowers near a source of direct heat, such as a fire or radiator, and do not subject it to hot, direct sunlight.

Preserving methods

The most active times for drying and preserving plant materials are summer and early autumn, when many plants are fully mature; however, some spring flowers should be treated earlier, and some autumn foliages later. The materials must be processed immediately after cutting, so allow plenty of time. As with flowers for fresh arrangements, they are best harvested in the morning or evening.

Air drying is a simple method of preserving leaf and flower stems, but there are significant changes to their shapes and colours. Material must be quite dry when cut, and only mature flowers should be selected. Wrap the stems in small bunches and hang them upside down in a cool, dark room with a good circulation of air. Air-dried flowers are fragile and should be stored in a box, covered with newspaper to keep them free of dust and discourage reabsorption of moisture.

Desiccants are used to dry individual flowers, leaves and small, delicate sprays. The available types of desiccant are sand, borax and silica gel. These granular materials absorb moisture from the flowers and leaves without changing their colour or structure. Silica gel is the best desiccant, more free-flowing than borax and easier to remove from the dried flowers than sand.

Use a rigid plastic container with an airtight lid. Cover the base of the container with a ½in (1.2cm) layer of desiccant. Lay the flowers on top, and use a spoon to sift the desiccant into and around the flower shapes. Continue building up in layers, ensuring that each flower is fully covered with the desiccant, tap the container to settle the granules and put on the lid.

The drying time varies, but it could take up to two weeks – check the container after one week, remove any materials that seem satisfactorily dried, and return the rest to the box. When the process is completed, it is important to store the dried materials in an airtight container so that they do not reabsorb moisture from the surrounding air.

Glycerining is a preserving process mainly applied to foliages, as flowers do not readily absorb glycerine. It causes colour changes, which is one way of checking that the preservation process is nearing completion. You can obtain glycerine from a chemist – for this purpose you need to dilute it with two parts warm water to one part glycerine. Trim leaves from the lower parts of the stems and place the stems in the glycerine solution to a depth of 2-3in (5-7.5cm). Keep them in a cool, but light place.

Different foliages vary in the time they take to complete the process of absorbing the glycerine, but shrub stems take from three to six weeks. Check frequently and once you notice the colour change, test the leaves by touch – they should be pliable, with a slightly oily surface texture. Before storage, allow the stem ends to dry, then put the glycerined foliage into a box lined with newspaper.

Pressing is a popular method of preserving flowers, with the obvious disadvantage to the flower arranger that, by definition, it flattens the flower shape and form. Pressed materials are therefore used mainly for picture-making. You can buy purpose-made flower presses from craft shops, but a simpler method is to press the flowers between the pages of heavy books – telephone directories are ideal – first folding them into blotting paper or tissues to absorb the moisture. If you need to store pressed flowers, keep them in an airtight box. A sprinkling of desiccant on the base of the box will ensure that they do not reabsorb moisture.

THE PLANT DIRECTORY

The Plant Directory categorizes flowering plants under eight individual colour sections – yellow, orange, red, pink, purple, blue, green, white – with a separate Assorted Colours section for plants commonly available in a range of colours, and another for shrubs of special interest for flower and foliage colours and other features such as berries and coloured stems.

A plant is categorized under a particular colour to draw attention to the dominant or most readily available flower colour, but in many cases the available range may include different-coloured species or cultivars which can also be highly recommended. A Colour Finder is included at the end of the Directory to cross-reference alternative flower colours described in various entries. This should be used as an additional colour guide when you are planning a garden scheme.

Each entry begins with a description of the recommended species and cultivars, followed by advice on cultivation and propagation of the plants. It also includes specialist commentary on using flowers, foliage and stems as cut materials for fresh and dried flower arrangements, with information on conditioning and preserving methods.

At the beginning of each entry is a graphic device highlighting the season of main colour interest and providing useful detail for flower arrangers. A key to the symbols is given below.

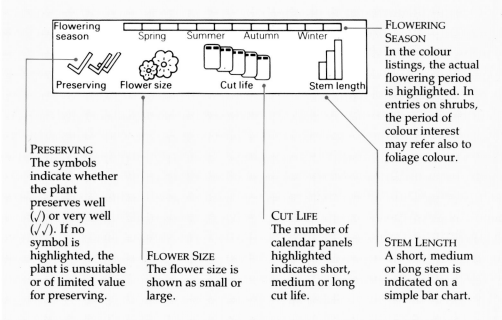

FLOWERING SEASON
In the colour listings, the actual flowering period is highlighted. In entries on shrubs, the period of colour interest may refer also to foliage colour.

PRESERVING
The symbols indicate whether the plant preserves well (√) or very well (√√). If no symbol is highlighted, the plant is unsuitable or of limited value for preserving.

FLOWER SIZE
The flower size is shown as small or large.

CUT LIFE
The number of calendar panels highlighted indicates short, medium or long cut life.

STEM LENGTH
A short, medium or long stem is indicated on a simple bar chart.

YELLOW

Achillea

Yarrow
Caucasus
Compositae

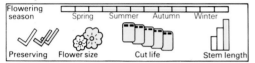

Achillea filipendula

A chillea filipendula has stout stems which rise erectly from a basal tuft of grey-green, feathery, richly pungent foliage. Densely packed, flat heads, or corymbs, of brilliant yellow flowers are produced through summer and autumn.

The most suitable hybrids to grow are 'Gold Plate', bright yellow flowers, midsummer, height 4-5ft (120-150cm); 'Coronation Gold', lemon yellow flowers, midsummer to autumn, height 3ft (90cm); and 'Moonshine', which has sulphur yellow flowers in midsummer, height 2ft (60cm).

These upright perennials are valuable border subjects and are commonly grown for use as cut flowers, both fresh and dried.

For highlighting in a single or mixed colour planting, there are also two very attractive white-flowered Achilleas, *A. ptarmica* 'The

Pearl', with sprays of button flowers from midsummer to early autumn, and 'W.B. Child' flowering in early summer. Both grow to 20in (50cm) high.

Cultivation and Propagation Achillea will grow successfully on a wide range of soils. It prefers a sunny situation. Propagation is by division of the roots in the late autumn or by seed in late spring. Germination will take some 14 to 21 days. When they are large enough to handle thin the resulting plants to 12in (30cm) apart in the row. Leave to grow on undisturbed until the late autumn when they are transplanted into their permanent position in an open sunny part of the garden. Leave plenty of space between the plants as their roots spread over a large area.
Uses As fresh material *A. filipendula* may be used as a focus for traditional arrangements in shades of yellow or as a highlight to a foliage design. *A. ptarmica* has white button flowers that are more suited to informal designs.
Conditioning Both varieties condition simply once they are mature. Crush the ends of the woody stems and stand them in deep water for at least 2 hours.
Preserving The flowers will dry on the plant but are susceptible to damage from rain. To keep the preserved flowers in good condition, collect them when all the flowers are fully developed and the stem has become woody. Tie them in very loose bunches and suspend them in a light airy atmosphere.

Anthemis

Ox-eye Chamomile
Europe
Compositae

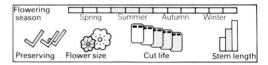

A nthemis tinctoria has lovely single daisy-like, golden yellow flowers up to 3in (7.5cm) across carried above a clump of fern-like foliage. It grows to 2½ft (75cm) high and flowers from mid to late summer. Useful hybrids with a slightly more upright habit are 'Mrs E.C. Buxton', light lemon yellow flowers; 'Beauty of Grallagh', golden yellow flowers; and 'Kelayi', rich yellow flowers, height 2ft (60cm).

Cultivation and Propagation This is a very easy plant to grow on any ordinary garden soil which is reasonably well drained and enjoys full sun. It needs support if you want it to be of neat appearance and produce good straight flower-stems for cutting. Plant them 20in (50cm) apart

Anthemis tinctoria

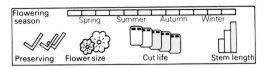

Coreopsis grandiflora 'Mayfield Giant'

in the row, with the rows 2½ft (75cm) apart. Regular weekly cutting of the flowers encourages flower production. Immediately flowering ceases in late summer cut the plants back to approximately 5in (12.5cm) above ground level to encourage fresh root development before activity ceases for the winter.

Propagation is usually by division of the roots in spring when fresh growth is commencing. New plants can also be produced from seed sown in the open ground in late spring. The resulting plants are thinned to stand 5in (12.5cm) apart in the row where they are left to develop. Transfer into their final flowering positions the following spring.

Uses Anthemis is not a flower that demands a dramatic or modern setting. Its unsophisticated appearance is best appreciated in a simple arrangement using an earthenware jug. Arrange them on their own or with a small amount of fern or grasses to extend the informal country atmosphere.

Conditioning They are undemanding to condition. Cut the open flowers at the coolest part of the day and remove any lower stem foliage. Stand them in cold water in a shaded area for 2 to 3 hours.

Preserving Desiccant and pressing are the only methods of preserving this flower. Its informality makes it a suitable subject for textural dried flower designs.

Coreopsis

North America
Compositae

There are excellent perennial and annual species of this plant, giving a range of strong yellows and interesting bicolours. The perennial *Coreopsis grandiflora* (Tickweed) is a robust plant native to the southern United States. It produces yellow daisy-like flowers, about 2½in (6.2cm) across, on long stems.

Good cultivars of this species include *C.g.* 'Badengold', with golden yellow flowers 3in (7.5cm) across, height 3ft (90cm), which will grow on very poor soil; *C.g.* 'Mayfield Giant', deep yellow flowers, height 2½ft (75cm); and *C.g.* 'Perry's Variety', with semi-double, clear yellow flowers, height 2-2½ft (60-75cm). All flower during summer.

The annual *C. tinctoria* (syn. *C. bicolor* and *C. elegans*), a native of the eastern United States, has smaller daisy-like flowers that are bright yellow with a scarlet-maroon central zone, height 2-2½ft (60-75cm).

C.t. 'Hybrida Double Mixed' has flowers which are fully double and semi-double in the colour range yellow, orange, crimson and maroon, height 3ft (90cm). These are carried on stiff stems and are ideal for cutting.

The dwarf cultivar *C.t.* 'Tiger Star' is a real beauty, with its bronze-striped and mottled yellow flowers, height 1ft (30cm). This succeeds everywhere, even in polluted areas such as road islands in the midst of busy city streets. *C.t.* 'Dwarf Mixed' provides compact plants up to 1ft (30cm) high, with flowers in vibrant reds and yellows freely produced through summer. These smaller strains are suitable for container growing.

Cultivation and Propagation Coreopsis likes a sunny situation and seems to thrive in almost any type of soil providing it is well drained.

Propagation is by seed. Sow under cloches in

early spring or in open ground in late spring. Seedlings of *C. tinctora* should be thinned to 9 to 12in (22.5 to 30cm) apart. They flower later the same year. Thin plants of *C. grandiflora* to 6in (15cm) again in late summer and early autumn. Watering may be necessary throughout the summer. In the late autumn the plants are transplanted into their permanent position in either a flower border with other perennials or in a special bed of their own. If growing them in rows the plants should be set out 2ft (60cm) apart in the row with the rows set 2½ft (75cm) apart.

Uses The simple form and clean colouring gives this flower an unsophisticated charm. The indented petals of the flower are an unusual change when arranged with other rounded forms. The intensity of colour associates well with preserved foliage, particularly glycerined beech with the addition of small amounts of the lighter *Choisya ternata*. Cut the flowers in the coolest part of the day, when they are charged with moisture.

Conditioning To condition them, simply stand them in deep water for up to 4 hours.

Preserving Individual flowers and petals may be pressed or dried in desiccant. Once dried they require careful handling as they become very brittle.

Doronicum

Leopard's Bane
Europe, Asia Minor
Compositae

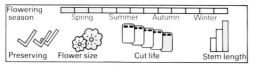

Doronicum is a useful source of bright colour in the earlier months of the growing season. The first species to flower in spring is *Doronicum cordatum*, 12in (30cm) high, with large golden daisies on 6in (15cm) stems. *D. caucasicum* has deep yellow flowers in late spring, height 16in (40cm); and *D.c.* 'Spring Beauty' has fully double, deep yellow flowers.

D. plantagineum provides a couple of very attractive cultivars in the form of *D.p.* 'Excelsum', which produces a profusion of bright yellow flowers during early summer, height 3ft (90cm), and *D.p.* 'Miss Mason', with light yellow flowers in late spring, height 18in (45cm).

Cultivation and Propagation *Doronicum* species are very hardy and will flourish in any ordinary garden soil providing that it is well cultivated before their introduction and given a moderate dressing of manure or garden compost. The

Doronicum caucasicum 'Spring Beauty'

roots benefit from being lifted and divided every third year to keep the young and vigorous plants. The best time to do this is just after flowering. Earlier flowering can be induced if some protection can be provided in the form of a coldframe, or plants can be carefully lifted and brought into a cool greenhouse.

Uses *Doronicum* will produce an abundant supply of flowers and if regularly dead headed will crop again in the autumn. Once the plant becomes established the flower stem length will increase in height from that originally advertised. The paler forms blend well with pastel colours of early summer flowers, while the brighter shades harmonize with light orange flowers and variegated foliage.

Conditioning Cut the fully opened flower when the central disc is young and fresh. It rarely presents any conditioning problems if stood in deep water for 2 to 3 hours.

Preserving To preserve the flower, select only those that are uniform in shape. Press them so that each petal is separated, for any that cross can't be adjusted once the process is complete. Though *Doronicum* is considered a spring flower, the preserved flowers associate perfectly with flowers and foliage in autumn colours.

Helenium

Sneezeweed
Canada and the eastern United States of America
Compositae

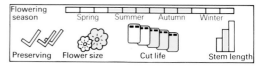

Helenium 'Butterpat'

flower is still young. Remove any excess foliage and stand the stems in water for 3 hours. Once they are fully charged with water the flowers will last a long time.

Preserving The shape of the flower makes it impossible to press, but it can be dried in desiccant.

Heliopsis

North America
Compositae

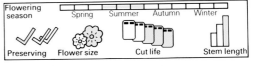

Helenium autumnale **is a free-flowering perennial plant with bright yellow daisies, each about 1½in (3.75cm) across, borne in clusters on long stems, height 4-6ft (120-180cm). Its flowering time is late summer to autumn.**

Two hybrids that produce a dependable source of rich yellow flowers are 'Butterpat', large, rich yellow flowers, height 3ft (90cm); and 'Madame Canivet', golden yellow flowers, height 3½ft (105cm).

For a warm gold and red colour scheme, there are several other hybrids that provide a range of rich, related hues: 'Bruno' has dark red flowers, height 3½ft (105cm); 'Chipperfield Orange', orange-yellow flowers, height 4½ft (135cm); 'Coppelia', deep copper-orange flowers, height 3ft (90cm); 'Moorheim Beauty', rich crimson flowers, height 3½ft (105cm); and 'Riverton Gem', red and gold flowers, height 4½ft (135cm).

Cultivation and propagation All the heleniums like a good rich moist soil and will grow equally well either in full sun or partial shade. Once clumps of plants are established they should be lifted and propagated by the division of the plants in winter every third year, so as to keep the stock young and vigorous. At this time dig in a generous dressing of manure, or well-rotted garden compost. Mulch annually in spring.

Uses The petals of this free-flowering plant reflex around a central disc rather like a shuttlecock. The colours are rich and bright which gives it a formal appearance. Plain green foliage would accentuate the brightness, so try using a variegated leaf to calm the vivid colour of the flower. The addition of a small amount of preserved foliage such as beech would also temper its luminosity.

Conditioning Cut the flowers before the central disc has changed colour, which means that the

Heliopsis 'Golden Plume'

The name Heliopsis means, appropriately, sun-like. The perennial species *Heliopsis scabra* **has yellow sunflower-like blooms, some as large as 3in (7.5cm) in diameter, during late summer, height 4ft (120cm). It has several useful cultivars:** *H.s.* **'Gigantea' produces rich yellow flowers throughout summer, height 4ft (120cm);** *H.s.* **'Golden Plume' has double yellow flowers, particularly good for cutting, in late summer and autumn, height 4ft (120cm); the summer-flowering** *H.s.* **'Incomparabilis' has large double, orange-yellow flowers, height 3ft (90cm); and** *H.s.* **'Patula', chrome yellow flowers in late summer, height 3ft (90cm).**

Cultivation and Propagation Heliopsis will grow in a wide range of moderately fertile soils providing it is planted in a sunny position. It is naturally sturdy and erect, except on over-rich soil, when it becomes weak and floppy. Plants should be set out to 3ft (60 to 90cm) apart in each direction, when they are planted out either in the autumn or spring, with their fibrous roots placed barely beneath the soil's surface. Once planted they should remain undisturbed for a number of years at a time. Newly planted heliopsis generally prove rather disappointing during their first year of establishment, with their flowers being borne on shorter stems than was expected, but it is worth being patient with them until their second year.

Propagation is either by division of the plants or by basal cutting in the early spring.

Uses This is a very vigorous plant that produces a large terminal flower and smaller side flowers. The flowers are a dull yellow and make good companions for the brighter *Helenium*. As they are multi-petalled and can reach a diameter of 3in (75cm) they are flowers for large designs or pedestals. Their atmosphere is decidedly rustic and they need the companionship of other unsophisticated garden flowers to look their finest. The dull yellow compliments blue flowers, particularly delphiniums, when they are used in arrangements for church where large flowers are needed.

Conditioning The stems are fragile and need to be handled carefully. Always give them some support during conditioning which should never be less than 3 hours.

Preserving I have tried several times to dry this flower and I must confess with very little success. The multi-petals make it difficult to dry in desiccant and the result can be dull and disappointing.

Inula

Fleabane
Europe, Africa and Asia
Compositae

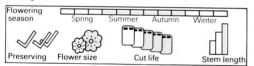

Flowering season	Spring	Summer	Autumn	Winter
Preserving	Flower size		Cut life	Stem length

These sturdy perennials create a profusion of fine-petalled daisy-like flowers from summer into autumn.

Inula ensifolia compacta has deep yellow rayed flowers on strong stems in summer, height 10in (25cm); the cultivar *I.e.* 'Golden Beauty' is similar but taller-growing, height 2ft (60cm). *I. orientalis* is also a summer-flowering species, with finely rayed, orange-yellow flowers, height 2ft (60cm).

I. hookeri carries its pale yellow flowers late in the season, and *I. royleana* also flowers from late summer to autumn, in deep golden yellow. Both are strong-growing, bushy plants that will achieve a height of 2ft (60cm) with equal spread.

Inula hookeri

Cultivation and propagation Inulas are all easy to grow and often succeed where other plants fail, particularly in clay loams. Any ordinary garden soil will do, providing that it does not dry out too quickly during the warmer summer months. On sandy soils, introduce some old garden compost or peat to improve the moisture-holding capability. Planting is best undertaken in the early spring, setting the plants out 1ft to 1½ft (30 to 45cm) apart in each direction according to the height of the species. Once established *Inula* should be given the benefit of a spring mulch each year.

Propagation is by division of the plants in the spring, or by seed which is sown in a coldframe in early spring or in the open ground in late spring. The resulting plants are planted in the open, in a nursery bed, 6in (15cm) apart in each direction, as soon as they are large enough to handle, and transferred to their permanent positions either in the autumn or the following spring.

Uses *Inula* will provide masses of flowers on long stems that may be used in abundance in any style of arrangement. They are unsophisticated to look at and always seem to me to be out of place in arrangements where the colour scheme is pastel. They are an ideal flower to include in a design of preserved foliages, and you can replace any that fade from the constant supply in the garden.

Conditioning To condition remove any lower foliage and stand the long stems in deep water for up to 3 hours.

Preserving I have always considered the flower to be too coarse to preserve, though the rather fascinating shaggy appearance is interesting as a component when the flowers are pressed.

Narcissus

Europe, North Africa, China and Japan
Amaryllidaceae

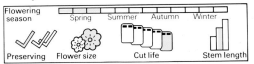

Flowering season	Spring	Summer	Autumn	Winter

Preserving Flower size Cut life Stem length

Narcissus jonquilla 'Bobbysoxer'

Apart from the many different species of the hardy bulbous plant Narcissus, there are also countless hybrids which have been produced in the wild, plus thousands of cultivars of garden origin.

There is often confusion as to the difference between the narcissus and the daffodil. In fact, there is no difference. Narcissus is the name of the genus, and the name daffodil is merely used to indicate narcissi with long trumpets, such as the clear yellow 'Dutch Master', 'Golden Harvest' with deep yellow, very large trumpets, and 'Mount Hood', which is a white-flowered daffodil. All these grow some 16in (40cm) high, making a fine display in the garden in late spring, and supplying fresh, large flowers on single stems for cutting.

There are some species which are not only delightful to look at but are also fragrant, and it is well worth introducing some of these into the garden. Narcissi are also easy to grow in containers to provide early colour on a windowsill or patio. The following flower in spring unless otherwise indicated.

Narcissus jonquilla has single yellow, sweet-scented flowers, height 1ft (30cm). *N.j.* 'Baby Moon' has light yellow flowers carried three or four to a stem in late spring, height 9in (22.5cm); *N.j.* 'Bobbysoxer' also carries several flowers to a stem, with yellow petals and orange cups, height 9in (22.5cm); *N.j.* 'Sugar Bush' has white petals surrounding white-edged yellow cups, height 10in (25cm); *N.j.* 'Suzy' is primrose yellow with orange cups, height 16in (40cm); and *N.j.* 'Treviathan' has large, clear yellow flowers, several per stem, height 16in (40cm).

Using the protection of cloches, all may be induced to flower several weeks earlier than those grown in open ground.

N. obvallaris is only slightly scented, but worth including because it flowers early in spring. Commonly known as the Tenby daffodil, it has golden yellow flowers and grows 12in (30cm) high. This species is particularly good for naturalizing in the lawn or side borders.

For a variation on the yellow theme in early summer, *N. poeticus* (Pheasant's eye) has white petals and a small deep red cup, height 14in (35cm). Its slightly larger cultivar 'Actaea' is white with a yellow cup edged in orange-red.

Narcissus jonquilla 'Suzy'

Narcissus 'Actaea'

Narcissus 'Dutch Master'

Narcissus 'Cheerfulness'

N. tazetta is a bunch-flowered form with many splendid cultivars. One of the finest is N.t. 'Cheerfulness', with creamy, fully double flowers, height 16in (40cm): it has an excellent sport, N.t. 'Yellow Cheerfulness', with primrose yellow, double flowers.

Two good white-petalled forms with orange cups are N.t. 'Cragford', height 1ft (30cm), which with protection can be induced to flower early; and the large-flowered N.t. 'Geranium', height 14in (35cm). N.t. 'Sir Winston Churchill' is a beautiful sport of 'Geranium' that has white double flowers, height 16in (40cm).

Cultivation and propagation *Narcissus* likes a heavy well drained loam of some depth but can be grown quite successfully on a wide range of soils providing that they are not too shallow. Good drainage is important so that the bulbs

will not rot during the cold winter months. However, they do appreciate a moisture-retentive soil and on gritty and sandy soils, where the drainage is excessive, well rotted garden compost or peat should be introduced to improve the water-holding potential. They may be grown either in full sun or partial shade with the exception of *N. jonquilla* which requires a sheltered sunny situation, if it is to flourish. Plant the bulbs 3 to 5in (7.5 to 12.5cm) deep and 6 to 9in (15 to 22.5cm) apart. Once established they call for very little attention. When flowering has ceased cut all the seed heads from the top of the flower stems, so that the bulbs do not waste their energies trying to produce seeds. Do not remove foliage until it has died down. Quite large colonies are produced over the years. In time the soil will become exhausted and unable to maintain the *Narcissus* in flowering condition. Instead lots of leaves are produced. To prevent this apply hoof and horn meal at the turn of the year. Simply dust it over the surface of the soil or lawn and leave the rains to wash it down into the soil.

Narcissus propagates itself by offsets and by seed. Offsets can be removed from the parent bulb and grown on to flower in 1 or 2 years. Seeds are not a reliable way of propagation as the resulting plants take several years to flower and are variable in quality.

Uses *Narcissus* is the true herald of spring for gardeners and arrangers, and is the most popular of the spring-time flowers. The colour and form of the narcissus has certainly changed dramatically over the years. The leaves are long and slender, strap like, green in colour. The flower bud is quick to develop, extending beyond the leaves when it is fully grown. Once the flower was simple to describe, a yellow trumpet at right angles to the stem surrounded by six petals. Today that is not always so, as some *Narcissi* have no recognisable trumpet, 'White Lion' for instance, has broad white petals with a fully double centre of cream and white petals. Narcissus makes a good subject for a spring landscape. All that is required is a suitable branch to represent a tree, and a well pinholder to arrange the flowers in. Incidental pieces of moss and stone may be added to carry the theme through. Don't attempt a complicated linear design; the flowers should be arranged in a natural manner. Vary the length of the flower stems and include some still in the bud stage. I generally use other foliage, preferring to leave as much *Narcissus* foliage on the bulb to help feed it for next year's flower. If your grouping will allow you cut a generous quantity, simply place them in a clear glass vase. Cut the stems to varying lengths to prevent the flowers from being packed tightly in the vase.

Narcissi show a dislike for water-retaining foam – the foam particles block the cut stem and reduce the intake of water. Whenever possible arrange them on pins or directly in water. To use them in a basket, place a deep dish inside the basket and cover it with a cap of wire netting, 2in (5cm) gauge, crumpled into a loose ball is ideal. Arrange the flowers through the mesh of the wire making sure that they all make contact with the water. A basket of mixed spring flowers is a delightful arrangement for the breakfast table.

Conditioning The cut stem of the *Narcissus* exudes a glutinous liquid, which continues to flow for a short while. As you cut them dip each stem in the surrounding soil to staunch the flow. To make full use of this generous flower cut them when they are still in bud; they will develop and open in the arrangement. When you are ready to condition them, cut off the staunched end and stand them in cool water until you need them. Flowers that are not to be arranged, may be placed directly into the chosen vase. To hasten the opening of flower buds stand them in a warm atmosphere or use warm water in the container.

Preserving The trumpet of the *Narcissus* prevents it from pressing successfully. Experiment with the small-cupped varieties, *poeticus*, 'Polar Ice', or 'La Riante'. Snip the cup at three equidistant intervals with a pair of fine nail scissors. This will allow the cup to flatten during the pressing operation. Drying the flowers in desiccant is most rewarding. Remove the stem and fill the trumpet with desiccant. Lay the flower on to a bed of drying compound and sift the desiccant around the flower until it is covered. The petals are paper thin and will reabsorb moisture, so the dried flower should be arranged under glass to avoid any distortion.

Rudbeckia

Coneflower
North America
Compositae

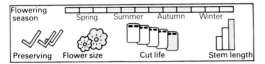

S everal species of Rudbeckia are widely grown, both for their showy contribution to the garden display and as excellent flowers for cutting. They all have large daisy-like flowers, some of which are fully double; in single-flowered forms each bloom has a conspicuous central disc. Heights range from 2ft (60cm) to 6ft (180cm) and their flowering season stretches from midsummer to late autumn. They provide a rich crop of yellows, but there are some interesting colour variations among the cultivars.

Rudbeckia hirta 'Double Gloriosa'

Rudbeckia fulgida, syn. *R. deamii*, is a perennial bearing deep yellow, dark-centred flowers in autumn, height 2ft (60cm).

R. hirta (Black-eyed Susan) is an annual with large daisy-like, yellow flowers that have dark brown cone-shaped centres, height 1½-3ft (45-90cm). The cultivar *R.h.* 'Irish Eyes' is without equal, its yellow flowers having emerald green central cones, height 2½ft (75cm). *R.h.* 'Double Gloriosa' is a double-flowered strain, height 3ft (90cm); some of its rich golden yellow flowers are so fully double that they are ball-shaped, up to 5in (12.5cm) in diameter and they are borne in profusion all summer long.

R.h. 'Marmalade' is very free-flowering, height 22in (55cm); the golden orange flowers have black cone-shaped centres. *R.h.* 'Rustic Dwarf' displays flowers of rich yellow, gold, bronze and mahogany shades, all with the characteristic black central cones, height 20in (50cm).

R. lacinata is a perennial growing to 5ft (150cm) high; the golden yellow flowers with greenish centres appear during early autumn. Two excellent cultivars have been produced: *R.l.* 'Golden Glow', with double chrome yellow flowers, height 6ft (180cm); and *R.l.* 'Goldquelle', also double-flowered but golden yellow, height 2½ft (75cm). Another good yellow cultivar for autumn flowering is *R. sulivantii* 'Goldsturm', 2ft (60cm) high and bearing clear yellow, dark-centred flowers.

In complete contrast to rudbeckia's wide range of handsome yellow flowers, *R. purpurea* and its cultivars provide strong red and purple shades for summer. The perennial species *R. purpurea* has purplish-crimson flowers, height 3ft (90cm). In *R.p.* 'Robert Bloom' the flowers are a glowing carmine-purple, while *R.p.* 'The King' blooms a rich rosy red. Both of these cultivars are slightly taller growing, at 3½ft (105cm).

Cultivation and propagation *Rudbeckias* are easy plants to grow, in any well drained garden soil. Choose a sunny situation. Although the stems of *Rudbeckias* are naturally stiff and erect, the taller growing ones are best staked to prevent damage by the wind. Indeed, if they are to grow to their full height during the spring and summer months they must be watered in dry spells.

The earliest flowers of R. *hirta* and its cultivars are produced from sowings made under coldframes and cloches in early spring. Germination takes two to three weeks. When the seedlings are large enough to handle prick them out into other boxes and harden them off for planting out in late spring. When sowing in the open do so where flowering is to occur. Set the plants out 15in (37.5cm) apart in each direction.

Perennials should be lifted and divided every third year, with the opportunity being taken to incorporate a moderate dressing of manure or garden compost. Mulch annually.

Propagation of perennials is by division of the roots during the late autumn and early winter, as the plants become dormant. The setting out of new plants from the nursery may take place any time then. Planting distances will depend upon the height the plants are expected to grow and will be anything from 15in (37.5cm) apart for the smallest, up to 2½ft (75cm) apart for the tallest.

Uses These simple but bold flowers with their rich colouring of yellow to red bronzes are much used in their season. They are particularly suitable for harvest festivals in church where they blend well with vegetables and fruits. Some varieties grow very tall and can be useful in a pedestal arrangement. The round form of the flower may be used purely as a focal area or if the scale is correct they can be used throughout an informal design. By using soft variegated foliage you can tame some of the more brilliant lemon yellows.

Conditioning To condition them I prefer to stand them in deep water overnight. Cut them late in the evening when the flowers are open. Remove any stem foliage.

Preserving The flowers are large and are not sufficiently attractive to press or dry in desiccant. Allow a number to set seed in the garden. The petals fall to leave a conical-shaped seed head. Harvest them when the stem has started to dry. Suspend them from a line in a warm atmosphere to continue drying.

Sisyrinchium

Satin Flower
Asia and North and South America
Iridaceae

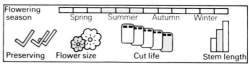

Sisyrinchium striatum

S. striatum is a perennial species with iris-like foliage and slender spikes of abundant primrose yellow flowers, height 2ft (60cm).

Cultivation and propagation Can be grown equally well either in a sunny or partially shady spot in the garden in any well-drained soil containing some humus. Regular division is necessary to keep the plants floriferous.

Propagation is by division of the roots during the dormant season or by seed sown in autumn or spring. Grow on the seedlings before planting out in their flowering positions the following year.

Uses The flowers are arranged quite loosely along the long slender stem, and growth is strong and upright. The pale cream to primrose colour is both cool and tranquil when arranged in a low dish where an appreciable amount of water is exposed. In this style of arrangement they need no accompanying flowers, just a little of their own sword-like foliage.

Conditioning Pick early in the day as the flowers often close up during the hottest time. Condition them in deep water for at least 2 hours.

Preserving I very rarely attempt to preserve the flowers as they produce a very fine seedhead later in the season. After the flowers have faded and dropped from the stem the small round seedpods are a bright green colour. At this point collect them and stand them in a glycerine solution. The process may take up to two weeks to complete, and they change colour to a rich mahogany brown. The stems can be used to make an arrangement with other preserved foliages.

Solidago

Golden Rod
North America
Compositae

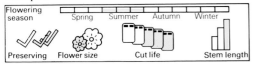

Solidago canadensis 'Crown of Rays'

Cultivars of *S. canadensis* provide fine quality plants with a delightful display of feathery golden plumes in late summer and autumn. The species is extremely vigorous and grows up to 6ft (180cm) high, but dwarf forms make these spectacular but tolerant plants suitable for inclusion in small gardens.

S.c. 'Golden Baby' has golden yellow sprays of flowers on stiff, erect stems in late summer, height 1ft (30cm). *S.c.* 'Crown of Rays' has wide, bright yellow flower heads in late summer, height 1½ft (45cm). *S.c.* 'Goldenmosa' carries golden yellow, mimosa-like flowers of neat habit in autumn, height 2½ft (75cm), and also has attractive yellow foliage; *S.c.* 'Mimosa' is a taller cultivar at 3½ft (105cm), but with the same fine feathery plumes as the smaller forms, bright mimosa-like yellow flowers borne in late summer.

Cultivation and propagation These are easy to grow in any ordinary garden soil in a sunny place. To get the best from them lift and divide the roots every second year, in the spring. This is also the normal way of propagation. Flowers are best cut when just showing colour.

Uses The tall elegant spires of *Solidago* are bright yellow, with a warmth that is sometimes missing from other yellow flowers. They are quite stiff growing and are best used to establish the height of an arrangement. The smaller varieties such as 'Golden Baby' may be used as transitional material. The foliage generally is of little use with one brilliant exception. *S. c.* 'Goldenmosa' leaves are a bright yellow/green and should be left on the stem to add colour and bulk to the design.

Conditioning The flower spike may be cut when the flowers are in bud, though the colour is brighter when the flowers are fully developed. Remove any leaves that will be below water and condition the flowers for up to 3 hours.

Preserving The small flowers are arranged along separate stems springing from the main stem. These can be removed from the growing plant with a pair of small scissors and pressed or dried in desiccant. The fine form of the curving spray can be used to excellent effect as outline material in a dried flower picture.

There are two methods of air drying the entire flowering stem. In both cases the stem foliage should be removed, as it becomes brittle and will disintegrate in time. The first way is to stand the mature stem in a jar containing 1in (2.5cm) of water. Let the stem absorb the water, don't top it up, it will continue to dry. An appreciable amount of colour loss will occur but the pale creamy yellow it attains is not unattractive. The second method is the conventional air drying process. Pick the flowers when they are fully developed, discard the leaves, tie them into loose bundles and hang them in a warm, airy atmosphere. Again a certain amount of fading will take place but the job will be considered worthwhile when you arrange them with preserved *Choisya ternata*, fresh trails of ivy and variegated holly in the winter.

Tellima

North America
Saxifragaceae

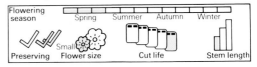

Tellima grandiflora is a good ground cover plant forming clumps of attractive bright green, round, hairy leaves. The spikes of bell-shaped flowers are light green turning to pale yellow with pink fringes as they mature in late spring, height 1½ft (45cm).

Tellima grandiflora

Cultivation and propagation *Tellima grandiflora* is a subject for the shadier parts of the garden. It will grow quite happily in any ordinary garden soil and being fully hardy will live for many years undisturbed. However, its mat of roots must have room to spread naturally. If you wish to keep it at its most floriferous it is best to lift and divide the roots every three or four years, selecting the younger clumps for replanting and discarding the remainder. This is the easiest method of propagation and it may be undertaken at any time during the dormant season. The new plants are then set out with their roots just beneath the surface 15in (37.5cm) apart in each direction. It is also possible to produce new plants from seed, which is sown in the open ground in spring. Sow the seeds very thinly and thin out the seedlings, when they are large enough to handle, to 8in (20cm) apart in the row. These plants are then transferred to their flowering places in the autumn or the following spring.
Uses As an evergreen plant this will prove useful in the winter when you need a change from preserved foliage. The leaves grow to a satisfying size, slightly rounded with a scalloped edge. Late in the season they change from green to a delightful marbled maroon colour. The flowers which grow above the foliage are very delicate in appearance. This delicacy is more visible when they are used in limited numbers for small pastel-coloured arrangements.
Conditioning Though they look fragile, they are amongst the easiest of flowers to condition. Simply stand them in water for 2 hours. The spring foliage should be floated in water before being stood in a glass of water to continue conditioning.
Preserving Choose the more striking leaves for pressing. It is possible to press the complete flower stem, but as the stem will dry at the same rate as the flower more benefit will be gained from drying them in desiccant.

Trollius

Globe Flower
Ranunculaceae

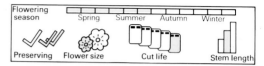

Trollius europaeus 'Superbus'

Trollius is a distant and much improved relative of the common buttercup. Two species provide good garden cultivars for flowering through late spring and summer, particularly suited to damp, shady sites.
Trollius europaeus 'Earliest of All' produces lemon yellow flowers in spring; *T.e.* 'Orange Princess' carries bright orange-yellow flowers in early summer; and *T.e.* 'Superbus' also flowers in early summer, in rich sulphur yellow. All grow to 1½-2ft (45-60cm) high. *T. ledebourii* 'Golden Queen' produces a deeper orange flower colour for summer, height 3ft (90cm).

Cultivation and propagation Both species will grow in any soil which is well supplied with organic matter and retentive of soil moisture. However, they will not survive for long under dry soil conditions. Choose a shady situation and ensure that the soil is supplied with lots of organic matter, e.g. compost, manure or peat, when preparing the ground. One should also water these plants during dry spells. Established plants should be lifted and divided every third year, in the autumn. They produce thick fibrous roots which can be easily propagated at this time, if further plants are required. This method is much quicker than propagating the plants from seed. Incorporate additional organic matter to maintain the soil's fertility and moisture-retention potential.

Plants should be set out 1ft (30cm) apart in each direction. In the spring following planting, it is advisable to provide a mulch of compost or peat. If starting from seeds, they should be sown, outdoors, in the autumn in a shady part of the garden. Growth is only slow at first and it will be two to three years before flowering may commence.

Uses This globe-shaped flower resembles a large buttercup, though the stem is much longer. It is often found in gardens growing along the edges of a pond. This sympathy with water can be extended by arranging them in a low dish, large enough to leave an area of water exposed. Use them on their own or with the addition of a little iris foliage.

Conditioning Cut the flowers when they are open or about to open, stand them in water for 2 hours to condition them.

Preserving The leaves, which are of little use in an arrangement, can be pressed. Once the leaf is mature the shape is quite intriguing, oval with deeply divided lobes. The central disc of stamens makes the flowers difficult to press. Ideally, they should be dried in desiccant.

Verbascum

Southern and Central Europe and the Mediterranean region
Scrophulariaceae

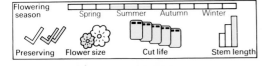

Verbascum 'Chaixii'

The tall flower spikes of Verbascum hybrids make a spectacular feature in the summer garden. In some types the flowers' central anthers add colour contrast. 'Chaixii' has

Verbascum 'C.L. Adams'

mauve-centred yellow flowers, height 5ft (150cm); 'C.L. Adams' has yellow flowers with magenta centres, height 6ft (180cm). 'Gainsborough' has delightful primrose yellow flowers rising above grey leaves, height 4ft (120cm). The flowers of 'Cotswold Beauty' are pale bronze, and those of 'Cotswold Queen' reddish-buff; both have lilac anthers and grow to about 4ft (120cm) high.

Cultivation and propagation Any fertile garden soil containing a little lime will do for these plants, providing that it is reasonably well drained and not subject to winter wetness. Choose a sunny site for them and dig this deeply, incorporating sand or other gritty material to improve the drainage, if necessary, and introducing just a little manure or garden compost, if there is any doubt about the humus content of the soil. Planting may take place at any time during the dormant season. Plants will need setting out some 16 to 20in (40 to 60cm) apart in each direction, depending upon their vigour.

Verbascums are not long lived herbaceous perennials but they are readily propagated from root cuttings, secured during the late autumn and winter time, and this is the method used to maintain the stocks of the named hybrids. They may also be propagated from seed, sown in the open ground in the spring. Germination will take 14 to 21 days. When the seedlings are large enough to handle thin them out to 8in (20cm) apart in the row and transfer the resulting plants to their flowering places in the autumn.

Uses For a while it was widely held that *Verbascum* was too tall to be of any use to the flower arranger. Luckily arrangers are now aware of its arranging quality, particularly when it is dried. True, the main stem is of statuesque proportions but it flowers at a prolific time of the gardening year and is useful for pedestal arrangements. The side spikes are of a more manageable length, arching gracefully in a range of pastel colours for traditional style designs.

Verbascum bombyciferum is one species to search out for its foliage and seed head. The foliage forms a rosette of pointed ovate grey leaves, covered with downy silver hairs. This looks splendid grouped in limited numbers in silvered driftwood. The effect is luminous. Once the flowers have faded and the seeds start to form the stem colour changes from green/ grey to a silver grey. Like the leaf it has a fine covering of hairs which gives it a ghostly quality. I would always advocate waiting for the seed stem to develop, instead of using it in its fresh state. If you are fortunate it may adopt some of the interesting twists and fasciations that are peculiar to *V. bombyciferum*. It is an eyecatching stem for modern arranging
Conditioning Cut the flower stem when the sun has gone from the plant. The flower head is most susceptible and wilts badly in excessive heat. Place the stem in cold water for 2 hours in a cool room. They are sometimes difficult to revive from a wilted condition, though treating them in boiling water should be successful. When conditioning foliage the leaves should be stood in shallow water. Any water touching the felted surface will discolour it. Check the water level often so that it can be topped up when necessary. Any of the leaves that start to wilt should be recut and the end treated in boiling water. Immature foliage responds to the boiling water treatment. Mature leaves may have the ends burned in a flame. The charred tip of the leaf can be left on for arranging, an advantage with this short stemmed leaf. A minimum of 2 hours should be allowed to fully condition the foliage.
Preserving Separate open flowers may be pressed or dried in desiccant. The real beauty of *Verbascum* is in its seed head, a slight contradiction as the seeds form the major part of the stem. When they set and begin to dry, the side stems straighten, moving closer to the main stem giving it a more attractive uniformity. Collect them when the seed pods have opened and the seeds have dispersed. The colour of the stem is dark oatmeal. A light spray of gold aerosol paint for a Christmas festival arrangement greatly enhances the colour. The alternative drying method is in glycerine. This must be accomplished as the flowers fade, while the seeds are still green. Stand the cut stem in glycerine solution, in a shady room. The process may take up to a fortnight to complete. When the stem is fully preserved, a change in colour will occur. The seed calyx and stem will darken and the seeds will become olive green with a slight oily sheen to them.

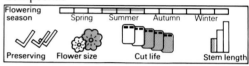

ORANGE

Calendula

Marigold
Southern Europe
Compositae

Calendula officinalis 'Art Shades'

*C*alendula officinalis, the well-loved pot marigold, is a hardy annual, an old-fashioned cottage garden flower which is as popular today as ever. The orange flowers appear from early summer onwards on plants up to 2ft (60cm) high. The cultivar 'Art Shades' provides a delightful range of shades of orange, apricot and cream, with various coloured centres, height 1½ft (45cm).
It flowers reliably even in poor conditions. Other recommended cultivars are 'Orange King Improved' with large, fully double flowers, height 16in (40cm), and 'Apricot Queen', height 2ft (60cm).

Cultivation and Propagation *Calendula* is very easy to grow. It does best on well-drained soils. The very earliest flowers are produced from seed sown in the open in early autumn. Except in mild districts plants should be given the protection of cloches or coldframes through the winter. Choose a well-drained moderately fertile soil, not too rich, for this will lead to soft sappy growth which will be susceptible to frosts. Spring sowing should be as soon as soil conditions are suitable. Thin out the resulting seedlings to 12 to 15in (30 to 37.5cm) apart. A second sowing should be made in summer, as this crop will flower during the autumn and in the succeeding spring.

Uses With its simple form, rough texture and bright colour, this is not a flower to use with cut glass or silver against elegant velvet furnishings. Marigolds are immediately associated with informality and lend themselves to simple arrangements in unglazed pottery or terracotta containers. Following this rural direction of arrangings, *Calendula* could be used in conjunction with dried grasses, preserved foliage, berries, even fruit or vegetables possibly in a basket design.

Conditioning The usual conditioning process will keep them fresh for up to 5 or 6 days.

Preserving There is no satisfactory method of preserving, though some attempt can be made to press them.

Crocosmia

South Africa
Iridaceae

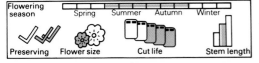

Crocosmia 'Lucifer'

Crocosmia × crocosmiiflora **(Montbretia pottsii) is a cross between the species C. aurea and C. pottsii. There are several superb named cultivars that provide glowing colour through summer and into autumn. The mid-**

Crocosmia 'Vulcan'

green, sword-like foliage offsets orange, yellow or scarlet flowers borne in arching panicles on stiff, wiry stems.

The strong orange-red flowers of C. 'Vulcan' appear in summer, height 2½ft (75cm), while C. 'Jackanapes' has striking deep orange and yellow flowers in autumn, height 2ft (60cm). Another good summer-flowering subject for a colour scheme of strong, hot hues is C. 'Lucifer', a brilliant flame red, height 3ft (90cm).

Cultivation and Propagation It grows best in light sandy soils which have been well enriched with a generous dressing of either manure or well rotted garden compost. Choose a sunny site. The corms are best planted some 3 to 4in (7.5 to 10cm) apart and 4in (10cm) deep. *Crocosmia* is not completely hardy and in more exposed areas is best lifted in the late autumn, when dormant. The corms are then kept in a cool dry frost free place until they are planted out again in the early spring. They multiply fairly rapidly and it is necessary to lift and divide the clumps of corms every third or fourth year. This is best done towards the end of the dormant season in early spring.

Propagation can also be by seed, sown in the autumn, as soon as it is ripe. Sow the seed in a seed pan containing a sandy soil, which is then placed in a coldframe or greenhouse. When the seedlings are large enough to handle they are pricked off singly into individual pots.

Uses The leaves of *Crocosmia* are as useful to the arranger as the flowers. They are sword-like, pleated like a partly closed fan, eminently suitable for modern and vertical arrangements. The flowers are carried on graceful arching stems, ideal for creating an outline for traditional arrangements. The colours range from yellow to flame/orange which contrast sharply with a background of plain green.

Conditioning The flowers open from the bottom of the spike upwards. Cut them when the lower flowers are open. The leaves can be left attached to the stem. Stand the stems in deep water for 2 to 3 hours.

Preserving The individual flowers can be preserved in desiccant, the luminous colour a striking item for a flower picture. During the autumn seed heads will develop, which should be collected when the seed has dispersed.

Gaillardia

Blanket Flower
Western North America
Compositae

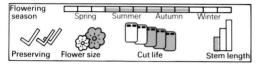

Gaillardia aristata 'Mandarin'

Gaillardia grandiflora

Gaillardia's bright daisy-like flowers are an asset in herbaceous borders and they are ideal subjects for cutting, providing a generous quantity of blooms through summer and into autumn. The most popular choices are hybrids of *Gaillardia aristata* (syn. *G. grandiflora*), which have a vivid colour range from bright yellow and orange through bronze to deep red. The following grow 2½-3ft (75-90cm) high: 'Dazzler', orange-yellow with maroon centres; 'Ipswich Beauty', bright yellow zoned in crimson; 'Mandarin', orange-flame.

Cultivation and Propagation *Gaillardia* likes a sunny position and a moderately light, well-drained soil, which has been supplied with a dressing of bulky manure or well rotted garden compost before planting. Planting takes place during spring and it is wise to set the plants out at least 2½ft (75cm) apart in each direction, if good results are to be achieved. A surface mulch of peat or garden compost should be spread on the ground between the plants during late spring to help to conserve soil moisture during the summer. When cutting flowers do not remove any foliage from the plant as this continues to provide further material. Immediately flowering ceases in the autumn, all the remaining flower stems should be cut back and a top dressing of bonemeal applied. A similar dressing should be repeated the following spring.

In mild districts, propagation is by the division of the plants in spring, established plants being lifted and divided every third year. If plant material is in short supply, root cuttings can be taken during late spring. In the early summer the resulting plants may be planted out in a small nursery bed where they can remain until the following spring, when they are planted out into their flowering positions. In colder areas plants are propagated from seeds which are sown in a warm greenhouse in winter. The resulting seedlings are pricked off into seed boxes as soon as they are large enough to handle. Later they are put out in a coldframe to harden off before being planted out in their flowering positions in late spring.

Uses *Gaillardia* is a typical cutting flower, bright and showy on stems of a useful arranging length. The broad petals set round a central disc have a luminous quality which will highlight the focal area of any traditional design. The more intense colour varieties such as 'Wirral Flame' can be used to great effect in a modern arrangement.

Conditioning Cut them when the flower is fully opened, no preconditioning is needed, just stand them in cold water for about 2 hours.

Preserving Little loss of colour will occur if you dry them in desiccant. This happy situation is emphasized when they are used in a design of dried materials as a study in colour.

Gazania

South Africa
Compositae

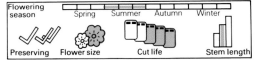

Gazania 'Golden Margarita'

Gazania × *hybrida* 'Sundance Mixed'

The various Gazania hybrids all carry large daisy-like flowers on sturdy stems. They are tender perennials, so the usual practice is to treat them as half-hardy annuals except in the mildest districts where they may survive the winter. They make useful summer bedding and are also suitable subjects for growing in pots, tubs or window boxes. The large, brilliantly coloured flowers are exotic-looking, with their clear-cut petal shapes and luminous hues, and different F1 hybrids provide single and mixed colours, plain and striped forms.

In G. × *hybrida* 'Golden Margarita', the large, clear-cut flowers have bright yellow outer petals and orange central zones, height 8in (20cm). G. × *h*. 'Sunshine Yellow Striped' mixes red and yellow in the form of brightly striped petals on flowers 3in (7.5cm) across, height 8in (20cm). G. × *h*. 'Sundance Mix' provides huge flowers up to 5in (12.5cm) across on strong stems 12in (30cm) long, in a range of bright colours – copper, yellow, mahogany and red. A tolerant hybrid that will succeed on dry or poor soils is G. × *h*. 'Chansonette', again in a mixed range of very fine, vivid hues,

height 10in (25cm).

In the mixed hybrid 'Carnival', orange is combined with pink, red and bronze, height 14in (35cm). 'Sunshine Red Shades' provides rich, deep red flowers, height 8in (20cm).

Cultivation and Propagation *Gazania* requires a sheltered sunny position in a well-drained fertile soil. Sow the seed in a greenhouse or on a windowsill in early spring. If the temperature can be maintained at 60°F (15°C) germination will be fairly even over the surface of the seed tray and take place within 2 to 3 weeks. If the temperature is lower than this then the germination will be erratic and take place over a longer period. When the seed lines are large enough to handle prick them out and, once they have had a few more days in the warmth to settle down, transfer them to a coldframe or cloches to be grown on without any heat. Protect the plants each night, for the first few days. The plants are hardened off in late spring and transferred to their flowering places in early summer setting them out 10in (25cm) apart. Cuttings can also be taken in late summer and overwintered in a warm greenhouse.

Uses Though the basic colour of *Gazania* is orange the garden hybrids have produced some very striking yellows and pink to ruby colours. The form of the flower is rounded with a distinct petal shape generally revealed through the marking at the base of the petal. As the stem is relatively short they are best used as a focal flower in a traditional design or as an individual flower in a modern container.

Conditioning This flower closes in the evening so it must be cut in the morning and immediately stood in water for 2 hours to condition.

Preserving The only method of preserving this brightly coloured treasure is by pressing.

Kniphofia

Red-hot Poker
South and East Africa and Madagascar
Lilaceae

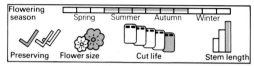

Flowering season	Spring	Summer	Autumn	Winter
Preserving	Flower size		Cut life	Stem length

Kniphofia 'Bees Yellow'

Kniphofia 'Royal Standard'

The stately inflorescences of Kniphofia, on sturdy, erect stems, create an imposing sight in borders or as isolated plantings from midsummer into autumn. As the common name 'Red-hot Poker' suggests, the colour range of the torch-like flower heads includes hot yellows, oranges and reds. Autumn-flowering types provide a range of clear oranges: *Kniphofia galpinii*, orange-yellow, height 2ft (60cm);. *K. nelsonii* 'Major', orange-flame, height 2ft (60cm); *K. uvaria grandiflora*, brilliant orange, turning to yellow late in the season, height 4ft (120cm).

Of the summer-flowering hybrids, recommended plants are 'Bees Yellow', with bright yellow flowers freely produced, height 3½ft (105cm); 'Fiery Fred', living up to its name with fiery orange flower spikes from early to late summer, height 3ft (90cm); 'Royal Standard', red and yellow flowers in late summer, height 3ft (90cm); 'Samuel's Sensation', deep orange, height 5ft (150cm).

Cultivation and Propagation *Kniphofia* prefers a light sandy loam containing a fair amount of humus, in a sunny part of the garden. Good deep cultivation is essential when preparing the site, as this plant likes to send its fleshy roots well down into the soil. Add sharp sand and other gritty material to heavy soils. Water during dry spells. Plants should be set out some 15 to 20in (37.5 to 50cm) apart in each direction. When once established they are best left undisturbed for a number of years. Plant in the dormant period.

Propagation is by the division of the roots in the early spring. These plants also produce suckers, which may be detached from the parent plants, which has the advantage that you don't lose a year's flowers from the parent. *K. uvaria* 'Mixed Hybrids', may also be propagated from seed. Sow in the late spring under glass. Germination will take about 4 to 6 weeks. When the seedlings are large enough to handle prick out into a coldframe. During warm weather the glass should be removed. Protect through the winter and plant out in permanent positions in the following spring.

Uses The stems of the *Kniphofia* curve slightly, and this will allow you to consider space as a design principle where two stems are used to create an oval void between them. The thicker-stemmed large-flowered varieties are particularly useful for creating this type of modern design. Smaller-flowered types that are not so strident in colour may be used in traditional arrangements. Arranged with lilies and light green foliage, they look most effective.

Conditioning Collect the stem when the lower flowers begin to open and the top buds are showing colour. Stand them in deep water for 2 hours; any flowers that die can be removed from the stem using a pair of scissors.

Preserving The flowers will not react to glycerine and are too fleshy to air dry. Single flowers can be removed from the stem and filled with desiccant to preserve them. The tubular shape of the flower is a contrast to round preserved flowers and leaves.

Physalis

Chinese Lantern
Japan
Solanaceae

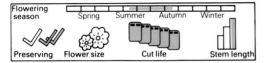

Flowering season	Spring	Summer	Autumn	Winter
Preserving	Flower size		Cut life	Stem length

Physalis

***P**hysalis franchetii* **is attractive for the orange-red lanterns which it displays in the autumn. The actual flowers are whitish and insignificant, hidden for the most part behind the leaves. The plant grows to 2½ft (75cm) tall and the roots are invasive. It can be grown in a tub or container to prevent this being a problem.**

Cultivation and Propagation This plant loves a deep fertile, moist soil containing plenty of decayed organic matter. If growing it in a tub or other receptacle, it is important to water it well in the warm summer months, as the plant is surface rooted and will soon begin to suffer. Stems have a habit of becoming too heavy, therefore some support with canes and string is needed, to provide long straight stems.

Propagation is commonly undertaken by division of the plant in the spring. Plants may also be propagated from seed sown in a coldframe in late spring. Germination takes up to 28 days. When the seedlings are large enough to handle prick them out into 4in (10cm) pots and transfer to permanent situation in the autumn 2ft (60cm) apart.

Uses Anyone already possessing this invasive plant will realize its worth as dried plant material. The leaves are of little use to the

arranger as are the rather insignificant flowers. It is the striking lantern shaped calyx which develops in the autumn that appeals. The lanterns are green at first, then turn yellow and finally orange-red. Cutting should commence when the lowest lanterns have turned orange-red. Choose the straightest stems for cutting and make the cut just above ground level. Fresh stems, with their leaves removed, can be used in an arrangement with Dahlias and Chrysanthemums that flower at the same time. Once a stem has been arranged it will start to dry, so don't throw it away with the rest of the flowers. In its dried state, the lantern colour is so striking that few flowers need to be used with it. Arrange it with preserved foliages and dried grasses. If the arrangement is exposed to direct light the colour will begin to fade but in some cases a less vibrant note might be desirable.

Conditioning Remove all but the terminal rosette of leaves, as they rarely remain turgid once the stem has been cut. Stand the stems in cold water for at least 2 hours (this only applies to the fresh stems). Often *Physalis* will dry in the arrangement if the stem is mature.

Preserving Towards the end of autumn, the stem and lanterns will start to dry naturally. Collect them before any of the fruits are damaged by the weather. Remove all the remaining foliage and tie the stems into loose bundles. Hang them from a line to continue drying; one or two lanterns may fall but sufficient remain to make the harvest viable.

Naturally dried stems are brittle and the lanterns are crisp and unyielding, often getting crushed in store. Preserving Physalis in glycerine relieves this problem. The fruits remain pliable. Any that inadvertently become squashed can be reflated to their former shape, a form of floral kiss of life. Glycerine the stems when the calyx is still green. Remove the leaves and stand the cut stems in glycerine for 6 to 7 days. The lanterns will change colour to a light beige, a pleasant alternative to the usual orange. They can be preserved after the fresh calyx has started to turn orange. The success rate is not as high, but any that do preserve are worth it.

Tagetes

Marigold

Mexico
Compositae

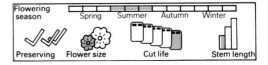

Flowering season	Spring	Summer	Autumn	Winter
Preserving	Flower size		Cut life	Stem length

Tagetes erecta 'Orange Jubilee'

Tagetes erecta 'Gay Ladies'

*T*agetes erecta (African marigold) provides a wide range of orange, gold and yellow flowers, some strongly scented. These undemanding plants brighten up any border or mixed planting, and where space is limited they can be grown in containers to provide splashes of intense colour on a patio or beside a pathway or lawn. There are some marvellous carnation-flowered and chrysanthemum-flowered cultivars available that bloom profusely all summer long, making a brilliant display of colour in the garden and providing excellent material for flower arranging.

The Jubilee F1 hybrids are very free-flowering. 'Orange Jubilee' has light orange flowers up to 4in (10cm) across, height 20in (50cm); 'Golden Jubilee' carries slightly smaller, pure gold flowers, height 20in (50cm).

In the F1 hybrid Climax series, the plants grow 2½-3ft (75-90cm) tall and have huge, almost globular flowers up to 5in (12.5cm) across and about the same in depth. They may be purchased as straight colours or a mixed blend of gold, orange, primrose and yellow.

The Lady series F1 hybrid produces fully double carnation-type flowers about 3in (8cm) across, and is well noted for the large number of blooms. Plants are particularly fine for bedding, as they are compact, height 1½ft (45cm). 'First Lady' has clear yellow flowers; 'Gay Ladies' flowers in bright orange-yellow or gold: 'Crackerjack' is a favourite early-flowering type, with giant fully double flowers in a superb mixed blend covering the full colour range, height 2½ft (75cm).

Chrysanthemum-flowered varieties are shorter, growing to about 1ft (30cm) high. These are useful plants for low-growing displays in island beds and as edging to borders and pathways.

T. patula (French marigold) provides good dwarf double forms for summer bedding. 'Bonita' and 'Boy-O-Boy' are mixed strains, with flowers in orange, yellow and mahogany, up to 1ft (30cm) high.

Cultivation and Propagation *Tagetes erecta* is a half-hardy annual which can be sown in a greenhouse or other warm place in spring. Germination takes 7 days. The resulting seedlings are then pricked out into other seed boxes, containing potting compost, and the boxes of seedlings are then placed within the protection of a coldframe or cloche until the frosts are passed, when the plants are transferred to their flowering position. In the open ground sow in late spring where they are to flower. Thin out the resulting plants to the appropriate distance apart. Choose a fairly fertile spot for these plants in a sunny part of the garden.

Uses The large bright solid coloured flowers are most useful and can be used with dramatic effect, creating blocks of colour in both traditional and modern arrangements. They are most accommodating in their growth pattern; partly open buds can be cut when small flowers of intense colour are needed. Fully developed blooms will last a considerable time once cut and can be used to vary the size of form where only one type of flower is being used.

Conditioning These flowers transpire heavily and need a lot of water, so it is necessary to give them an overnight drink to condition them. Remove all the lower leaves.

Preserving The smaller flowers should be dried in desiccant. They will add a note of vibrancy used in a picture or collage.

RED

Amaranthus

Love-Lies-Bleeding
Widely distributed
Amaranthaceae

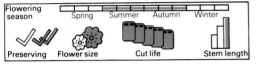

Amaranthus 'Molten Fire'

*A*maranthus caudatus is native to the tropics and is grown as a half-hardy annual. It produces long drooping racemes of crimson flowers from late summer to autumn, among large ovate green leaves, height 24-36in (60-90cm). The form 'Viridis' has unusual pale green flowers.

Cultivation and Propagation Choose an open sunny situation and any well drained soil. Sow the seed directly into the site where flowering is to occur, during late spring. Germination will take 2 to 3 weeks. Once the resulting seedlings are large enough to handle, thin them out to 18in (45cm) apart in each direction. The cut flowers have a long vase life.
Uses The long rope-like racemes of *Amaranthus* do not have a specific position in a flower arrangement. The longer, mature flowering

stems can be used to hang gracefully down the sides of a pedestal design, where the spectacular elegance can be seen without interruption. Smaller pieces, cut from the main plant during the growing season may be used throughout a traditional arrangement to introduce a different shape and texture. The foliage is of little use and should be removed from stems when used fresh or fry drying.
Conditioning Remove excess foliage and stand the mature stems in deep water for at least 2 hours.
Preserving To dry them, collect the mature stems when the flower colour is just starting to fade. Tie them into loose bunches and hang them in a light airy atmosphere. They will change from a deep scarlet or pale green to a pale beige.

Astilbe

Japan and China
Saxifragaceae.

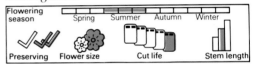

Astilbe × arendsii 'Fanal'

*A*stilbe comprises several hardy species of feathery-plumed, ferny-foliaged plants. Many hybrids have been produced, particularly by Herr Arends of Rondorf in Germany, hence the name *Astilbe × arendsii*. These shade from strong reds through a range of pinks to white. Recommended hybrids include 'Dusseldorf', brilliant cherry red, of compact growth and height 2ft (60cm); 'Fanal', intense deep red flower plumes appearing early in the season, height 1½ft (45cm); 'Federsee', rose red, height 2½ft (75cm);

Astilbe 'Bressingham Beauty'

'Ostrich Plume', arching plumes of rich coral-pink flowers, height 2ft (60cm); **'Bressingham Beauty'**, rich pink, and **'Bressingham Charm'**, clear pink, both 2½ft (75cm) high; **'Amethyst'**, rose-lilac flower plumes on stiff, erect stems, height 3ft (90cm); **'Irrlicht'**, pure white, and **'White Gloria'**, creamy white, both 2ft (60cm) high.

Other species have provided useful cultivars that increase the colour range: *A. chinensis* 'Pumila' is a dwarf form at 1ft (30cm) high, with small lilac-rose flower plumes in late summer.

Cultivars of *A. simplicifolia* are also smaller-growing: 'Atrorosea' has graceful plumes of pink flowers in late summer, and grows to 15in (37.5cm) high; 'Sprite' carries dense plumes of pearly pink flowers in late summer and early autumn, height 10in (25cm). A valuable tall-growing form is *A. taquetii* 'Superba', with superb, erect flower plumes of intense purple-rose in late summer, height 4ft (120cm).

Cultivation and Propagation *Astilbe* will succeed in any deep fertile, moist soil, either in full sun or partial shade and do particularly well on clay loams. Sandy soils will need a heavy application of bulky organic matter in the form of manure, well rotted garden compost, particularly well rotted grass mowings, if available, or peat. Astilbes may be planted at any time during the dormant season. Plants should be set out 1 to 2ft (30 to 60cm) apart in each direction, according to the height of the plants concerned. Once planted, Astilbes may be left undisturbed for some three to five years before they become too crowded and require lifting and dividing. Mulch annually in spring. On sandy soils they will need frequent watering in hot weather. The best solution if you have a pond or stream in the garden, is to plant them close to the water's edge, where they will feel most at home.

Propagation is by the division of the roots in spring, with a sharp knife, just as fresh growth is about to commence. Keep divided plants well watered. Alternatively, you can divide the roots late autumn and pot these up and keep them in a coldframe throughout the winter ready for planting out in spring.

Uses The shape of the flower spike restricts its use to being outline material in an arrangement, but this can be a very welcome change from foliage. Both the flower and the leaf are of considerable use to the arranger, not only for the range of colour but for longevity as cut material.

Conditioning Immature foliage should be floated in water before conditioning in deep water. Cut the flower spike when the panicle looks fluffy and bright. Remove any excess stem foliage and stand the stem in water for at least 2 hours. It prefers a cool atmosphere for conditioning.

Preserving Astilbe will dry naturally on the plant, so if the weather is kind they will grace the garden well into the winter with their brown feathery spikes. To reduce any weather damage they may be air dried. Collect them when the flower head looks crisp with a slight dullness of colour. Strip away any stem foliage and hang them to dry in a light airy room.

Geum

Avens
Chile
Rosaceae

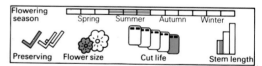

Geum chiloense 'Mrs Bradshaw'

*G*eum chiloense is a very easily grown and rewarding plant. It produces a dense clump of mid-green crinkled leaves which make good ground cover and help to preserve moisture about its roots. The panicles of flowers are borne on long slender, wiry stems up to 2ft (60cm) in height. This herbaceous perennial is a useful cut-and-come-again plant suitable for planting in borders and mixed beds; the more the flowers are cut, the more the plant will go on producing flowers throughout the summer.

G.c. 'Mrs Bradshaw' is a popular cultivar with vivid, deep red, semi-double flowers; 'Fire Opal' is another semi-double form, in glowing scarlet. Alternative colours include 'Lady Stratheden', golden yellow, and 'Prince of Orange', with orange-yellow, double flowers.

Cultivation and Propagation It seems to grow quite happily in any ordinary garden soil, preferring moist rather than dry conditions and flowers equally well in full sun or partial shade.

Propagation is generally by the division of the plants in the late autumn and this regular splitting-up of established clumbs of *Geum* keeps the plants so floriferous each year. New plants can also be produced from seed but these will not flower until the second year after sowing. The seed is best sown in a coldframe or cloche in spring. Once the seedlings are large enough to handle thin them out so that they are some 5in (12.5cm) apart in the row. Ventilate the plants whenever possible, so that by the end of spring the glass can be removed and the plants continue growing in the open ground. In the autumn these plants are transferred to their flowering positions and they should be spaced out some 15in (37.5cm) apart.

Uses The double, self-coloured flowers are extremely bright, carried at the top of slender stems. They are an eyecatching highlight when used in an arrangement of monochromatic colours. The soft ruffled petals lack sufficient dramatic impact to be of any use in a modern design, though the strength of colour may be desirable. It may be an advantage to reserve them as side pieces for inverted crescent shapes as the flower hangs in a most graceful manner.

Conditioning Select the flowers for cutting as they open and condition them in water for at least 2 hours.

Preserving Pressing would destroy the shape of the double hybrid flowers, drying them in desiccant will keep the shape and the colour.

Heuchera

Coral Flower
North America
Saxifragaceae

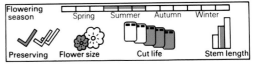

Heuchera 'Red Spangles'

Heuchera is a very hardy perennial plant which bears panicles of small flowers on slender wiry stems 1-1½ft (30-45cm) long. Its evergreen foliage clumps make useful ground cover and edging. The species *Heuchera sanguinea* has bright red flowers, but its crossing with *H. micrantha* and *H. americana* has resulted in a number of very attractive hybrids, in a range of colours and heights up to 3ft (90cm). These retain their role as ground cover, but are more free-flowering than the parent plants. The following flower throughout the summer:

'Red Spangles' carries flowers of brilliant crimson, and 'Shere Variety', blooms in vivid scarlet. 'Rhapsody' is glowing pink; 'Coral Cloud' a bright coral pink; the flowers of 'Pearl Drops' are pearly white; and those of 'Greenfinch' are a delicate greenish-white.

Cultivation and Propagation *Heuchera* is extremely easy to grow, in any well-drained soil, in sun or partial shade. Heuchera are tough drought-resistant plants which cling tenaciously to the ground they have colonized over many, many years. However, they are inclined to lift themselves out of the ground after they have been there for some time. One solution here is to place well-rotted garden compost around the plants, which also stimulates the more vigorous production of flowers. The alternative is to replant more deeply every four or five years.

Propagation is by the division of established plants in the spring or by the rooting of offsets in a coldframe in the late summer ready for planting out the following spring. Plants should be set out 18in (45cm) apart in each direction.

Uses Heuchera is a long-lasting cut flower, particularly suited to water-retaining foam, as the stem is so fine. The small flowers extending down the stem make attractive material to use for establishing height in small arrangements. Though the stem is fine it can be coaxed between thumb and finger to form a gentle curve. The foliage is vaguely hairy, a bright green in the spring turning to greeny/bronze in the autumn. It is a very useful leaf to reflect focal area flowers in a massed design.

Conditioning Cut the stems with a pair of scissors as the plant is shallow rooted and will be disturbed by the slightest tug. Condition them in water for 2 hours. The leaves may be floated in water for an hour. Shake off any residual moisture and continue the conditioning in deeper water for a further hour.

Preserving The leaves are a fine medium for pressing. Be selective and search the plant for any leaf that displays an unusual colour or figuration. The fastest method of drying the flowers is in desiccant, the stem will not distort and the resultant flower can be arranged with other preserved material instead of being glued and crafted as with other pressed flowers.

Incarvillea

Western China and Tibet
Bignoniaceae

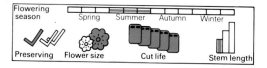

There are two exotic-looking species of this herbaceous perennial. The first is *Incarvillea delavayi*, which bears five or six deep pink, large, trumpet-shaped flowers on each stem, height 1½ft (45cm). These beautiful flowers appear in midsummer and look particularly attractive against the dark ash-like leaves.

The other species is *I. grandiflora*, smaller-growing at only 1ft (30cm) high. It has the same large trumpet-shaped flowers in midsummer, but these are a deep rosy red and the centre of the tube is suffused yellow. There is a cultivar, *I.g.* 'Brevides' which bears carmine-red flowers.

Incarvillea grandiflora

Cultivation and Propagation *Incarvillea* is easily grown in any rich, well-drained soil in a sunny position. Good site preparation requires deep cultivation and a generous incorporation of well-rotted organic matter, for once planted these plants resent any further disturbance, having fleshy fanged roots which penetrate deeply into the soil. Planting is best undertaken in the spring, setting the plants out some 6 to 10in (15 to 20cm) apart in each direction. Incarvilleas are particularly slow into growth in the spring, but when they do start development is very rapid indeed! Provide an annual mulch of well rotted organic matter about the roots of these plants in late spring or autumn.

It is possible to propagate established plants by division of their roots in the spring but the easier method is to propagate plants from seed sown in a coldframe in spring. Plant out in their flowering position the following spring. It takes two years to produce flowering plants by this means.

Uses This is a flower to challenge the arranger, as it is not the easiest subject to include in a mixed arrangement. The flowers are arranged at the top of a short stem, signpost fashion. They often interfere with or conceal adjacent flowers and leaves. However, the strong colour and unusual shape may be used in free form or modern arrangements. The flowers are produced before the stem has finished growing. Check the quality of the flower before you pick. Any that wither can be removed and this will encourage any buds to open.

Conditioning Cut them at the cool part of the day and condition them for at least 2 hours in a shaded area as the flower petals are paper thin and scorch easily.

Preserving Allow a number of flowers to set seed as the dried pod is extremely handsome.

Monarda

Bergamot
North America
Labiatae

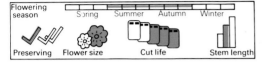

Monarda didyma 'Cambridge Scarlet'

*M*onarda didyma **bears clusters of scarlet, ragged honeysuckle-like flowers and its foliage is aromatic. Named cultivars of this perennial species provide a range of strong flower colours excellent for borders and mixed plantings.**

M.d. 'Adam' has immense cherry red flowers, height 2½ft (75cm); the flowers of 'Cambridge Scarlet' are brilliant scarlet, height 3ft (90cm). Attractive alternatives to the reds are 'Blue Stockings', violet-blue flowers, height 3ft (90cm); 'Croftway Pink', a delightful salmon pink, height 3ft (90cm); and 'Snow Maiden', with pure white flowers, height 2½ft (75cm).

Cultivation and Propagation All are very easy plants to grow on any ordinary fertile garden soil which retains summer moisture and is in a sunny situation. Sandy soils will require the addition of lots of manure or garden compost to improve their moisture-holding capacity.

Monarda forms a mat of fibrous roots, fairly quickly, and in order to keep the plant young and floriferous it will require lifting and dividing every second year, either in the late autumn or in the early spring. Plant out 15in (37.5cm) apart in each direction, with the tops of the crowns barely beneath the soil's surface. A mulch of peat or well rotted garden compost

should be placed around the roots of the plants each spring to help to retain soil moisture. Water in warm sunny weather.

The propagation of the named cultivars is by the division of their roots in the early spring or by seed. The older parts are discarded and the more recent roots are retained. If propagating from seed sow in a coldframe. When the seedlings are large enough to handle, they are pricked out 2in (5cm) apart in seed trays. The seedlings are then placed back into the coldframe and gadually hardened off. They are then planted outdoors in a nursery bed for the summer, with the young plants set out 9in (22.5cm) apart in each direction. In the autumn the plants are lifted from this nursery bed and transferred to their flowering positions.

Uses The loose, shaggy appearance is very informal and it is most useful as a transitional flower for relaxed designs of summer flowers. It associates well with *Physostegia, Penstemon* and garden pinks. In the wild, *Monarda* inhabits woodlands and water edges. Provided the cultivated flower colour is appropriate it can be included in landscape designs.

Conditioning Allow the main flower to open fully with the side buds showing colour. Stand them in water to condition for as long as possible.

Preserving The mature flowers will air dry, though the success rate is not high, so dry more than you will need. Hang them in a dry atmosphere as any moisture in the air will cause the square stem to twist.

Paeonia

Peony
Siberia, Mongolia, Caucasus
Ranunculaceae

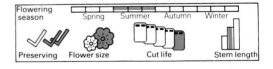

*P*eonies **have grown in popularity not only because of their flowers and fragrance, but more particularly because of their hardiness and reliability; once they have been given a suitable place in the garden, they may remain undisturbed for many years. Planting a peony is rather like planting a tree, because a peony's life expectancy can be 50 to 70 years, or even longer. Flower colours range from deepest red through a range of pinks to white, cream and yellow, and including some interesting bicoloured forms.**

The single-flowered Chinese peony (*Paeonia lactiflora*, syn. *P. albiflora*) offers cultivars

Paeonia 'Chief Justice'

Paeonia 'Felix Crousse'

officinalis and its cultivars. The species has large, single, crimson flowers. *P.o.* 'Rubra Plena', with dark crimson flowers, has attractively divided leaves.

For cut flowers early in the season, *P.o.* 'Alba Plena', with double white flowers, or *P.o.* 'Rosea Plena', double pink blooms, are suitable choices. Both of these grow to a height of 2ft (60cm).

P. mlokose witschii produces single, lemon yellow flowers even earlier in spring, height 1½ft (45cm).

Cultivation and Propagation The peony is most at home in the heavier loams, providing that they are well drained, deep and fertile. The lighter loams can give good results also, if they are deep and have been well fortified with a generous dressing of organic matter prior to planting peonies. So be generous with the preparatory work, as once planted the plants resent being disturbed. Choose a site which enjoys partial shade, so that the flowers are not affected too much by strong sunlight, which curtails the flowering season. Dig the soil to a depth of 18in (45cm) and ensure that the manure, garden compost or peat is well dug in. Peonies need plenty of space, as they become quite bushy when fully established, so set them out 3ft (90cm) apart in each direction. The most suitable time to plant out is in autumn. When planting, place the crowns of the peonies 1in (2.5cm) beneath the finished surface of the soil. If one plants more deeply than this then flowering may be much delayed. In the spring when the young shoots appear, dust the soil about the plants with a dressing of finely ground bonemeal, and lightly rake this in. This dressing encourages the development of the peony roots. Water during dry warm weather, especially in late summer, as this is when the buds are being formed which will produce the

with large, fragrant, mainly double flowers borne in midsummer, height 2½-3ft (75-90cm). Particularly fine choices among the reds are 'Eve', semi-double, bright crimson flowers; 'Karl Rosenfeld', double, dark crimson flowers; 'Felix Crousse', double, bright rose red flowers; and 'Torpileur', single, bright cherry red to lighter rose pink flowers.

A popular choice among the lighter hues is 'Sarah Bernhardt', with double, apple-blossom pink flowers. 'Bowl of Beauty' has semi-double, pale rose pink flowers with prominent yellow stamens; 'Edulis Superba' has double, bright rose pink flowers; and 'M. Jules Elie' double flowers of light silver-rose. 'Couronne d'Or' and 'Duchesse de Nemours' have fragrant white flowers, and 'Festiva Maxima' is an attractive double form with crimson-centred white petals.

For early flowering in summer, choose *P.*

Paeonia lactiflora

flowers during the subsequent year. Provide a surface mulch about the plants each autumn and lightly fork this into the soil each spring, taking great care not to damage the roots.

Newly planted peonies take a year or two to settle down to flower. While the flowering season is short, it is possible, by making a judicious selection, to have a supply of peony flowers for cutting late spring to midsummer. Furthermore, they can be forced in the greenhouse. Dormant plants are lifted in the autumn and placed in a well ventilated garden frame until they are required. Maintain the greenhouse at a temperature of 62°F (17°C). Flowering will commence some eight weeks after the peonies are planted. Peony roots which have been forced need time to recover again in the garden.

Propagation is by division of the roots, with a sharp knife, while they are dormant in the autumn. Select only strong roots for this purpose.

Uses The peony provides a mixture of handsome flowers and attractive foliage. The leaves are composed of several leaflets irregular in size and shape growing on a single stem from the plant. A limited amount grows on the flowering stem. Be selective when you use peony leaves from a young plant, some must be left on to provide food for the plant. Autumn colour is another good reason for delaying the removal of foliage. The leaves develop streaks of bronze, red and brown as the season progresses.

The flowers are sumptuous in colour and form, rounded or bowl shaped, averaging 4in (10cm) in diameter. The bowl-shaped flowers have exposed stamens, and in some hybrids these have become ribbon-like filaments, increasing the novelty and beauty of the flower. Two superb examples are 'Bowl of Beauty' and 'Globe of Light'. As the flower is so large it requires an arrangement of suitable proprtion to accommodate it. Until your plant is able to produce lots of flowers use only a few in the focal area of the design. It has a soft, silky quality and should be used with flowers that harmonize with this. Surprisingly, it looks attractive when arranged lightly with driftwood, to create a design outline. Both the single and double flowers may be included in a modern arrangement. They should be positioned at the centre of the design or below centre, for placed any higher the size of the flower may upset the balance of the arrangement.

Conditioning Peony flowers and foliage suffer badly from high midday temperatures. They must be cut at the coolest time of the day, preferably in the morning. Cut the single flowers as they are about to open and the double flowers when they are about three-quarters mature. The flower will continue to unfurl after it has been cut. Stand them immediately in cold water in a cool room for 4 hours. Autumn foliage will not require such a long period to condition, but the spring leaves should have about the same as the flowers.

Preserving The leaves can be encouraged to absorb glycerine. I am not entirely satisfied with the result and prefer to use them in the autumn when they have changed colour. The seeds in the open mature pod are highly coloured and worth collecting. If you can resist the urge to pick *P. mlokosewitschii* flowers they will reward you with an array of scarlet/orange seeds spilling from five fat pods.

Penstemon

Bearded Tongue
Mexico
Scrophulariaceae

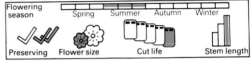

Penstemon hartwegii 'Garnet'

There are several good cultivars of *Penstemon hartwegii*, including *P.h.* 'Firebird', with graceful spikes of tubular scarlet flowers, height 2½ft (75cm), and *P.h.* 'Garnet, with deep garnet red flowers, height 1½ft (45cm). Both flower throughout summer. The mixed seed strain 'Bouquet Mixture' provides a variety of colours from pink, red and violet to shades of blue.

P. barbatus carries glossy green leaves and drooping coral pink flowers on long stems, height 2-3ft (60-90cm).

Cultivation and Propagation It requires a sunny situation and a well-drained soil, containing just a little organic matter. Water during the warm summer months to prevent

Penstemon 'Early Bird' mixed

the roots from becoming too dry and encourage the continued development of the flower spikes. If the tubular flowers drop from the flower spikes it is generally because the soil is too rich in organic matter. If you transfer the plant to a poorer soil this problem will disappear.

Propagation is by seed or by basal cuttings secured in the spring. Only the second method is suitable for the named cultivars. These basal cuttings are inserted in a sandy soil in a coldframe during spring or early summer and transferred to their flowering positions during the autumn, with the plants spaced 1ft (30cm) in each direction. When once planted they are best left undisturbed for a number of years. Add a little soil around the roots of the plants in the late autumn to provide them with some extra protection during the winter..

Uses *Penstemon* produce a continuous supply of flowers during the summer for the arranger. This and their splendid colour range is a good reason for growing them. The flowers are arranged loosely along a tall graceful stem. The rich colours of wine and ruby red add a note of distinction to an arrangement of pink flowers. The tall stem is an elegant piece of outline material arranged with grey foliage, roses, *Erigeron* and the young flowers of *Eryngium*.

Conditioning Pick the stem when most of the tubular flowers are open, strip any foliage away that is likely to be under water and stand the flowers in water for about 3 hours.

Preserving The complete flowering stem cannot be preserved. Remove single flowers from the growing stem and dry them in desiccant or press them. When the flowers are pressed arrange them in such a way that the finest profile will result.

PINK

Agrostemma

Southern Europe
Caryophyllaceae

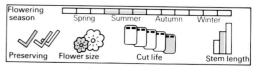

Agrostemma 'Milas'

A grostemma coeli-rosa has purplish-pink flowers shading to white in the centre, carried individually on slender stems, height 1½ft (45cm). Its rather insignificant foliage is grey-green. There are two good cultivars of this summer-flowering annual: 'Milas', with large soft pink, white-centred flowers, height 2½ft (75cm); and 'Purple Queen', with rosy purple flowers, white at the centre, height 1½ft (45cm).

Cultivation and Propagation *Agrostemma* grows easily in a sunny situation in well-drained soil. It is propagated by seed. Sow seeds in their flowering positions in late spring. Germination will occur in two to three weeks, and the resulting plants should be thinned out to 9in (22.5cm) apart. Seed may also be sown in the open ground in autumn in sheltered areas, but do not use over rich soil, as this will induce soft sappy growth which will not overwinter well. If young plants are given some protection in winter they will bloom earlier, thus prolonging the cutting season.

Uses This delicate flower has long, practically leafless stems which makes them highly desirable as outline material for both large and small arrangements. In very large designs the whole plant can be used. Remove the root system and place the stem directly in the oasis or into a water-filled cone. The soft pink colour is welcome as the flowering period coincides with peonies, stocks, dianthus and roses.

Conditioning The flower will continue to open after it has been cut, so do this when the flower is about to unfurl. Stand them in cold, deep water for 2 to 3 hours.

Preserving Fully developed flowers can be pressed or preserved in desiccant. The stem may be left attached when drying in desiccant as it is sufficiently fine to dry without distortion.

Armeria

Sea Pink
Europe including Britain
Plumbaginaceae

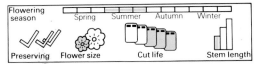

Armeria 'Bees Ruby'

*A*rmeria maritima **is a low-growing, tufty, grass-like perennial plant, found growing wild in coastal districts. It displays lilac-pink flower heads on thin, wiry stems 6in (15cm) high, in early summer. It is a sun-loving,** drought-resistant plant which can be depended upon to provide its attractive flowers regardless of prevailing weather conditions. It makes an excellent edging plant for paths and can be grown in cracks between paving; it is also suitable for container gardens.

There are also several delightful named cultivars in a varied colour range: *A.m.* 'Alba' has neat white flowers, height 6in (15cm); 'Dusseldorf Pride' has carmine red flowers; 'Ruby Glow' is slightly taller-growing, with flower stems up to 10in (25cm) and red flowers; 'Vindictive' is a smaller form with rich rose-crimson flowers on 4in (10cm) stems. Frequent cutting encourages further flowering.

Another useful cultivar which grows considerably taller is *A. pseudoarmeria* 'Bees Ruby', with bright ruby red flowers, height 16in (40cm).

Cultivation and Propagation *Armeria maritima* is one of the easiest plants one could possibly wish. It will grow on a wide range of soils, providing that they are not badly drained during the winter. Once established the plants can be left for years without being disturbed.

Propagation is by division of the plant roots in the spring. Seed can be sown in a coldframe, also in spring. Transplant to the flowering position in the autumn. Cuttings may also be taken in midsummer and rooted in a sandy soil in a shaded coldframe or cloche. Plant out rooted cuttings the following spring.

Uses The colours vary from soft pink to the rich ruby of *A.p.* 'Bees Ruby'. This range of colour makes them ideal companions for grey foliages. The association with the seashore makes *A. maritima* an obvious choice of flower for a seascape design. The pale pink colour blends well with wood that has been silvered by salt water.

Conditioning It is a greedy drinker and quickly becomes charged to capacity.

Preserving Its generosity of flower compensates for its disappointing preserving quality. Towards the end of the season the flowers will dry on the plant, but they tend to look a little dishevelled so collect them before they become weather damaged.

Bergenia

Elephant Ear
Siberia
Saxifragaceae

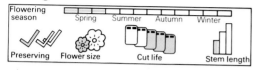

Bergenia 'Silver Light'

B*ergenia cordifolia* **makes interesting evergreen ground cover, with large, glossy oval leaves which are green during summer and flushed with metallic purple-bronze during the colder months. This is a really tough plant which in spring bears drooping racemes of bell-like, deep pink flowers on thick, erect stems, height 1ft (30cm). The flowers have a light fragrance best appreciated after cutting.**

B.c. 'Purpurea' has purple-pink flowers on longer stems, height 16in (40cm). B. 'Silver Light' is a delightful cultivar with white flowers delicately tinged with pink, height 1ft (30cm).

Cultivation and Propagation *Bergenia* will accommodate itself to a wide range of soil conditions and is happy in either sun or shade. Once established it will survive for many years without being disturbed. However, it is better to lift and divide every several years, as younger plants bear more flowers. Division of the plants is best done immediately after they have finished flowering in the spring. Remove the old flower stems after flowering has ceased.
Uses Flower arrangers reached the decision a long time ago that the *Bergenia* is a useful foliage plant, though the flowers that grace the garden in spring are an elegant inclusion in an

arrangement of spring flowers. The leaf is large and smooth often with a shiny texture, perfect material to act as a foil for special flowers used to create a focal area in a traditional or modern design. Look out for the varieties that change colour as the season progresses; some turn the most delicious mahogany red that links perfectly with Chrysanthemums and Dahlias..
Conditioning The leaf will condition perfectly well if floated on water. It is a temptation to use very young leaves that are a bright glossy green, but these wilt very quickly. Burning the end of the stem before the leaf is conditioned will help to counteract this, though it is better to allow the leaf to mature a little more.
Preserving The *Bergenia* leaf will preserve in glycerine. Use only perfectly fresh leaves and float them in a shallow dish of glycerine solution. The process is lengthy, but eventually the entire leaf changes colour to a dark brown almost black.

Clarkia

Western North America
Onagraceae

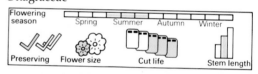

Clarkia pulchella

Clarkia has flowers which may be either single or double, and the colour range covers pink, purple, scarlet, orange and white. Two species of this annual plant are well suited to border planting or container growing: *Clarkia elegans* and the smaller-growing *C. pulchella*.
C. elegans 'Royal Bouquet Mixed' is a

particularly good strain with double flowers 2in (5cm) across in a superb blend of colours, height 2ft (60cm). The trend is towards selling seeds in mixed colour blends, but single colours may be available.

C. pulchella is usually only available as a mixed strain of white, lavender and carmine-pink flowers. It has both double and semi-double flowers, and grows to a height of 1-1½ft (30-45cm).

Cultivation and Propagation Clarkia will grow quite happily in any ordinary garden soil which is well drained and is in an open sunny situation. Over-rich soils should be avoided otherwise foliage will be produced at the expense of the flowers. Seed is sown thinly where flowering is to occur, either in autumn or spring. It may also be sown under cloches, during early spring. Thin the resulting plants out to stand 10in (25cm) apart. The autumn sowing will produce plants which flower from the end of spring onwards. In cold districts the plants may need some protection against frosts. Spring sowings will flower about three months later.

Uses *Clarkia* is a flower with a rural feel. Arrange it in an informal way with other flowers that generate a similar feeling. It tends to dislike water-retaining foam, so if mechanics are necessary a pinholder or chicken wire is more suitable. I favour a container that will hold plenty of water where the flowers can be placed to arrange themselves.

Conditioning They have a long cut life. Condition them in deep water for about 6 hours if they are to be arranged in oasis. Where there is no artificial mechanics they may be placed directly in the vase. It is wise to keep them in a cool place for the first few hours.

Preserving Any side shoots or small flowering stems can be dried in desiccant.

Dianthus 'Doris'

Dianthus barbatus

Dianthus

Carnations, Pinks, Sweet Williams
Africa, Asia and Europe including Britain
Caryophyllaceae

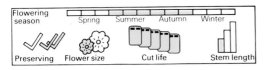

The Greeks were very fond of this particularly fragrant flower, regarding it as the 'flower of love' and using it in garlands and coronets for festivals. The common name carnation is said to be a corruption of the word 'coronation'.

Dianthus 'Doris Majestic'

Dianthus provides a generous range of flowers from midsummer to late autumn. The various forms provide a range of plants for different uses, from tall-growing border carnations to dense-flowered Sweet Williams of medium height to small-scale garden pinks perfect for edgings and rock garden planting. The flowers are very decorative, including simple colours and bicoloured forms, some distinctly banded or edged with the second colour, others irregularly splashed and striped.

MODERN PINKS

These fast-growing, versatile plants derive from *Dianthus × allwoodii*, a hybrid resulting from a cross between an old-fashioned garden pink and a hardy carnation. The following cultivars can be depended upon to flower continuously from midsummer to the onset of cooler autumnal weather.

'Cilla', pure glistening white flowers with red eyes, height 10in (25cm); 'Doris', pale pink flowers with distinct red eyes, height 12in (30cm); 'Helen', bright salmon pink, scented flowers on a plant of bushy growth, height 14in (35cm); 'Ian' very large double, glowing crimson, scented flowers lasting well into autumn, height 12in (30cm); 'Susan', pale lilac flowers with deeper eyes and lacing on each petal, height 13in (32.5cm); 'Thomas', deep rose flowers with darker central zoning, height 12in (30cm).

There are three good sports of the popular *D. allwoodii* 'Doris', all of which have flowers more than 2in (5cm) across. 'Doris Majestic' has fragrant salmon pink flowers with slightly serrated petals, produced in large sprays on strong stems; 'Doris Supreme' has scented flowers in a delicate shade of pink, marked with carmine flakes and stripes; 'Doris Elite' is similar to the original 'Doris', but has deeper red eyes and a longer flowering season.

SWEET WILLIAM

Dianthus barbatus (Sweet William) is an old favourite; the attractively clustered flowers have a tantalizing fragrance. This is a perennial species native to southern Europe. *D.b.* 'Scarlet Beauty' and 'Pink Beauty' are popular choices, but there are others as good, including *D.b.* 'Giant White', *D.b.* 'Auricula-Eyed Mixed', which has white or pale flower centres, and *D.b.* 'Messenger Early', which flowers about a fortnight earlier and has a fine mixture of colours. All these plants grow to a height of 18in (45cm).

OLD WORLD GARDEN PINKS

The old-fashioned clove-scented pinks need little or no attention and thrive in any well-drained soil in a sunny position, where they can be left undisturbed for years. The following all flower in midsummer and grow to about 12in (30cm) in height.

'Earl of Essex', double rose pink flowers, in great profusion; 'Freda', bluish-mauve flowers; 'Inchmery', exquisite shell pink flowers; 'Mrs Sinkins', double white, heavily scented flowers; 'Pink Mrs Sinkins', a pink-flowered form of the previous cultivar; 'Sam Barlow', large double white flowers with almost black eyes; 'White Ladies', pure white flowers, which are produced in abundance and possess an intense fragrance.

HARDY BORDER CARNATIONS

These are every bit as accommodating as pinks and will thrive in any sunny, well-drained spot in the garden. There is a great number of hardy border carnations and the following is a brief selection. All grow 1½-2ft (45-60cm) tall and flower during late summer.

'Alie Forbes', white flowers marked with rosy mauve; 'Beauty of Cambridge', large sulphur yellow flowers; 'Bookham Lad', exquisite white flowers striped with scarlet; 'Eudoxia', superb pure white flowers; 'Fiery Cross', brilliant scarlet flowers; 'Leslie Rennison', beautiful purple flowers with a rosy sheen; 'Lord Grey', heliotrope grey flowers with a silver sheen; 'Sunstar', distinguished yellow flowers which are edged and marked with scarlet.

Cultivation and Propagation Carnations, Pinks and Sweet Williams will grow in a wide range of garden soils, providing that they are well drained and not acid. If in doubt about the need to add lime, don't hesitate for one moment, as its presence may well do some good, and it will certainly not harm one's plants. Carbonate of lime can be raked into the soil immediately prior to planting. On established beds, apply a top dressing of carbonate of lime between the plants, in the spring. If the soil is heavy, it should also have a good dressing of sand worked into its surface, to further improve its drainage capability. Established plants will benefit from a dressing of general fertilizer in spring. Do not mulch as this leads to stem rot. When setting out the plants they should be spaced out 12in (30cm) apart in each direction. The soil into which they are to be planted needs to be fairly firm and it is desirable to 'tread' the soil prior to planting. Avoid over deep planting. Disbudding of the flowers on carnations is commercially practised but for flower arranging they look much more attractive if the side-buds are left to develop naturally. Pinks are not disbudded. The flowers are ready for cutting as soon as the terminal bud opens; the side buds will open as a matter of course.

While pinks do not require any form of support the taller growing carnations do. Wire hoops are the simple answer to this problem.

The named cultivars of both Carnations and

pinks are best propagated by means of cuttings or pipings. Pinks, with a naturally tufted habit of growth, may also be propagated by division of the plants best undertaken in the autumn or the spring. Propagation by cuttings or pipings takes place during midsummer. When propagating from cuttings, it is important to select healthy plants. Choose young non-flowering shoots around the base of the old plant and detach these with the aid of a sharp knife. Pipings are simply young shoots which are removed from the parent plant by pulling the top growth of a stem from out of its joint

When grown for cut flowers and for summer bedding purposes, *D. barbatus* is treated as a biennial plant. The seed is sown in the open ground in spring. Germination takes about two weeks. When the seedlings are large enough to handle, they are thinned out to stand 6in (15cm) apart and then left to continue growing there until autumn. The resulting plants are then transferred to their flowering places and planted out 10in (25cm) apart. Flowering occurs during midsummer of the following year. Alternatively, sow the seeds in a warm greenhouse in the early spring to produce plants which flower later the same year. It is quite hardy and will set seeds freely.

In the case of hardy border carnations, cuttings and pipings should have their lower pair of leaves removed and have their bases trimmed up just beneath a leaf joint (node). They are then inserted in either a coldframe or cloche in a well drained cutting bed composed of light sandy soil or a seed compost. Shade the cuttings to prevent wilting. Under the cool shady conditions rooting will take place in four to five weeks. Hardy border carnations may be planted out in their permanent positions during the autumn. Pinks may also be planted out at this time in the milder southern and western parts of the country, but elsewhere they should be given the protection of a covered coldframe during the colder wintry weather and be planted out in the following spring.

Uses These are well worth a place in an arrangement for their perfume alone. The range of colours extends their use into all areas of design. Paler shades are well suited to arrangements for informal parties, particularly as table arrangements where they highlight the colour of napkins and glassware. More sumptuous colours, crimson, scarlet and purple, are most effective in designs for formal occasions. The rounded, solid shape of *D. barbatus* makes it appropriate for the focal area of smaller arrangements. *Allwoodii* cultivars associate well with roses of a similar colour. Border carnations offer an interesting colour selection, on tall stems.

Conditioning *Dianthus* has the happy habit of quickly reviving in water whatever the time of day that you cut it. Cut the stem between the nodes to facilitate easier water absorption and stand them in deep water for up to 4 hours.

Preserving The old-fashioned single pinks have been for a long time firm favourites for pressing. Those with a coloured edge to the petal look delightful as the focal point in a pressed flower picture.

Dicentra

Bleeding Heart
North America, China, Japan
Fumariaceae

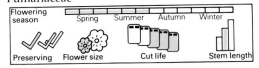

Dicentra spectabilis

This genus of hardy herbaceous perennials provides graceful flowers and foliage from late spring to early summer.

Dicentra eximia carries drooping, branched racemes of rose-purple flowers and fern-like, grey-green foliage. It grows to 12in (30cm) high. *D.e.* 'Alba' is a good white-flowered cultivar.

D. formosa is similar in appearance to *D. eximia*, but larger at 18in (45cm) high, and with pink flowers and coarser ferny foliage. *D.f.* 'Bountiful' has carmine-pink flowers; the flowers of *D.f.* 'Luxuriant' are bright red.

D. spectabilis is an outstanding herbaceous plant and the best known of the Dicentra species, with rose pink, white-tipped flowers borne on arching stems in early summer. Its glaucous, finely divided, fern-like foliage forms an attractively shaped mound, height 1½-2ft (45-60cm).

Cultivation and Propagation *Dicentra* likes well drained, deeply cultivated soils which have been well supplied with organic matter, such as manure or well rotted garden compost, and prefers a slightly shady position in the garden.

Propagation of these species is by division of the roots or by root cuttings taken in early spring. Plants are set out 12 to 14in (30 to 35cm) apart in each direction. For some extra early flowers, *D. spectabilis* can be pot grown, in the cool greenhouse.

Uses It is easy to be carried away with enthusiasm and recommend every plant that grows, but this is one plant that all arrangers should have. The foliage is light and delicate, very much like a robust maidenhair fern. Its arching graceful manner is perfect in an all-foliage design. The heart-shaped flowers are also carried on arching stems. To see and appreciate the true beauty of the flower, place two stems in a tall glass vase with a little of foliage. Stood in front of a mirror they accurately reflect flower glory.

Conditioning Always cut these flowers during the cool part of the day and condition for at least 3 hours in a cool area. Arrange them away from direct heat as they are susceptible and will quickly wilt.

Preserving Cut the flowers from the plant with a pair of fine scissors. They may be dried in desiccant or pressed. The heart-shaped profile of the pressed flower can be added to dried vine tendrils to reproduce an arrangement for a flower picture. Selected pieces of foliage should be pressed. The stem is fleshy and does not dry satisfactorily in desiccant.

Erigeron

Fleabane
Western North America
Compositae

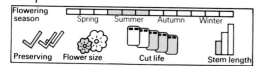

*E*rigeron speciosus resembles a Michaelmas daisy (*Aster novi-belgii*) in appearance, with the same daisy-like flowers, but this is a summer-flowering plant. There are a number of very good cultivars available that provide a generous display of flowers throughout the summer.

E.s. 'Charity' has light pink flowers, height 2ft (60cm); 'Dimity' is also light pink, height 1ft (30cm). The flowers of 'Forester's Darling' are large and semi-double, carmine pink, height 18in (45cm).

As with Michaelmas daisies, the colour range shades from pink into mauve and blue:

Erigeron 'Forester's Darling'

Erigeron 'Sincerity'

'Azurfree' has lavender-blue flowers, height 20in; the flowers of 'Prosperity' are semi-double, light blue, height 18in (45cm); 'Serenity' is later flowering, with blue-mauve flowers, height 2ft (60cm); and 'Strahlenmeer' has soft blue flowers with yellow eyes, height 2½ft (75cm).

Cultivation and Propagation This is a very easy subject to grow, in any ordinary well drained soil, preferably in a sunny situation, although it will tolerate light shade. Over-rich soils are not desirable as this stimulates over lush growth at the expense of the flowers. While this plant is a sun lover, its fibrous roots must be kept moist during the warm summer months. Every third year lift and divide the roots of the plants in the late autumn. Discarding the older parts of the roots, replant some of the young, more vigorous pieces, to stimulate flowering in the following year. In the intervening years, cut back the plants to within 4in (10cm) of the ground immediately flowering ceases in autumn, as this helps to strengthen the roots before the onset of the dormant season.

Propagation is either by division of the plants, as just described or by seed. When propagating from seed this is sown outdoors, during late spring. Germination will occur within 14 to 28 days. When the seedlings are large enough to handle, these should be pricked out in rows some 8in (20cm) apart with the seedlings 6in (15cm) apart in the row. The resulting plants should be moved to their permanent positions in the late autumn and planted out 1ft (30in) apart in each direction.

Uses *Erigeron* is very tolerant of salt-laden atmosphere; some cultivars can even withstand sea spray. The taller cultivars come in soft shades of lilac/mauve through to clear purple, while the shorter types are generally yellow to yellow/orange. This colour range adds a further dimension to a summer arrangement. The short cultivars are ideal for landscape designs as the stems are erect and easy to handle.

Conditioning Cut the stems when the flowers are open as any buds usually fail to develop. Any stem foliage that remains will not affect the cut life of the flower. Stand them in water for 2 to 3 hours.

Preserving Pressing and drying in desiccant are the two methods of preserving this flower. The lilac and mauve shades are suitable companions for pink and light red dried flowers and the pressed leaves of *Senecio* and *Eucalyptus*.

Helipterum

South Africa, Australia and Tasmania
Compositae

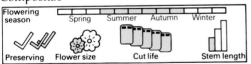

Annual species of Helipterum make attractive small border plants, and their bright daisy-like flowers are often grown for cutting because they dry well and remain so decorative when dry.

Helipterum roseum, syn. *Acroclinium roseum*, has large daisy-like flowers of pink, red or white, with yellow button centres, borne on stiff, erect stems, height 1½ft (45cm). Seed may be obtained in straight colours or as a mixture.

H. manglesii, syn. *Rhodanthe manglesii*, is very different in character, having clusters of

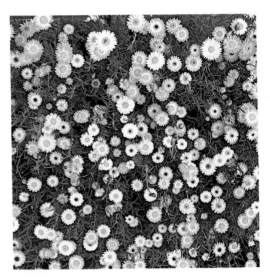

Helipterum roseum

drooping daisy-like, papery-textured flowers, each about 1½in (4cm) in diameter. The flowers may be bright rose, carmine or silver-white in colour, with yellow button centres. Seeds of this species may also be available in straight or mixed colours.

H. humboldtianum is a species with clusters of fragrant golden yellow flowers against silver foliage, height 1½ft.

Cultivation and Propagation All three species prefer dry poor soil in a sunny sheltered position. Sow the seed in the open ground where flowering is to take place, during late spring. Germination may take anything from 14 to 28 days, so be patient. When the seedlings are large enough to handle, thin them out to stand some 6in (15cm) apart. Flowering commences in late summer and continues to late autumn.

Uses Like the *Helichrysum*, this is also a flower for its preserving quality rather than for use as a fresh flower. Wait until the majority of the flowers are fully open and then cut the whole plant. Strip off all the foliage and tie the stems into small bundles. Suspend them in a warm, airy atmosphere for 2 to 3 weeks. Check them periodically to tighten any bundles that have become loose. The scale of the flowers somewhat restricts their use to smaller arrangements and collage or picture work. They make effective additions to Christmas decorations either in their natural colour or lightly gilded. Very inexpensive ornaments for a Christmas tree can be made by wiring the heads into a garland. Glass or plastic tree decorations can be given a face lift by glueing on a pattern of these flowers.

Lavatera

Mallow
Mediterranean
Malvaceae

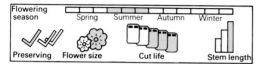

Lavatera trimestris 'Loveliness '

Tthe annual species *Lavatera trimestris* and its cultivars are highly attractive summer bedding plants, and given a sunny location will flower freely throughout the season. *L. trimestris* bears large, trumpet-shaped, rose-coloured flowers 4in (10cm) in diameter, height 3-6ft (90-180cm).

L.t. 'Loveliness' has glistening rich rose pink flowers, height 3-4ft (90-120cm); it may need some discreet support from twiggy branches pushed into the soil.

L.t. 'Mont Blanc' has glistening white flowers, height 2ft (60cm); 'Silver Cup' has glowing rose pink flowers lasting into early autumn, height 2ft (60cm); *L.t.* 'Splendens Sunset' produces even deeper rose pink flowers and grows to a height of 2-2½ft (60-75cm).

Cultivation and Propagation Any reasonably fertile soil will do for these plants, but they must be planted in an open sunny situation.

The seed should be sown where flowering is to take place in late spring. Germination will be sporadic over three to four weeks. When there is a good stand of seedlings, and they are large enough to handle easily, thin them out 18 to 24in (45 to 60cm) apart according to height. One can also sow the seeds earlier in spring in boxes in coldframes and cloches and prick these out into boxes. Harden off before planting in the open in early summer.

Uses This is a very popular flower for the border and for cutting and arranging. The flowers are on the large side and this restricts them to arrangements of that scale. Although a particular shape can be achieved through artificial mechanics this flower lends itself to a simple massed grouping in a glass or china vase.

Conditioning The flowers are delicate and should not be cut during the hottest part of the day. Immediately after cutting place them in deep water for at least 3 hours to condition. Do this in a shaded room well away from direct light.

Preserving The flowers may be pressed or dried in desiccant, but the size of the individual flowers may not make this a viable proposition.

Lychnis

Campion
Caryophyllaceae

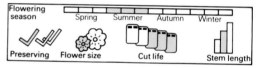

Lychnis chalcedonica 'Salomon'

Lychnis chalcedonica, originating from eastern Russia, bears flat clusters of brilliant scarlet flowers on leafy, bright green stems in summer, height 3ft (90cm). There are attractive pink and white cultivars of this species, a particularly fine example being the delicate salmon pink *L.c.* 'Salomon'.

L. × *arkwrightii* is the result of a cross between *L. chalcedonica* and *L. haageana*, with red flowers and purplish leaves, height 1ft (30cm).

L. coronaria, native to southern Europe, bears single flowers in pink, red, purple, magenta or white, height 2½ft (75cm). Good cultivars are *L.c.* 'Alba', white flowers, height 2ft (60cm), and *L.c.* 'Abbotswood Rose', bright pink flowers, height 1½ft (45cm). All flower during late summer.

L. viscaria is another native European species with rosy red flowers in midsummer, height 1½ft (45cm), but the more popular form is *L.v.* 'Splendens Plena', with large, double cerise flowers, height 15in (37.5cm).

Cultivation and Propagation With the exception of *L. chalcedonica*, all Lychnis need a deep, well-drained soil. If necessary improve the drainage by the introduction of sharp sand or other gritty material. Very sandy soils will need some well rotted manure or garden compost to bind the soil and help moisture retention, otherwise the *Lychnis* will wilt during warm spells and the flowering be affected. *L. chalcedonica* prefers a moisture-retentive soil and will grow quite happily in clay loams and in boggy conditions.

All the Lychnis have sturdy stems and no support be will required. However, the soil must be kept moist during the summer months, if they are to flower vigorously. A surface mulch of peat or well rotted garden compost should be applied during late spring.

Planting is best undertaken in the early spring when new growth is about to commence. Actual planting distances will depend upon the height the plants grow and may be anything from 12 to 60in (30 to 50cm) apart. *Lychnis* will need lifting and dividing every third year and this should be done during the dormant season. Choose young vigorous pieces of root when replanting, as these will prove to be the most floriferous.

Propagation of named cultivars is by division of the roots as just described. New plants can also be propagated from seeds as *Lychnis* sets its seeds quite freely. Sow seeds in early summer. When seedlings are large enough to handle prick off into nursery beds. Plant out in autumn in flowering positions.

Uses *Lychnis chalcedonica* is one of the most brilliant scarlet herbaceous plants. The large multi-flowered head can measure up to 5in (12.5cm) in diameter. This shape and size easily satisfies the modern flower arranger. The bright colouration restricts its use in arrangements in mixed summer flowers but when possible it makes a fine focal area flower. *Coronaria* has a much smaller flower head in a wide colour range that is more suited to massed arrangements of an average size.

L. viscaria 'Splendens Plena' with double cerise flowers grows in an ovoid spike and blends perfectly with other blossom and roses in the pink range.

Conditioning Cut the flowers when they are

open. Remove any stem foliage and stand the flowers in water for 2 to 3 minutes.

Preserving The petals of *L. coronaria* are a particularly fine shape and are worth pressing. To maintain the shape and strong colour preserve in desiccant.

Nerine

South Africa
Amaryllidaceae

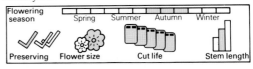

Nerine bowdenii

Nerine is a genus of bulbous plants. *Nerine bowdenii* is the hardiest, able to withstand slight frost, and can be grown in the open ground in many areas. It produces its elegant clusters of finely curled pink flowers, on 1½ft (45cm) stems, during autumn each year. The cultivar *N.b.* 'Triumph' displays extra large pink flowers and attains a height of 2ft (60cm).

Cultivation and Propagation The bulbs are globose at the bottom but taper to a thin neck at the top. These need planting in a well-drained light soil with their tops just beneath the surface and some 4in (10cm) apart. Choose a site with a southern aspect and, if possible flanked by a south-facing wall. If the soil conditions are heavy one can incorporate suitable gritty materials to improve drainage or, better still, excavate the unsuitable soil and replace this with a mixture of soil, peat and sand. Planting takes place in the late autumn to early winter. Once planted the bulbs are

immediately covered with a mulch of peat,
leafmould or straw to protect them from the
worst of the winter frosts. This needs to be
some 4in (10cm) deep and remains in position
until new growth commences in the spring. At
this time the leaves appear and do not die
down again until late summer. When these
leaves are seen to be dying one should give the
bulbs a topdressing of bone meal, followed by a
light mulch of garden compost. And when
flowering has finished provide that protective
mulch once more for the winter. Once planted
these bulbs should be left undisturbed until
such time that they become overcrowded and
flowering begins to decline. They are then lifted
and divided. They can also be propagated from
seed but this is a slow process taking some five
years before flowering can be expected.

Uses This is a flower of striking beauty. It
extends all that is elegant in a summer garden
through the months of autumn. Most of the
hybrids are pink, some being deep, darkening
to scarlet. The elegant lily form should be
retricted to the choicest area of a massed design
or used as a point of impact in a modern
design. As it flowers late in the year it is an
ideal companion to roses that are producing a
last valiant flush of colour.

Conditioning Cut them when most of the
flowers are open and stand them in deep water
for 2 hours to condition. Any buds will develop
in a warm room after they have been arranged.

Preserving The flowers are star-shaped with six
slightly crimped petals, the most satisfactory
method of preserving them is desiccant. The
dried flowers can be fixed to false stems with
adhesive and used in small arrangements or
flower pictures.

Physostegia virginiana 'Vivid'

**18in (45cm); and for highlighting in summer
there is a pure white cultivar, *P.v.* 'Summer
Snow'.**

Cultivation and Propagation *Physostegia* grows
on any ordinary garden soil, providing it is
reasonably fertile and well drained, either in a
sunny or partially shady situation. *Physostegia* is
best lifted and divided every year or two in
early spring. Plants are set out in their
flowering positions some 18 to 24in (45 to 60cm)
apart, according to their height. A surface
mulch of garden compost or peat between the
plants will help to retain moisture around their
roots, during the summer.

Propagation is by division of the fibrous,
creeping roots, or by cuttings of the young
shoots 3in (7.5cm) long, in the spring each year.
When propagating from cuttings, these are
inserted in a sandy compost and given the
protection of a coldframe.

Uses *Physostegia*, known as the obedient plant,
has hinged snapdragon-like flowers that will
remain in an altered position if they are moved.
The stem is upright, with the flowers on
opposite sides, tapering up to a point. The spire
effect puts them in the range of outline
material. The flowers might be considered
fussy and will benefit from an association with
plain green foliages, *Griselinia* or *Hosta lancifolia*.
The cut flowers are long lasting.

Conditioning Collect them when at least one-
third of the flowers are open. Remove the lower
stem foliage and condition the flowers for about
2 hours.

Preserving My only success in preserving the
plant is to collect the seed head and this is
mainly Nature's work, not mine. The result is
not outstanding but it can be useful as a point
element in a dried material design.

Physostegia

False Dragon's Head
North America
Labiatae

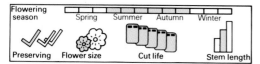

The densely clustered snapdragon-like
flower spikes of Physostegia are an
attractive addition to border plantings from
summer into autumn. *Physostegia speciosa*
'Rose Bouquet' carries rose-purple flowers in
autumn, height 2½ft (75cm).

 P. virginiana has stiff spikes of deep pink
flowers in summer and autumn, height 3ft
(90cm). A good smaller cultivar is *P.v.* 'Vivid',
with bright pink flowers in autumn, height

Pyrethrum

Poor Man's Chrysanthemum
Persia and Caucasus
Compositae

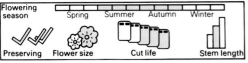

Flowering season	Spring	Summer	Autumn	Winter
Preserving	Flower size		Cut life	Stem length

Pyrethrum 'Eileen May Robinson'

Pyrethrum roseum **is an invaluable plant for early summer, when the main crop of flowers is produced. It forms a clump of much-divided, fern-like foliage at ground level, from which arise long leaf-clad flower stems, each bearing just one single or double, daisy-like flower. A second, much lighter flush of flowers may appear in autumn.**

Several cultivars of this hardy herbaceous perennial are available, in the height range 2½-3ft (75-90cm):

'Bees Pink Delight', large, semi-double flowers of deep, rich pink; 'Eileen May Robinson', single, soft pink flowers; 'Jubilee Gem', large single, bright cerise flowers; 'Vanessa', double, rich pink flowers; 'Kelway Glorious', single, scarlet flowers; and 'Madeleine', double pink flowers, 'White Madeleine', double white flowers.

Cultivation and Propagation *Pyrethrum* is very easy to grow in any well-drained sandy or loamy soil but heavy soils are not suitable unless they can be lightened by the addition of sandy or gritty material. Choose an open sunny position but not an unduly exposed one. Prepare the ground in the winter cultivating deeply and incorporating well-rotted manure or compost. Plants are set out 18in (45cm) apart in each direction in spring. Mulch annually.

Established pyrethrums should be lifted and divided every third year in spring in order to keep them vigorous and floriferous. They will flower very little that summer but more heavily in autumn. This can help to spread the flowering season, as can protecting the plants with cloches in the spring.

Propagation is by division of the plants and is usually done in spring. However, it can be done several times during the summer if plants are in short supply and one wishes to increase one's stock rapidly. For this it is important that the plants are kept growing vigorously and prevented from producing any flowers.

Uses The flowers are daisy-like, with bright pink or red petals surrounding a yellow disc. The informal form is useful as a filling-in flower in a massed arrangement. Some of the strident colours can be used in a modern arrangement. Bunch the flowers tightly together and use them as elements of colour. My earliest recollection of this flower was seeing them massed in a redundant milk jug.

Conditioning An easy flower to condition. Stand them in water for 3 hours, though they will not suffer if they are left for much longer.

Preserving The flowers are large and they can be bulky subjects for pressing or drying in desiccant. Restrict yourself to the more interesting colour forms.

Saxifraga

Saxifragaceae

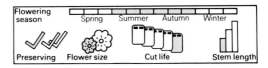

Flowering season	Spring	Summer	Autumn	Winter
Preserving	Flower size		Cut life	Stem length

Saxifraga umbrosa primuloides 'Elliot's Variety'

Saxifraga umbrosa

There are hundreds of Saxifraga species, providing attractive edging and rock garden plants. In the following selection, the delicate, bright flowers mostly appear in early summer, and some types grow particularly well in shade.

Saxifraga umbrosa, the familiar London Pride, bears sprays of deep pink, tiny star-like flowers in early summer, height 12-16in (30-40cm). A useful dwarfer cultivar is *S.u. primuloides* 'Elliot's Variety', which has deep pink flowers and grows to a height of 10in (25cm). *S.u.* 'Aurea Punctata' has sprays of pale pink flowers, and it flourishes in shade, height 1ft (30cm).

S. aizoon, syn. *S. paniculata*, produces star-shaped white flowers in early summer, as does the cultivar *S.a.* 'Correvoniana', height 10in (25cm). An attractive alternative is *S.a.* 'Lutea', with sprays of dainty yellow flowers appearing in early summer, height 6in (15cm). *S.a.* 'Rosea' has pale rose pink flowers, height 10in (25cm).

S. fortunei, originating from China and Japan, flowers in the autumn and prefers a shady spot. It bears drooping clusters of white flowers, height 1ft (30cm).

Cultivation and Propagation The above species are all hardy, easily grown perennials which will thrive in any semi-shady spot in the garden. They require a well-drained gritty soil to which has been added some peat and a little lime. Be careful not to choose a spot which lies wet during the winter time as *Saxifraga* will not survive long under such conditions.

Plants may be propagated by the division of their roots either in the autumn or the spring or they may be increased from seed. When producing plants from seed they must be sown in seed pans containing gritty soil, in spring. These are then placed in a coldframe or under a cloche where germination will occur in 3 to 5 weeks. When the seedlings are large enough to handle they are pricked out into pots or boxes and grown on in these until the autumn, when they are transferred to their permanent flowering places. The plants are then set out 9in (22.5cm) apart in each direction.

Uses Most of the species are associated with rock gardens, an area that is often overlooked by the arranger. Do consider creating a miniature rock garden in a suitable dish that can be left outdoors and brought inside when the flowers are blooming. *S. umbrosa* is, however, an arranger's plant eminently suitable for outlining a small arrangement. The leaves of the larger *Saxifraga* can be put to good use as a disguise for water-retaining foam.

Conditioning As the flower stems are fine, harvest them with a pair of scissors. No preconditioning is required; simply stand them in water for 2 hours.

Preserving The smaller alpine varieties have always been a subject for pressing. Those that grow in clusters can be dried in desiccant, the stems left attached. With their own stems they can be arranged in the same way as their fresh counterparts.

Senecio

Compositae

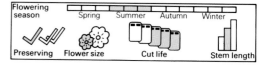

Senecio elegans

Senecio elegans is a half-hardy annual from South Africa, height 1½ft (45cm), well worth growing for its double daisy-like flowers in pink, purple, mauve and white

appearing in late summer. Seed is usually sold in assorted colours.

Cultivation and Propagation It is quite easy to grow. It requires a sunny sheltered situation and a well-drained soil. Some support with twiggy sticks may be necessary.

Sow the seed in the flowering position in spring. Germination takes 2 to 3 weeks. When the seedlings are large enough to handle thin them out to 9in (22.5cm) apart in the row.

Uses The form and colouring of this plant make it most suitable for filling in a design of high summer flowers. Used in profusion, it provides blocks of colour as a contrast to more dominant blooms such as lilies. The colour is sufficiently deep to recess them into the arrangement to create the necessary visual depth without the design looking too heavy.

Conditioning The flowers require about 3 hours conditioning. Strip away any foliage that will be submerged and stand them in deep water.

Preserving The flowers have a loose appearance that is quite informal. They can be successfully pressed to form rather striking components in a collage of textures.

The delicate flower sprays of *Vaccaria pyramida*, syn. *Saponaria vaccaria*, look particularly effective when massed. This annual species displays small, dainty pink flowers in sprays on fine branching stems in summer, height 1-2ft (30-60cm).

There are two equally pretty cultivars: *V.p.* 'Pink Beauty', similar to the parent but even more colourful and free-flowering; and *V.p.* 'Alba', with star-like white flowers, height 1½-2ft (45-60cm).

Cultivation and Propagation Plant in a sunny situation in any ordinary garden soil. Propagation is by seed. Sow in spring where flowering is to take place. Thin the resulting seedlings to 8in (20cm) apart. Flowering is throughout the summer.

Uses These delicate flowers growing on a stem of a desirable length for arranging blend perfectly with the pastel shades of summer. Both the white and pink forms can be used, especially with roses and grey foliages.

Conditioning Cut the flowers when the majority are open, remove the lower stem foliage and stand them in deep water for 4 hours.

Preserving Small sprays of flowers preserve well in desiccant and they provide useful background material for miniature arrangements or dried flower pictures.

Vaccaria

Siberia to Persia (Iran) and eastward to Southern Europe
Caryophyllaceae

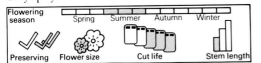

Vaccaria pyramida

Xeranthemum

Southern Europe, the Mediterranean region and Persia (Iran)
Compositae

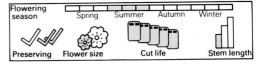

Xeranthemum annuum

*X*eranthemum annuum is an annual which bears single or double, daisy-like flowers in the colour range pink, rose, purple and white. These are borne on upright, branching stems 2ft (60cm) high in summer. Seeds are usually sold as a colour mixture. With its fine grey-green leaves, this species makes attractive summer bedding and a good cut-flower subject. The papery flowers keep their shape and colour well when dried.

Cultivation and Propagation Choose a sunny place in which to cultivate this plant, as it is a true sun lover. Any well drained garden soil will do. The seed may be sown in coldframes and cloches in spring or in the open ground in early summer. If sowing in the flowering situation, sow the seeds very thinly as the resulting plants will need thinning out when they are large enough to handle. Germination usually takes about 2 weeks. Seed can be sown earlier either in the greenhouse or under cloches. Ventilate well on warm days and harden off prior to removing the protective covering. The plants are set out 1ft (30cm) apart. The flowering period is summer..
Uses The scale of these useful flowers is small. Though their value is as a dried flower, they do look most attractive as a fresh component in a posy of mixed coloured flowers.
Conditioning When used fresh, pick the flowers as they open and stand them in water for at least 2 hours. They have the ability to dry in the arrangement, so don't be in haste to discard them when the other flowers have faded.
Preserving They dry remarkably easily. Cut the thin, wiry stems as the flowers open and insert them in a block of dry water-retaining foam. This method prevents the stems being damaged. Keep them in a shaded place to prevent the colour from becoming bleached.

PURPLE

Hosta

Plantain Lily
Liliaceae

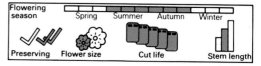

Flowering season		Spring	Summer	Autumn	Winter

Preserving Flower size Cut life Stem length

Hosta fortunei 'Albopicta'

Hostas have bold, heart-shaped leaves, on stout stalks, which may be green or strikingly variegated. These tough, long-lived plants are much valued for the foliage display, which forms weedproof ground cover once established. The short-lived flower spikes, produced from summer to late autumn in the forms described below, come in white, lilac, violet and purple. As Hostas enjoy a shady position, the light leaf variegations and pale flowers provide colour in what may otherwise be dull areas of the garden.
  Hosta fortunei has blue-green leaves and lilac-blue flowers in summer, height 2½ft (75cm). It provides several good cultivars, including *H.f.* 'Albopicta', green-margined yellow leaves and lilac flowers in late summer, height 2ft (60cm); *H.f.* 'Aurea', with leaves at

Xeranthemum annuum mixed

first yellow and turning to light green, and purple flowers in late summer, height 2ft (60cm); and *H.f.* 'Aureomarginata', green leaves edged with golden yellow and mauve flowers in summer, height 2½ft (75cm).

H. 'Frances Williams' has glaucous green leaves with yellow margins which deepen in colour in late summer, and mauve flowers, height 3ft (90cm). 'Royal Standard' is green-leaved, with sweet-scented ivory white flowers in autumn, height 18in (45cm); 'Thomas Hogg' has fine emerald green leaves broadly edged in white, and deep purple flowers in late summer, height 1ft (30cm).

H. undulata has white-streaked leaves and pale lilac flowers, height 1½-2ft (45-60cm).

H. ventricosa is a reliable species with glossy green leaves and purple flowers in late summer, height 2½ft (75cm).

Cultivation and Propagation All species will grow quite happily in any ordinary garden soil, even relatively dry soils, though then they take some years to develop to any size. They prefer moist shady sites. Apply a generous dressing of manure or well rotted garden compost to such soils to improve their moisture retention prior to planting.

Propagation is by division of the crowns in the spring time when new growth begins. Once planted, hostas may remain undisturbed for a number of years. Lifting and dividing takes place in early spring. Plant 12 to 18in (30 to 45cm) apart in each direction depending on the height of the plants.

Uses Most *Hosta* flowers are in the white, white/lilac to rich purple range. They are informally arranged on strong straight stems hanging like bells, with just the tip of the anthers showing. When they are used in massed designs of pastel colours they are an ideal component for establishing height. In this type of colour scheme they may be used in generous quantities as the shape of the flower is not bold or likely to distract from the overall effect. In a scheme of darker shades use fewer numbers, sufficient to create an interesting change of colour. For those of you who prefer the sparse effect of driftwood and a few flowers, this one is perfect. The flowers last a long time, and any faded lower blooms can be carefully removed with little adverse effect. Though you will find the flowers of use, the leaf of the *Hosta* is what will give you the most pleasure. Once your affection for the *Hosta* family has been established you will soon be collecting more than have been named here. The leaf has its own qualities, colour, form and texture. These will instantly tell you where to use them. Fortunately the leaves come in a good range of sizes. Generally they are used to create the focal area. They are unsurpassed as a foil to the delicate tracery of fine ferns or the exquisite shape of a sweet pea.

Conditioning New growth should be cut cleanly from the plant and floated in a dish of water for at least 1 hour and then stood in deep water for a further 2 hours. Mature foliage may be stood in water immediately it has been cut. Flower stems should be cut when the lower flowers are open, as the flowers continue to develop in a limited way after they have been arranged.

Preserving I have not been successful at preserving the leaf of this noble plant. Many will change colour in the autumn, and these can be used in any design providing they have access to a limited amount of moisture. They generally last several weeks before the stem softens and flags permanently.

The flowers may be preserved individually in desiccant. The inside should be filled with desiccant before the flowers are completely covered. Pressing the flowers will give you a rather fine bell-shaped profile.

Hosta 'Thomas Hogg'

Liatris

Kansas Feather
East and South USA
Compositae

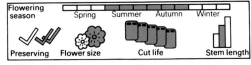

These interesting late-flowering border perennials produce spikes of thistle-like, tufted flowers that open from the top downwards. *Liatris callilepis* carries lilac-purple flowers in late autumn, height 3ft (90cm). *L. pycnostachya* has purple-rose flowers in autumn, height 3-5ft (90-150cm); being tall-growing, this species may need

Liatris pycnostachya

staking or support from wire netting.

The red-purple flowers of *L. spicata* appear in late summer, height 2ft (60cm); this species will tolerate damp soil conditions. *L.s.* 'Alba' is a white-flowered cultivar, *L.s.* 'Kobold' is lilac-mauve.

Cultivation and Propagation Choose a well drained soil in a sunny situation for the fleshy corm-like roots of *Liatris* and set them out 8in (20cm) apart in each direction, taking care that the tops of the corms are only just covered with soil. Planting may be undertaken any time in the dormant period. Plants are left undisturbed for several years before being lifted for division and subsequent replanting once more. Division merely calls for the pulling apart of the clumps of corm-like basal buds which have developed, best done in early spring. You can also treat this plant as a biennial, by growing it from seed sown in a coldframe in late spring, sowing the seeds as thinly as possible. When the seedlings are large enough to handle, set them in a nursery bed in the open 6in (15cm) apart. The resulting plants are transferred to their flowering positions in the autumn.

Uses *Liatris* is a feathery thistle-like flower that has the rare quality of opening from the top of the stem first. It is of an upright nature and can be used for establishing the outline of a formal arrangement. Its lilac-mauve colouration is good with silvered wood and grey foliage to recreate the feeling of the seashore.

Conditioning Wait until about the top inch (2.5cm) of flower has opened before you cut them. Remove any stem-borne foliage and condition the stem in water for about 2 hours.

Preserving To dry them select the flowers when the majority have developed, tie them into small bunches and hang them in a cool dry room away from direct light to preserve the original colour.

Lythrum

Northern temperate regions and Australia
Lythraceae

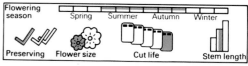

Lythrum salicaria 'Firecandle'

Lythrum salicaria 'The Beacon'

Lythrum has two herbaceous perennial species that have given rise to several cultivars commonly grown. These are useful large plants for damp conditions, all bearing spires of small flowers in summer, some continuing into autumn.

Lythrum salicaria (purple loosestrife) grows wild beside rivers and ponds in Europe. It displays purple-red flower spikes on erect stems, height 3ft (90cm), in summer and autumn. *L.s.* 'Firecandle' has intense purplish-rose, slender spikes in summer, height 3ft (90cm); *L.s.* 'Lady Sackville' flowers from early to late summer in a beautiful rose pink, height 5ft (150cm); *L.s.* 'Robert' has clear pink flowers in summer, height 2ft (60cm); *L.s.* 'The Beacon' has deep carmine flowers in summer, height 2½ft (75cm).

L. virgatum, native to Turkey, is a more slender and compact plant than *L. salicaria*, but is otherwise similar. The cultivar *L.v.* 'Dropmore Purple' has slender, graceful spikes of rose-purple flowers in early to late summer, height 2½ft (75cm); *L.v.* 'Rose Queen' is a fine, bright rose red, flowering in late summer to autumn, height 1½-2ft (45-60cm); and *L.v.* 'The Rocket' is deep magenta-pink, height 3ft (90cm).

Cultivation and Propagation All the *Lythrum* are very easy plants to grow in any ordinary garden soil especially in damp places. They are gross feeders and will require a good dressing of organic matter annually, during the dormant season. They also appreciate the application of a mulch of garden compost, leaf-mould or peat about their roots in spring. Given this kind of treatment they will thrive equally well either in full sun or partial shade and provide lots of cut flowers over many weeks.

Planting may take place at any time during the dormant season. Large growing cultivars of 3ft (90cm) or more should be set out 16 to 18in (40 to 45cm) apart in each direction, while the smaller growing cultivars may be set out 12 to 14in (30 to 35cm) apart in each direction. Keep the plants young and vigorous by lifting and dividing the roots every three to four years. No staking is required for these plants.

Propagation is generally by division of the roots either in the spring or the autumn. It is also possible to propagate by securing half-ripe cuttings in midsummer. These are inserted in a shaded coldframe and rooting will take place in three to four weeks. The resulting plants are then transferred to their flowering places in spring of the following year. *Lythrum* hybrids can also be propagated by seed sown in the open in spring and the resulting plants are thinned out when they are large enough to handle, so that they are left standing 6in (15cm) apart in the row. Transfer to their flowering places in following spring. When flowering commences discard the inferior plants.

Uses *Lythrum* grown in large clumps is a dazzling haze of pink to purple flowers. As the stem is erect and grows quite tall, its chief use in arranging is as outline material. The colour range will blend with most other garden flower colour though I would exclude it from a design that is predominantly yellow.

Conditioning Wait until the lower flowers have started to develop before you cut them. Remove any excess foliage and stand the

flowers in deep water for 3 hours.

Preserving Mature flowering stems can be air dried in the usual way. The small star-shaped flowers can be individually dried in desiccant. Whilst *Lythrum* is notorious for self-seeding the seed head is not very attractive.

Salvia

Perennial sage
Temperate regions
Labiatae

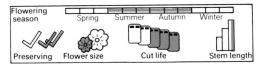

Salvia

Perennial species suitable for borders and mixed plantings include *Salvia haematodes*, with blue-violet flowers in summer, height 3ft (90cm); the flower spikes of the cultivar *S.h.* 'Indigo' are branched and deep blue, height 3½ft (105cm). *S.* × *superba*, syn. *S. nemorosa*, carries violet-blue, branching spikes and red bracts which persist after flowering has ceased, height 32in (80cm). Its flowering period is late summer to autumn. *S. turkestanica* is paler-tinted, with blue-white flowers and pink bracts during summer, height 4ft (120cm).

Cultivation and Propagation *Salvia* will grow in any well drained soil in either full sun or partial shade.

Propagation is by division of the roots during the dormant season.

Uses The value of growing *Salvia* for arranging is in the long life of the cut material. The colour is in the bracts, perhaps the most useful one is *S. turkestanica* where its size and the varying

blend of colour adds considerable interest to any design. The tall species are excellent for creating the outline of a shape and the smaller ones can be used throughout the arrangement.
Conditioning Once the bract has matured and the colour is at its most intense stems should be cut and conditioned in water for 2 hours.
Preserving At the peak of the growing season *Salvia* should be collected and air dried. It is essential to pick only those in perfect condition. Tie them in small loose bundles and hang them up in a dry room. Avoid strong light as this will drain the drying bracts of their colour.

Thalictrum

Meadow Rue
Ranunculaceae

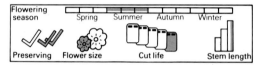

Thalictrum aquilegifolium

Perennial species of Thalictrum are grown for their attractively divided foliage as well as for the unusual fluffy flower heads. *T. aquilegifolium* bears loose, spreading panicles of purple-mauve flowers in summer, height 3ft (90cm). It has two useful cultivars, both 2½ft (75cm): *T.a.* 'Album' with white flowers and *T.a.* 'Thundercloud' with rich purple flowers. The flowers of *T. dipterocarpum* are deep lavender, with prominent yellow anthers, produced from mid to late summer on tall stems up to 6ft (180cm) high. There is also the cultivar *T.d.* 'Hewitt's Double', which has fully double, deep lavender flowers in late summer, height 3ft (90cm).

T. flavum **provides a complete colour contrast, with fluffy heads of lemon yellow flowers rising above deep green leaves during midsummer, height 4ft (120cm).**

Cultivation and Propagation *Thalictrum* requires a fertile, well-drained soil. *T. flavum* prefers a sunny position whle *T. aquilegifolium* and *T. dipterocarpum* are better suited to partial shade. They all need some support from pea stakes and require shelter from strong winds. Plants are set out 1½ to 2ft (45 to 60cm) apart according to the height of the species being planted. If some greenhouse space is available *T. dipterocarpum* can be greatly forced. Roots are potted up in the autumn and brought into the greenhouse. They flower a month earlier than plants outside.
Uses A most useful combination of flower and leaf for the arranger. The foliage is fine and delicate rather like maidenhair fern, a perfect foil for the large plain leaves of the *Hosta* or *Bergenia*. It is a splendid inclusion to an all-foliage design, though it loses impact when too closely associated with variegated leaves. The small flowers are arranged in a loose pyramid shape on the main stem. I prefer to include them around the focal area of a massed arrangement to lighten the effect.
Conditioning Condition them in a cool position. Any stems that show signs of wilting should be removed and the lower section held in boiling water for about 10 seconds. Return it to the water immediately.
Preserving The fern-like leaves are an excellent medium for pressing, the more so when they are young as they are a delightful bright green. Panicles of flowers can be pressed or dried in desiccant.

Thalictrum dipterocarpum

BLUE

blue flowers in summer, height 40in (100cm).

A. orientale produces exquisite ivory-white flowers tinged with lemon, in summer, height 5ft (150cm).

A. carmichaelii, syn. *A. fischeri*, is a reliable species bearing amethyst blue flowers in autumn, height 5ft (150cm).

A. autumnale 'Kelmscott Variety' is another autumn-flowering type with fine lavender-violet flowers, height 4ft (120cm).

Cultivation and propagation *Aconitum* grows most satisfactorily in damp shade, although it will also grow in sun, providing its roots can be kept moist in summer. Any ordinary garden soil will do, if it is well supplied with humus. Incorporate a generous dressing of manure or well rotted garden compost before planting. Established plants should be provided with a mulch of compost or peat early in the sring.

Propagation is by seed sown in the spring either in a coldframe or cold greenhouse. Established plants can be divided either in the autumn or the early spring. Planting may take place at any time during the dormant season. Plants should be set out 2ft (60cm) apart in each direction with their crowns barely beneath the soil's surface. Tall growing cultivars will need some form of support, unless they are growing in a sheltered place.

Uses An exquisite flower for those that favour blue. Used as fresh material it is most useful for creating an outline to a traditional design. The intense colour contrasts well with orange *Kniphofia* or *Alstroemeria* and harmonizes with the steel blue of *Echinops* and *Eryngium*. *A. orientale* is a stunning ivory form, ideal for arranging with pastel shades.

Conditioning To condition the flowers, remove the lower stem foliage and stand them in water for at least 4 hours.

Preserving The flowering stem will air dry. Remove all the stem foliage and hang them upside down in a dry atmosphere. Most of the flowers will be brittle so will need careful handling once the process is complete. Individual blooms can be dried in desiccant.

Aconitum

Monkshood
Europe, Asia
Ranunculaceae

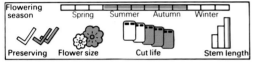

Aconitum napellus 'Spark's variety'

Although a useful garden plant which provides fine spikes of flowers in strong blue shades, Aconitum is poisonous to both man and beast; it should be planted well out of reach of grazing animals, and you should wash your hands after handling any part of it. The following provide flowers from early summer through autumn; flowering is most prolonged if the plants are kept moist.

Aconitum napellus has dark blue flowers on erect spikes in summer, height 4ft (120cm). Its named cultivars include 'Blue Sceptre' with erect, tapering blue and white flower spikes in late summer, height 2ft (60cm); 'Bressingham Spire', violet blue flowers in late summer, height 3ft (90cm); 'Newry Blue', deep blue, flowering in midsummer, height 4ft (120cm); and 'Spark's Variety', deep violet-

Agapanthus

African Lily
South Africa
Liliaceae

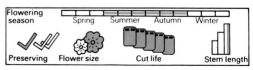

These elegant members of the lily family carry their pretty bell- or trumpet-shaped

Agapanthus 'Headbourne hybrid'

flowers in large, shapely umbels at the top of erect, sturdy stems. The flowers are various shades of blue or white, while the foliage is light green and strap-like.

Agapanthus campanulatus is a hardy species with blue flowers in summer, height 2-2½ft (60-75cm). *A.c.* 'Alba' is a strong-growing white-flowered form, reliable in cold districts, which produces its flowers in late summer, height 2½ft (75cm). *A.c.* 'Isis' grows to a similar height and its intense blue flowers appear during early autumn. There is also the exceptionally hardy race of Agapanthus hybrids, the 'Headbourne hybrids', with flowers in pale to deep blue, a little larger than those of *A. campanulatus*, borne in late summer to early autumn, height 2½-3ft (75-90cm).

A. praecox 'Blue Triumphator' has clear blue flowers in late summer, height 2½ft (75cm). It is not fully hardy, but makes an ideal subject for growing in a large pot or tub, given the protection of a greenhouse or coldframe during winter.

Cultivation and propagation *Agapanthus* flourishes best on light, rich, well-drained soil and requires a sunny situation. Heavy soils will require the introduction of plenty of sand or other gritty material to improve their drainage, and all types of soils will benefit from a good dressing of manure or garden compost. The brittle roots are best planted in the early spring just before growth begins and should be set out 20in (50cm) apart in each direction. Growth will be quite disappointing during the first couple of years, but once the roots penetrate deeply into the soil flowers will be produced quite freely, so be patient. The less hardy species should be protected in winter with a covering of bracken or straw.

Propagation is by root division in early spring.

Uses The larger flowers of the *Agapanthus* are of sufficient scale for use in pedestal or large designs. The smaller varieties make an interesting central feature in traditional arrangements for the home. The colour and sea urchin quality of the flower makes it easy to associate with bleached driftwood and coral in a seascape arrangement.

Conditioning To condition the strap-like leaves, cut them with a pair of sharp scissors, as secateurs would tear and bruise the broad leaves, shortening their cut life. The flowers should be cut when they display a proportion of open bloom. Stand them in deep water for about 3 hours.

Preserving Individual flowers will dry quickly in desiccant. Allow a number of stems to set seed. Collect them after the pod has burst open and the seed dispersed.

Camassia

Quamash
North America
Liliaceae

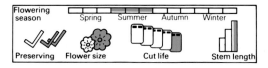

Camassia esculenta

Camassias are hardy bulbous plants with spikes of star-like flowers on upright stems, borne above clumps of fresh green, strap-like foliage in midsummer. They make good border plants but also thrive in a moist, partially shaded location.

Camassia cusickii has flowers of wisteria blue, height 2½ft (75cm). *C. esculenta*, syn. *C.*

raseri, flowers dark blue and is smaller, at 10in (25cm) high. *C. leichtlinii* is a vigorous species and strains are available with white, cream, blue or purple flowers on stems up to 3ft (90cm) high. *C.l.* 'Semiplena' is a particularly prolific, creamy white form.

Cultivation and propagation The bulbs are fairly large and should be planted 4in (10cm) deep and 9in (22.5cm) apart in a deep moist fertile soil, in a sunny or slightly shaded position, in the autumn. Once planted they may be left undisturbed for three or four years, before being lifted and divided. It sets seed quite freely. The seeds are sown as soon as they are ripe ½in (1.25cm) deep and the resulting plants commence flowering 4 years later. Established bulbs should be given a mulch of leaf-mould or peat each spring, and watered during the growing period.

Uses This exquisite flower is still rarely grown by the British flower arranger. The spikes of starry flowers are always noticed first in any arrangement where they are used. The colour is clear and distinct. Its tall growing habit places it in the range of outline material. The statuesque shape lends itself perfectly to formal, symmetrical arrangements.

Conditioning Cut the stem when most of the flowers are open and stand it in deep water for about 2 hours in a cool place. Any tip buds will open within a short period.

Preserving The *Camassia* flower almost demands to be preserved. Remove individual flowers and dry them in desiccant. The seed head, though not as striking as the fresh flower, will develop on the plant and dry naturally. Collect this before it is damaged by wind and rain.

Campanula

Bellflower
Northern hemisphere
Campanulaceae

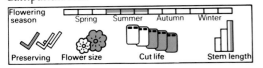

C ampanula is a large genus containing annual, biennial and perennial species variously suitable as border plants, summer bedding, and rock garden or edging plants. Two species and their cultivars are recommended here, both providing a generous display of their cup-shaped flowers through summer.

The biennial species is *Campanula medium* (Canterbury bell, or cup and saucer flower), which is native to southern Europe. This

Campanula medium

species carries its spikes of white, pink, blue or mauve flowers on strong, erect stems, height 1-3ft (30-90cm).

C.m. 'Calycanthema Mixed' is a splendid blend of all the available colours and the flowers are large, height 1½ft (45cm); it is also possible to buy the seeds in single colours.

C.m. 'Bells of Holland' is a dwarfer type, growing into a compact, conical plant 1½ft (45cm) high, with the same range of flower colours as the species. It is also available as seeds of straight or mixed colours.

C. persicifolia is a native British and European perennial species with spikes of blue bell-shaped flowers, height 3ft (90cm). There are several excellent cultivars, some with double flowers, including *C.p.* 'Alba', white flowers, height 3ft (90cm); *C.p.* 'Fleur de Neige', double white flowers, height 3ft (90cm); *C.p.* 'Pride of Exmouth', semi-double powder blue flowers on slender stems, height 2ft (60cm); *C.p.* 'Telham Beauty', single large china blue flowers, height 3ft (90cm); and *C.p.* 'Wirral Belle', double violet-blue flowers, height 3ft (90cm).

Cultivation and propagation *Campanula* needs a fertile, well drained soil. It grows well on chalky soils, so if you have any doubt about the lime status of your soil apply a dressing of lime prior to introducing these plants. Choose a sheltered yet sunny situation.

Sow the seed of *C. medium* where flowering is to take place. If you have a few cloches to protect and encourage early growth sow in early spring, otherwise wait till late spring. Early sowings will give bigger and better plants. Germination takes about three weeks. Thin the seedlings out to stand 9 to 18in (22.5 to 45cm) apart. The resulting plants will flower in midsummer the following year.

Campanula persicifolia 'Telham Beauty'

C. persicifolia and its cultivars are propagated by division of the roots in the spring. Established plants should be lifted and divided every third year, otherwise the plants will deteriorate. When preparing the ground incorporate some manure or well-rotted garden compost. The plants should be spaced out in their flowering positions 15in (37.5cm) apart in each direction. For earlier flowering, plants can be carefully lifted when they are dormant and be placed in large plant pots in a cool greenhouse for gentle forcing. Flowering should be about a month earlier than normal.

Uses The pastel shades blend well with other summer flowers especially in massed arrangements for weddings and garden parties. The annual species can be used as a complete plant, giving conical sprays up to 3ft (90cm) long for outline material.

Conditioning Cut the stems when the lower flowers are beginning to open. Remove any excess stem foliage and condition them in deep water for 3 to 4 hours. Avoid strong sunlight. If the whole plant is to be used, supply water liberally for several days before cutting.

Preserving The blooms are very delicate, but can be pressed with a certain amount of patience. The dimensional shape is lost, but the profile is most interesting.

Catananche

Cupid's Dart
Southern Europe
Compositae

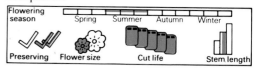

Catananche coerulea

Catananche coerulea produces long-lasting, semi-double, blue or white flowers, similar to cornflowers. These are carried throughout the summer on slender, wiry stems, height 2ft (60cm).

The cultivar *C.c.* 'Major' is most frequently grown; it has lavender-blue flowers with dark eyes and forms clumps of attractive grey-green grassy leaves. *C.c.* 'Bicolor' has blue and white flowers.

Cultivation and Propagation This herbaceous plant is not fussy about its soil. It likes good drainage for its roots and a sunny position. Plant in spring.

Propagation of the species is from seed sown in spring in a coldframe. Germination takes 14 to 21 days. Once the seedlings are large enough to handle prick them out into seedtrays and set out the resulting plants into their permanent places during June. Allow 1ft (30cm) between the plants in each direction. Named cultivars are best propagated by root cuttings taken in winter and placed in a coldframe. Set out resulting plants in late spring.

Uses Although this is a short-lived plant the flower has an extremely long cut life. The grass-like foliage is of little use to the arranger, but the lavender blue flowers are a very useful addition to an arrangement of pastel colours.

Preserving Its major use is as a dried component. The flower resembles a cornflower with short florets and papery bracts. Collect them when they are fully developed, tie them in loose bundles and hang them in a darkened room to prevent excessive loss of colour. To retain the distinct colouration preserve a number in desiccant. Pierce the flower with a wire before the process begins, this will allow you to attach a false wire stem easily when the flower is dry.

Delphinium

Larkspur
Europe
Ranunculaceae

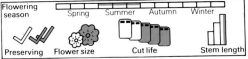

Delphinium 'Blue Bees'

Delphinium 'Blue Jade'

Delphinium 'Blue Tit'

The Delphinium genus includes popular annual and perennial plants with showy spikes of spurred flowers. Though notable for the range of beautiful blues, there are also fine pink and mauve tints, gentle colours appropriate to themed or mixed borders and informal cottage-garden style plantings. The height range also makes delphiniums adaptable to different types of planting schemes, varying from dwarf cultivars 1½ft (45cm) high to spectacular flower spikes up to 6ft (180cm).

The annual species include *Delphinium ajacis* and *D. consolida*, both often found in seed catalogues listed under their common name, larkspur. These have given rise to some good garden hybrids. 'Giant Imperial Mixed' has double flowers on erect stems in a wide

Delphinium 'Blue Nile'

range of colours, height 5ft (150cm). This is best treated as a biennial, with direct sowing in the open ground where the plants are to flower. Sow in late summer for early summer flowering in the following year.

'Giant Hyacinth Flowered Mixed', another double-flowered type, is best sown in spring. Flowers are white, violet, pink and carmine, height 2½ft (75cm). The characteristic form of hyacinth-flowered hybrids is the densely packed, blunt-tipped flower spike, which is sturdy and weather resistant. 'Dwarf Hyacinth Flowered Mixed' provides plants up to 1½ft (45cm) high with bright flower colours. In addition to mixed colours you may, with a bit of searching, find seeds of single colours.

Many perennial delphinium cultivars have been produced from *D. elatum*, including tall, large-flowered types such as 'Blue Nile', clear blue with white eyes, height 5½ft (165cm) and 'Loch Nevis', mid-blue flowers with white eyes, height 6ft (180cm). Listed below are recommended dwarf and hybrid forms. The flowering period is midsummer; if flower spikes are removed, there may be a second, somewhat inferior and lighter crop in early autumn.

DWARF DELPHINIUMS

'Baby Doll', pale mauve flowers with white eyes, height 4ft (120cm); 'Blue Tit', indigo blue flowers with black eyes, height 3½ft (105cm); 'Blue Jade', pastel blue flowers with dark brown eyes, height 4ft (120cm); 'Cinderella', bright mauve flowers, height 3½ft (105cm); 'Cupid', pale sky blue flowers with white eyes, height 3ft (90cm); 'Pageboy', brilliant mid-blue flowers with white eyes, height 3ft (90cm); 'Blue Fountain', blue, purple and white flowers, height 2ft (60cm).

DELPHINIUM BELLADONNA HYBRIDS

'Blue Bees', clear pale blue flowers with white eyes, freely produced, height 3½ft (105cm); 'Bonita', gentian blue flowers, height 4ft (120cm); 'Cliveden Beauty', sky blue flowers, height 3ft (90cm); 'Lamartine', deep violet-blue flowers, height 4ft (120cm); 'Moerheimii', pure white flowers, height 4ft (120cm); 'Peace', intense blue flowers, height 3½ft (105cm); 'Pink Sensation', light rose pink flowers, height 4ft (120cm); 'Wendy', deep gentian blue flowers flecked with purple, height 4ft (120cm).

DELPHINIUM PACIFIC HYBRIDS

'Astolat', flowers in shades of pink, height 4-5ft (120-150cm); 'Black Knight', rich purple-blue flowers with dark eyes, height 4-5ft (120-150cm); 'Blue Jay', mid-blue flowers with white eyes, height 4-5ft (120-150cm); 'Cameliard', lavender-blue flowers with white eyes, height 4-5ft (120-150cm); 'Galahad', snow-white flowers, height 5-6ft (150-180cm);

'King Arthur', royal purple flowers with white eyes, height 5-6ft (150-180cm); 'Silver Moon', exquisite silver-mauve flowers with white eyes, height 5½ft (165cm); 'Summer Skies', pale blue flowers, height 5ft (150cm).

Cultivation and Propagation These plants like a moist, deep, reasonably fertile soil in an open sunny position. They need shelter against strong winds. Taller varieties need staking. Established perennial plants are usually divided every other year to keep the plants vigorous. It is the usual practice to sow the seeds where flowering is to take place as these plants do not like being transplanted. If a frame or cloches are available sowing may commence in early spring, otherwise a few weeks later. Thin the resulting plants to 10in (25cm) apart in a row.

For perennial delphiniums the propagation of named cultivars is generally either by division of the plants or by basal cuttings taken in spring. Cuttings must be secured from the parent plant before the shoots become hollow at the base (about 4in (10cm) long). They are then placed in a sandy soil in a coldframe to root. Delphinium Pacific Giants can also be grown from seed sown early in the year, either in a greenhouse or in a coldframe. When the seedlings are large enough to handle they are pricked out into 4in (10cm) pots. They are then planted in the open ground that summer, and some flowering will take place in the autumn. Alternatively, sowing may take place in midsummer and the resulting plants are transferred to their flowering positions in the autumn. It is possible to obtain a good selection of delphiniums from a single packet of mixed hybrid seeds if one is willing to undertake some roguing of inferior plants when they show colour.

Uses The form of this flower makes it an ideal outline material for very large arrangements. The flower spikes are less solid than those of the *Antirrhinum* and can be used in a similar way to create a lighter effect. Happily their flowering period coincides with that of the *Campanula* which with their similar colour but contrasting form can be combined to make an harmonious design. After the main spike has flowered, shorter side spikes develop for using in smaller arrangements. The feathery foliage adds considerably to the charm of these flowers.

Conditioning Give them a good drink in deep water for at least 6 hours.

Preserving This is one of the best flowers for air drying. The stem should be cut when it is about two-thirds developed. Remove most of the foliage and tie the stems into loose bundles with sufficient space between each stem to allow the air to circulate. Hang them upside down in a light, warm atmosphere. The process will take between 3 and 4 weeks, then they can be stored in a box until needed. The flowers may look a little crushed after a while, but they can be restored to their original form by applying a jet of steam from a boiling kettle. Don't attempt to dry the flowers when they are damp, as they will invariably start to rot during the drying process.

Echinops

Globe Thistle
S. Europe, Asia
Compositae

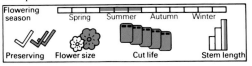

Echinops ritro

Echinops produces blue globe-shaped flowers, spiny until they open, on stiff, erect, branching stems bearing much divided thistly foliage. They have a striking sculptural presence in mixed plantings.

Echinops humilis and its cultivar 'Taplow Blue' flower in late summer; both are 5ft (150cm) high. *E. ritro* has steel blue flowers, also appearing in late summer, height 3ft (90cm).

Cultivation and Propagation Both species are equally easy to grow, as they are not fussy about soil and may be situated in full sun or partial shade. However, they do like to be able to thrust their fleshy tap-roots well down beneath the soil's surface, so some deep cultivation is desirable, with some bulky organic matter worked in.

Propagation is usually by the division of the existing roots in spring. Root cuttings can be taken when the plants become dormant in the autumn. *Echinops ritro* can be propagated by seed sown in the open ground in spring. Germination will take some three to four weeks. When the seedlings are large enough to handle one can either thin out or prick out the seedlings, so that they stand some 9in (22.5cm) apart in the row. The resulting plants are transferred to their flowering location in the late autumn and set out 2ft (60cm) apart in each direction. Once established these plants should be divided every third year.

Uses The mature flowers of the *Echinops* are metallic blue, arranged in a tight ball at the top of the stem. If you remove any side flowers, the central flower will develop considerably. It is coarse in apearance and generally looks at odds arranged with flowers of a delicate form and colour. Its most popular use is in seascape arrangements, the unusual formation of the flower resembles that of a sea urchin.

The flower has an unyielding, permanent quality, which harmonizes well with driftwood. Both foliage and flowers may be used at any stage of development. The leaves have a silvery reverse resembling the foliage of the common thistle.

Conditioning Remove any leaves that will be submerged during conditioning and stand the stems in deep water for about 3 hours.

Preserving The seed heads will mature and dry on the plant, though the calyx will fall in adverse weather. To prevent this happening, collect the stems as the flowers fade and preserve them in glycerine solution. The stem foliage should be removed as this will wither as the stem absorbs the preservative. The seeds are an unusual shape resembling a torpedo. Collect them after the flower has faded, to add textural interest to a seed collage.

Eryngium

Sea Holly
Europe
Umbelliferae

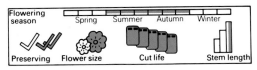

Eryngiums are grown for their beautiful foliage and bracts, which form stiff, spiky ruffs around the domed flower heads. There are several species that between them provide flowers from early summer through to late autumn.

Eryngium alpinum has light blue flowers produced early in the season, height 3ft (90cm).

E. bourgatii is another early-flowering type with steely blue heads, height 2ft (60cm).

Eryngium alpinum

Eryngium oliverianum

introduce any manure, as this plant seems to manage quite well without this.

The common method of propagation is by root cuttings taken in the winter. It may also be grown from seed sown in a coldframe in spring. Germination takes 4 to 6 weeks. Prick out seedlings into 3in (7.5cm) pots, when large enough to handle, and set out the resulting plants in their permanent flowering position in the autumn, allowing a space of 18in (45cm) between plants.

Uses *Eryngium* is a very long lasting cut flower. The head is domed with a frill of feathery but sharp bracts behind it. The visual texture is coarse and when used in traditional designs it should be used with restraint. Generally it is best displayed in free form or modern designs where its dramatic beauty can be seen without distraction. As the common name sea holly indicates, it is very much a part of the seascape arrangement. Flowers that are on the point of drying naturally can be pinned to the back of driftwood to heighten the effect of the seashore.

Conditioning It is an easy flower to condition. The more mature the stems, the less they seem to need to drink.

Preserving The flower bract can be successfully air dried. Collect them once the flower has faded and hang them in bunches in a dry atmosphere. To achieve a bleached effect suspend them close to a source of bright light.

Myosotis

Forget-me-not
Europe including Britain
Boraginaceae

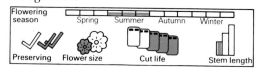

Forget-me-nots are frequently grown as carpeting plants in spring bedding displays, as the tiny blue flowers make a fine background against which the various types of tulips may be seen to advantage. They can be grown in rock gardens or as edging to paths or mixed plantings. The two species described here are perennial, but usually grown as biennials.

Myosotis alpestris produces dense clusters of bright blue flowers with pale yellow eyes. The cultivar *M.a.* 'Blue Spire' has vivid blue flowers on erect stems; *M.a.* 'Royal Blue' has pretty deep blue flowers. Both grow to 1ft (30cm) high and flower in midsummer. *M. oblongata*, syn. *M. sylvatica*, offers the beautiful cultivar 'Blue Bird', with dark blue flowers, height 1ft (30cm).

E. oliverianum and *E. planum* 'Blue Gnome' both flower in mid season: the former has very deeply cut leaves and deep blue flowers, height 2½ft (75cm); 'Blue Gnome' also has deep blue flowers and grows to 2ft (60cm) high.

Species that flower later in the summer are *E. tripartitum*, which has much-branched stems bearing small, spiny, grey-blue flowers, and grows to a height of 2ft (60cm); and *E. verifolium*, an evergreen plant with deeply cut, marbled silver leaves and silver-blue flowers, height 2ft (60cm).

Cultivation and Propagation It prefers a deep, well-drained sandy soil and a sunny situation. Heavy soils can be adapted by the incorporation of sharp sand or other gritty material to improve the drainage. Providing the soil is reasonably fertile there is no need to

Myosotis alpestris 'Royal Blue'

Nepeta

Cultivation and Propagation *Myosotis* will grow in any ordinary garden soil either in light or partial shade. The seeds of both species are sown in the open in early summer. Germination takes two to three weeks. When the seedlings are large enough to handle they are pricked out 6in (15cm) apart in each direction. The resulting plants are transferred to their flowering places in the autumn and planted out 9in (22.5cm) apart in each direction.
Uses Because of their small size these flowers have a somewhat limited use in fresh arrangements, except perhaps as a small posy of welcome on a dressing table. Whole plants may be used in landscape designs by lifting them from the garden and wrapping the root ball in polythene. They do provide the blue colour that is sometimes difficult to obtain and look very natural providing the polythene is well concealed.
Conditioning They only need a short drink of water to condition them. I find that generally they do not appreciate water-retaining foam, so when possible arrange them in water.
Preserving Individual flowers and short sections of stem can be dried in desiccant for using in small arrangements of grasses and blossom or flower pictures.

Nepeta

Catmint
Northern Hemisphere
Labiatae

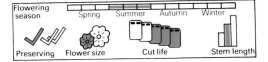

The hybrid *Nepeta* × *faasenii* is a useful ground cover plant, also suitable for edging and for growing among paving stones. It has fragrant grey foliage and lavender-blue flowers which it produces all summer long, height 1ft (30cm).
    N. × *f.* 'Six Hills Giant' is a similar but larger plant, height 2ft (60cm). There is also an intermediate form, *N.* 'Blue Beauty', with many erect lavender-blue flower spikes, height 1½ft (45cm); its grey-green leaves are longer and narrower.

Cultivation and Propagation *Nepeta* likes an open sunny place and will grow on a wide range of soils providing they are well drained. Cut back the stems in the late autumn and fork a small amount of old garden compost into the soil's surface. The roots normally need lifting and dividing every third year, and this provides an opportunity to cultivate the soil and provide a more generous application of manure, prior to replanting.
    Propagation is by division of the roots in spring, just as new growth is about to commence, by half-ripe cuttings taken in summer and rooted in a shaded coldframe, or by seed sown in the open ground during late spring. When the seedlings are large enough to handle they should be thinned out to stand 6in (15cm) apart in the row. They are then left to develop until the autumn, when they are transferred to their flowering places and set out 12in (30cm) apart.
Uses *Nepeta* has a soft colouration that will blend with most pastel colours. The flowers are small and tubular, growing in profusion along the stem. The tall spiky stem is often used as outline material for massed traditional arrangements. The fussy effect can be toned down by including flowers and leaves that are plain and bold. It is not a flower for modern

designs but as the plant is very generous with its flowers it can be used in profuse quantities in terracotta jugs to decorate the kitchen.

Conditioning Select the stems when the flowers are open. Pick them over to remove any dead flowers. No preparatory work is needed to condition them; just stand them in water for 2 hours.

Preserving As the flowers are so small they are best preserved by air drying. Do more than you will need as the flowers tend to become very crisp and fall from the stem.

Nigella

Love-in-a-Mist
Mediterranean
Ranunculaceae

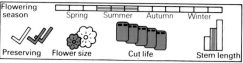

Nigella damascena 'Miss Jekyll'

The hardy annual *Nigella damascena*, with blue or white flowers, is a popular summer bedding plant, particularly suited to the informal cottage-garden style. Its balloon-like seed pods are used in dried flower arrangements.

N.d. 'Miss Jekyll' has semi-double, bright blue flowers and attractively fine, fern-like foliage; there is also a good dark blue strain. *N.d.* 'Persian Jewels' provides a beautiful colour mixture, ranging from rose and pink through mauve, lavender and purple. These plants grow to 18in (45cm) high. *N. hispanica* carries deep blue flowers, height 1-2ft (30-60cm).

Cultivation and Propagation This is a plant

which will flourish in any ordinary garden soil. It is very easily grown. Sow where it is to flower, taking care to sow as thinly as possible. When the seedlings are large enough to handle thin them out to stand 8in (20cm) apart. Seed may be sown in the autumn or the early spring. The earliest flowers are produced by the autumn-sown seeds, when flowering will commence in early summer. The spring sowing will flower later.

Uses A light airy effect is easily achieved with these flowers. The whole colour range blends well with other material that is in the garden at the same time. The cut life is not long but the plant is so prolific that further supplies are always at hand. The fine, fern-like foliage is an added bonus in enhancing the delicate appearance of the flower in a traditional design.

Conditioning They are very easy to condition. Cut them when they are fully open and stand them in deep water for about 2 hours. Do not cut all the flowers, but allow a certain number to develop their characteristic balloon-shaped seedhead.

Preserving The naturally dried heads can be brittle. To obviate this, collect them when they have reached maturity but are still green and preserve them in glycerine solution. The process is rapid; a complete colour change will tell you when it is complete.

Platycodon

Chinese Bellflower
China, Manchuria and Japan
Campanulaceae

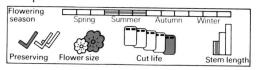

*P**latycodon grandiflorum* is a herbaceous perennial with wide, bell-shaped blue or white flowers 2-2½in (5-6cm) across, borne several to each stem in summer, height 1ft (30cm). *P.g.* 'Album' has blue-tinged white flowers in midsummer, height 2ft (60cm). *P.g.* 'Mariesii' has large, deep purplish-blue flowers in late summer, height 1½ft (45cm).

Cultivation and Propagation These plants grow in any well drained soil, either in light or shade, providing that it is of some depth to enable their brittle roots to penetrate deeply beneath the surface. What they will not tolerate is badly drained wet soil during the cold winter months. Good soil conditions are essential before planting, as once planted they resent any disturbance. On sites which are poorly drained in the winter time, it would be advisable, not only to incorporate sharp sand

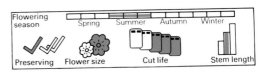

Flowering season | Spring | Summer | Autumn | Winter

Preserving | Flower size | Cut life | Stem length

Platycodon grandiflorum 'Mariesii'

Scabiosa atropurpurea 'Blue Moon'

and other gritty material, but also to plant on a raised bed, in order to solve the drainage problem. Planting takes place in the spring, setting the plants 14in (35cm) apart each way.

Platycodon is a bit late coming into growth in the spring and they die down completely in the autumn, so if one does not mark their exact position with a stake, it will be impossible to locate their position during the dormant season. Top dress with bonemeal in spring and mulch with peat or well-rotted garden compost.

Propagation is by division of the plants·roots in spring or from seeds sown at that time in a coldframe. The resulting plants are transferred to flowering positions the following spring.

Uses This is a plant whose fascination lies in its flower bud. The flower is cup shaped, with five pointed false petals. In the bud stage the points remain closed over each other and it resembles an inflated balloon. The open flower reflexes to reveal some remarkable colour shading. They can be used as a transitional flower or as a focal point in smaller massed designs.

Conditioning Pick the flowers as they are about to open and stand them in water for about 2 hours.

Preserving Only the opened flowers can be preserved either by pressing or drying in desiccant.

Scabiosa

Sweet Scabious or Pincushion Flower
Asia, Africa and Europe
Compositae

The annual species grown as summer bedding for its fragrant, fully double flowers is *Scabiosa atropurpurea*, height 3ft (90cm). The range of flower colours includes blue, purple, lavender, red, pink and white. Seeds are usually offered as mixed blends, but you may find some straight colours, such as *S.a.* 'Blue Moon', with large lavender-blue flowers, and *S.a.* 'Rosette', which is a fine, deep rose pink.

There are also dwarfer strains, such as 'Tom Thumb', growing to a height of 1½ft (45cm); these are more bushy in habit but the flowers are in the same colour range as those of the larger plants.

The commonly grown perennial species for herbaceous borders and mixed plantings is *S. caucasica*, height 2ft (60cm), with flowers in shades of blue and purple or white. Popular cultivars include 'Clive Greaves', with violet-blue flowers and 'Miss Wilmot', which is white-flowered. Among the paler tones, recommended cultivars are 'Moonstone', light blue, height 3ft (60cm); 'Edith', silvery lavender; and 'Bressingham White', a rich creamy white. All of these cultivars flower throughout the summer and as well as making fine garden plants, provide a rich supply of cut flowers.

Cultivation and Propagation *Scabiosa* prefers a well-drained light soil containing some lime, and an open sunny position. An annual dressing of lime may be beneficial. Taller growing *Scabiosa* may need some support with canes and string. Dead head regularly to stimulate new flowers and extend the period of flowering. Established plants of *S. caucasia* need lifting and dividing up in spring every second year, if first class cut flowers are to be assured. Choose young parts of the older plant which have lots of fibrous roots, not ones of a woody nature. If possible, select a fresh site for the plants to occupy. Take the opportunity of fortifying the soil with organic matter well dug in. In mild areas seeds of *S. atropurpurea* may be sown in the autumn and the plants generally survive the winter quite happily, but elsewhere sowing is delayed until the spring, after the frost unless some protection is available in the form of coldframes or cloches. The seed is sown where flowering is to take place. Germination will take 2 to 3 weeks. When the plants are large enough to handle they are thinned out to stand 10in (25cm) apart. Where autumn sowing is possible flowering will commence in early summer. Spring sowings will flower later in the summer.

Propagate *S. caucasica* by division or by seed sown in spring. The seed is sown thinly in seed-boxes containing a sandy compost and then placed in a coldframe to germinate. When the resulting seedlings are large enough to handle, they are pricked out individually into 3½in (8.75cm) pots containing the same compost. They are then placed in the open during the summer months and given the protection of a very well ventilated coldframe through the subsequent winter months.

Uses The shades of blue are beyond compare. Under strong artificial light each flower has a silvery sparkle. The long stems make these suitable for large arrangements, where the somewhat quieter colour shading will not clash with other more dominant materials. They give a natural feel to both landscape and seascape designs. The dwarf strains are excellent for interpretative designs where they can be used to introduce bold areas of colour and form without appearing too sophisticated.

Conditioning They are remarkably easy to condition. All they require is 3 hours in water away from direct sunlight.

Preserving Some of the smaller blooms are ideal for preserving in desiccant. Do this when they have reached their peak of maturity. A small length of stem can be left on.

Veronica

Speedwell
Europe, N. Asia
Scrophulariaceae

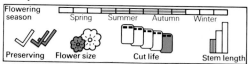

Veronica incana

Selected species of the herbaceous veronicas provide interesting spiky flowers from late spring through summer to autumn. All are easy to grow and need no staking. They all last well as cut flowers.

Veronica gentianoides produces dainty light blue flower spikes in late spring, height 2ft (60cm).

V. incana is particularly noteworthy, not only for its short spikes of deep blue flowers, but for the additional colour feature of its silvery-grey, lance-shaped foliage. This is a dwarf plant, 1ft (30cm) high, which flowers during summer.

V. longifolia bears graceful spikes of lilac-blue flowers during summer, height 2½ft (75cm). Its cultivar *V.l.* 'Forester's Blue' is a little shorter at 2ft (60cm), and has deep blue flowers.

V. spicata has bright blue flowers borne in dense spikes during summer, height 1½-2ft (45-60cm). This has a bright blue cultivar which is an earlier-flowering form, *V.s.* 'Kapitan', height 1ft (30cm).

Alternative flower colours come from *V.s.* 'Barcarolle', rose pink, late summer and autumn, height 2ft (60cm); and *V.s.* 'Heidekind', wine red flowers in summer, height 20in (50cm).

V. teucrium has lavender-blue flowers in

slender spikes in summer; a desirable cultivar is *V.t.* 'Crater Lake' with exquisite, vivid blue flower spikes, height 1ft (30cm).

Cultivation and Propagation These plants will grow in any reasonably fertile garden soil which is well drained. The presence of sand or other gritty material in the soil is very much to their liking. While they like a sunny situation they will also tolerate light shade. Once planted they may remain undisturbed for three or four years, before it becomes necessary to lift and divide their fibrous roots. Planting may take place at any time during the dormant season but, is best in the early spring. The roots of the plants should be set out some 12 to 16in (30 to 40cm) apart in each direction. When dividing old roots select some of the younger crowns and discard with the remainder. Established

plants should be provided with a light mulch of well rotted garden compost about their roots each spring and this should be forked in each autumn.

Propagation can be accomplished in one of three ways. First, by the division of the plants during the dormant season. Second, by cuttings secured in the spring or early summer. These are inserted in a coldframe or cloche to encourage rapid rooting and the glass is shaded to protect the cuttings. New plants can also be propagated from seeds. The seed is sown in the open, during the early summer. Germination will take 14 to 21 days. When the seedlings are large enough to handle they are thinned out to stand 8in (20cm) apart in the row. The resulting plants may then be transferred to their flowering positions either in the autumn or early the following spring.

Uses *Veronica* provides some of the deeper shades of blue that arrangers are fond of. The flower spike is erect with a luxuriant growth of glossy stem foliage. As outline material the darker shades such as 'Crater Lake' and 'Heidekind' link perfectly with *Penstemon*, *Scabiosa* and *Erigeron*. The pale colouration of 'Kapitan' is an attractive adjunct to a traditional design of pastel tones.

Conditioning The only conditioning problem that is likely to be encountered is with the stem foliage. Excessive amounts left on the stem tend to prevent an adequate supply of moisture reaching the flowers. Remove at least two-thirds of the leaves and stand the flower stem in water for 3 hours.

Preserving The very small flowers can be dried in desiccant, though it will be a tedious job. Allowing the seed spike to develop will give you suitable pieces of tall material for arrangements of preserved foliages.

Veronica longifolia 'Forester's Blue'

Veronica spicata

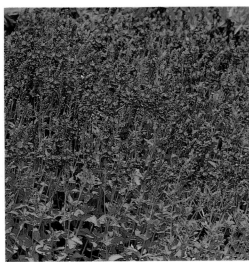

Veronica teucrium 'Crater Lake'

GREEN

Euphorbia

Euphorbiaceae

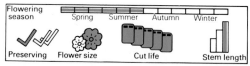

Flowering season	Spring	Summer	Autumn	Winter

Preserving   Flower size   Cut life   Stem length

Euphorbia robbiae

Euphorbia wulfenii

Euphorbia is a very large genus of about one thousand species with widely different habits. It embraces annual and perennial plants, shrubs and trees, which are distributed worldwide. Several of the herbaceous species provide unusual green flower heads that create a fine sculptural effect in an all-green or mixed colour planting.

Euphorbia epithymoides, syn. *E. polychroma*, is early flowering, its sulphur yellow flower bracts appearing in spring; these fade to green and stay green through summer. It is a trouble-free plant of neat bushy habit, height 1½ft (45cm).

E. griffithii 'Fireglow' has orange-red flower bracts during early summer, after which they fade to green, height 2½ft (75cm).

E. palustris has flattish heads of greeny yellow flowers and lush green foliage, height 3ft (90cm). The flowering period is early summer, and the plant grows best where the soil contains plenty of moisture.

The flower heads of *E. robbiae* are pale yellow to green, appearing in early spring, and the foliage is dark green, height 2-2½ft (60-75cm).

E. characias wulfenii has dense spikes of blue-green, evergreen leaves topped by sulphur yellow bracts during spring, height 3ft (90cm).

Cultivation and propagation All species grow quite satisfactorily in poor soil either in direct sun or partial shade. *E. robbiae* is inclined to run in good soil. Plants should be set some 1½ to 2ft (45 to 60cm) apart in each direction, during the dormant season. Propagation is either by seed, which is sown immediately it is harvested, or by division of the plants once the flowers have faded.

E. wulfenii is quite good at sowing its own seeds when they are ripe, in the immediate vicinity of where it is growing, and the resulting plants flower in their second year.

Uses The charm of this popular arranging plant lies in its acid green flower bracts. They are an excellent highlight when used as focal material in an all-foliage design. Some of the larger varieties make an ideal alternative flower for modern arrangements. As they have a long cut life one or two heads arranged on pins with a branch of foliage make a suitable design, and they can be quickly replaced as they fade.

Conditioning The cut stem exudes a caustic sap. This must be staunched immediately over a naked flame for 10 to 20 seconds and the stem then placed in water for 3 hours.

Preserving The fresh flowering stem will not preserve with any degree of success. Let a number of stems dry naturally in the garden and collect them before they are damaged by any adverse weather.

Ferns

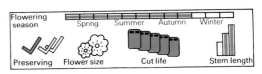

Flowering season	Spring	Summer	Autumn	Winter
Preserving	Flower size		Cut life	Stem length

Ferns are extremely useful plants for shady, moist areas of the garden where few other species can thrive. They may provide a feature in their own right, or a lush green background for flowering plants, which can be particularly rich during the growing season from spring to autumn. The following selection provides variations of colour and texture, and a range of heights.

Asplenium
Polypodiaceae

Asplenium scolpendrium (the hart's tongue fern) is a most adaptable subject with bright green, lacy fronds, height 1½ft (45cm). Once planted it needs the minimum of attention and will even grow successfully on chalky soil.

Athyrium
Polypodiaceae

Athyrium filix-femina (lady fern) is a temperate species native to Europe, with lovely large, lacy, pale green fronds, height 2-3ft (60-90cm).

Dryopteris
Polypodiaceae

Dryopteris filix-mas (male fern) is indigenous to Britain and Europe, and other temperate regions of the world. It has pale green, shuttlecock-like fronds, height 2-3ft (60-90cm). It grows robustly and makes good ground cover.

Osmunda
Osmundaceae

Osmunda regalis (royal fern) is a widespread species which requires a very moist situation near a stream or pond if it is to be grown successfully. It has graceful fronds divided into large leaflets, which are bright green in spring and summer; with the approach of autumn these become reddish-brown in colour, height 4ft (120cm) or more.

Polystichum
Polypodiaceae

Polystichum setiferum (shield fern) has elegant deep green, lance-shaped fronds, height 3ft (90cm), which in mild districts retain their colour during winter if planted in a sheltered site. This species does equally well in a sunny or shady location, provided the soil remains moist.

Cultivation and propagation Choose a site which gives some protection from the cold winds in the spring so as to protect the newly developing fronds. If there is any doubt about the soil's ability to retain moisture apply a generous application of well-rotted leaf mould, well-rotted garden compost or peat, before planting. Drought is the main enemy of hardy ferns. Planting is undertaken during the dormant season. In the spring mulch to retain soil moisture. This may be with rotted garden compost or peat. The mulching must be undertaken annually, so as to recreate the natural growing conditions to which ferns are accustomed.

Propagation is by division in spring.
Uses If you have the space to grow the five types mentioned, you will have a supply of interesting foliage that will be of use from the spring through to mid-autumn. They are foliages for use in traditional designs, landscapes and informal arrangements. The solid form is a useful outline material in bold designs. The finer form (Lady Fern) looks more

attractive in an arrangement that is at close quarters, as in a dinner table arrangement. Fronds that are in the process of unfurling may be arranged in a modern way, using a limited number with a piece of driftwood or other sculptured leaves.
Conditioning Immature foliage may be a little difficult to condition. Burn the end of the stem over a naked flame and stand it in deep water for about 4 hours. Mature stems will condition without reducing the stem end to charcoal, though I always play safe and burn them before conditioning.
Preserving Ferns can be preserved by pressing them between sheets of newspaper and laying them under a carpet. The fronds tend to be brittle and will disintegrate with careless handling. The pressing must be done when the fronds are fully mature.

Molucella

Syria and the Eastern Mediterranean
Labiatae

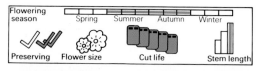

Molucella laevis

Molucella laevis (bells of Ireland) is a boldly shaped plant with tall flower spikes composed of large, pale green, bell-shaped calyces surrounding small white flowers. It makes an interesting and unusual border plant, height 1½ft (45cm) and is often grown particularly for the provision of cut flowers, which can be used both fresh and dried in arrangements.

Cultivation and propagation *Molucella* thrives best in light sandy soils of only moderate fertility and prefers an open sunny situation. If the weather is warm and dry during the early establishment of this plant watering will be necessary.

Although *M. laevis* is a perennial, it is treated as hardy annual and it can either be grown entirely in the open or an earlier start can be made with the aid of coldframes or cloches. The earliest sowing, with some protection, takes place in spring. Sowings in the open can take place in early summer. Germination is likely to be a gradual process over some 14 to 21 days, or even longer. The resulting plants are thinned out to stand 8in (22cm) apart. Early sowing will produce spikes ready for cutting during midsummer, while sowings made later in the open ground will be available for cutting in autumn. It is also possible to sow seeds in midsummer and give the plants some protection with coldframes and cloches to provide spikes for cutting in late autumn. The actual time of cutting is a matter of personal judgment for as the flowers develop it will be seen that the stems continue to lengthen with the calyces becoming further apart.

Uses Very few plants are as versatile as this. It is much prized by arrangers as fresh plant material, providing spikes of light green calyces up to 2ft (60cm) long as outline material for the largest arrangements. The smaller, side spikes are equally useful when working on a more modest scale. When the stem is growing in the garden it has a rather confused appearance, due to the presence of the leaf which obscures the calyces.

Conditioning Cut the fresh stems when they have reached their maximum development. Take off all the foliage and the lower calyces. Stand them in water for at least 4 hours in a cool room away from direct sunlight.

Preserving To preserve them again remove the stem foliage and lower calyces and stand them in a solution of glycerine and water. They are prone to wilting during the first few hours of preserving so it is essential to give them a certain amount of support. The process is quite rapid. After 3 days remove them from the solution. They will probably retain a certain amount of green colouring. Hang them upside down from a convenient line to continue the preserving, for any residual preservative in the stem will continue to act. If the position is against a window the colour will lighten even more. The tip of the stem often refuses to accept the solution, but this can be removed without damaging the stem. Store them in a box in a damp-free atmosphere. Should they get crushed they can be revived by a jet of steam from boiling water.

Ornamental grasses

Gramineae

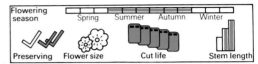

Flowering season		Spring	Summer	Autumn	Winter

Preserving   Flower size   Cut life   Stem length

Grasses are undemanding but pleasantly decorative plants, providing a colour range from various greens to gold and cream, foliage textures from fine feathery tufts to strongly delineated sprays of graceful lance-shaped leaves, and in some cases the added attraction of small plumed flower heads or pod-like seedheads.

Coix lacryma-jobi

Stipa pennata

As well as being useful garden features for a naturalized area or to add texture to a mixed planting, grasses provide plenty of valuable material for arrangements, particularly suited to dried flower work. The following subjects are recommended for both purposes.

Agrostis nebulosa (cloud grass) is a tufted grass with panicles of what look like lots of dainty flowers during late summer, height 1½ft (45cm). This species is a native of Spain.

Briza maxima (pearl grass) is another tufted form with mid-green foliage and panicles of nodding spikelets, pale green tinged with purple, from early to midsummer, height 1½ft (45cm). It is native to the Mediterranean region and the Canary Islands.

Briza minor (little quaking grass) is also a tufted type which produces panicles of erect spikelets during late summer, height 1ft (30cm). This is a native of western Europe and the Mediterranean.

Coix lacryma-jobi (Job's tears) is a species of vigorous growth. It produces thick maize-like mid-green leaves and decorative racemes of pearly grey seeds in autumn, height 2-3ft (60-90cm). A native of tropical regions of India and China, it is more tender than other species recommended here; it needs sowing in a warm greenhouse or frame in spring.

Hordeum jubatum (squirrel tail grass) is a tufted grass with arching, feathery, silver-grey flower plumes during midsummer, height 1½ft (45cm). This is native to both North and South America, and Siberia.

Lagurus ovatus (hare's tail grass) is a European and British native species which produces panicles of soft, furry, creamy flower heads during midsummer, height 16in (40cm). This is best treated as a biennial. Sow the seeds in pots in the early autumn and provide the plants with the protection of a cold frame or cloches during the winter months. Give ventilation during mild spells of weather. Harden the plants off and plant in the open in late spring, 9in (22.5cm) apart.

Panicum is a large genus of annual and perennial grasses which are mostly native to the warmer parts of the world. *Panicum virgatum rubrum* is a hardy perennial which is native to North America. It has crimson-tinged foliage and in autumn bears sturdy stems of much-branched flower sprays, height 3ft (90cm). It is propagated by division in spring.

Phalaris canariensis is a tufted grass commonly grown for its attractive ovate spikes. It flowers in midsummer, height 1½ft (45cm). This species is a native of the Mediterranean region.

Briza maxima

Panicum virgatum

Lagurus ovatus

Stipa (feather grass) is a native of Europe and Siberia. *Stipa pennata* is of erect habit and has bright green leaves, height 3ft (90cm). During summer it produces silky flower plumes in creamy buff, which are particularly good for drying. Seed should be sown in a greenhouse in spring and later planted in open ground.

Cultivation and propagation Any ordinary, reasonably well drained soil will do for growing the grasses. They do not need to be on full view, so a corner of the kitchen garden will do just fine, providing that it is in a sunny position. All one then has to do, is to wait for the grasses to flower. Immediately they are seen to be doing this, cut the flowering grasses with as long stems as possible and hang them up to dry in a cool dark place. Do not wait till the whole of the flowers are at their maturest, as by this time they will be past their best for drying for use in winter decorations.

With the exception of *Coix Lacryma-Jobi*, *Lagurus ovatus*, *Panicum* and *Stipa* the seed is sown in the open ground in spring where the grasses are to flower. Germination may take some two to three weeks. When the grasses are large enough to see quite clearly, one can take a hoe and leave small clumps of the young grasses at 9in (22.5cm) intervals.

At harvest time it is well worthwhile making a trip out into the countryside to collect a few heads of barley, oats, millet and wheat, as these also make an important contribution to the dried floral arrangements either in their natural colours or dyed.

Uses With enterprising seedsmen introducing new kinds for us to try there is really no excuse for not devoting a corner of your garden to grasses and wild flowers. Grasses will blend with any style of arrangement, though they are more at home in the natural landscape designs. The tall nodding heads of grass seed blend perfectly with preserved material. As the harvest will be most prolific, you will be able to create arrangements composed of grasses only.

The containers for this type of design should be unsophisticated and if possible unglazed to enhance the natural atmosphere.

Conditioning Grasses need almost no conditioning. *Stipa* benefits from 2 hours in deep water. They seem to suffer no ill effect if kept dry after cutting.

Preserving Some grasses are best left until they have dried naturally. Others, once they have ripened, tend to shed seed which reduces their value. Preserving them in glycerine when the heads are mature and still green will lengthen their effective life as dried plant material.

Considerable amounts of dried and dyed grasses are available today, but the colours are often harsh and strident. Experimenting with cold water dye, I am sure that you can produce a more tasteful effect at a fraction of the cost.

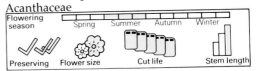

WHITE

Acanthus

Bears' Breeches
Southern Europe
Acanthaceae

Acanthus spinosus

This plant bears foxglove-like spikes of flowers on sturdy, erect stems and has attractive large, glossy foliage. *Acanthus mollis* and *A. spinosus* produce white and purple flowers in late summer, heights 3ft (90cm) and 4ft (120cm) respectively. *A. longifolius*, flowering in late summer, is a more compact plant, height 2½ft (75cm), with lilac flowers.

Cultivation and propagation These are deep rooted plants, requiring a soil rich in humus and well drained. They prefer a sunny situation but will tolerate partial shade. Once planted, Acanthus may be left undisturbed for several years so it is important that the soil is well prepared. Deep cultivation, to a depth of 18in (45cm), is a prerequisite. Heavy soils should have coarse sand and other gritty material incorporated at this time, and all types of soil should be given a good dressing of manure or well rotted garden compost. Planting may take place at any time during the dormant season. Set the plants 2ft (60cm) apart in each direction. Established plants should be mulched with peat or leaf-mould each spring.

Propagation can be by division, in the autumn or winter. Acanthus can also be propagated by root cuttings. The easiest way of all to propagate this plant is from seed. As soon as the seeds are ripe in the autumn, soak them in water for 12 hours and then sow them directly into the soil in a coldframe. Cover the frame with glass throughout the winter. Pot up the plants when they are large enough to handle and place them back in the coldframe. Remove the glass during the late spring and set the new plants out in the permanent positions early the following spring.

Uses The tall flowering stems are best suited to bold vertical designs. Their rough textural appearance associates well with driftwood and the large smooth leaves of *Hosta* or *Fatsia japonica*. They may be cut at any stage of growth, though those stems that you wish to preserve should be left to reach their maximum height.

Conditioning The flowers condition very easily. All they require is a deep drink of water for about 3 hours.

Preserving The stems will preserve automatically if left on the plant until the autumn. To prevent any damage by harsh weather they may be collected when the seed pods have developed and hung up in an airy atmosphere to dry. Preserving the stem in glycerine solution will extend the life of the preserved material considerably. Cut the stems when the seed pods have developed, remove any faded flower petals, and stand them in the solution. The stem will change colour to dark brown, while the calyx varies from pale biscuit to brown, and preserving may take up to a fortnight.

Astrantia

Masterwort
Asia and Europe
Umbelliferae

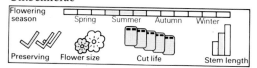

Astrantia is a herbaceous perennial with broadly ovate, glossy green leaves. *Astrantia involucrata* produces its near-white

Astrantia involucrata

star-like flowers continuously through summer and into autumn, height 2ft (60cm). *A.* 'Margery Fish' also produces white flowers over a similarly long period, height 32in (80cm).

Attractive colour variations are *A. maxima*, with shell pink flowers in summer, height 1½ft (45cm) and *A. rubra*, dark crimson, height 16in (40cm).

Cultivation and propagation *Astrantia* likes a moist soil, and will grow equally well in sun or shade. Propagation is either from seed which is sown under glass during the spring or by division of the roots of established clumps in winter.

Uses The flower of the *Astrantia* is small but exquisite and for this reason should be confined to small delicate designs where the full beauty can be seen. The shell pink and wine crimson blend with most colours and look particularly fascinating arranged in a seashell. The flower resembles a pin cushion with numerous filaments growing in a dome on a frill of false petals.

Conditioning Cut the flower stem when the top flower is fully developed. Stand them in a container of water for about 2 hours to condition.

Preserving The flower is too intriguing not to preserve. The ideal method is desiccant. Providing the stem is reasonably thin it can be left attached to the flower for drying. If the stem appears fleshy it will not preserve at the same rate as the flower and is best removed.

Convallaria

Lily of the Valley
Europe
Liliaceae

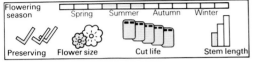

Convallaria majalis

Convallaria majalis is a hardy British native
plant which thrives in any moist, shady
place. It produces its fragrant, white, bell-
shaped small flowers during early summer,
height 6in (15cm).

Cultivation and propagation This is one of
those perennial plants which can be depended
upon to flower regularly each year in the
garden and requires the minimum of
attention. Ideally, it prefers a heavy loam. If
the soil is light you will need to incorporate a
copious dressing of manure or well-rotted
garden compost, prior to planting. The site
cultivation should be deep and thorough. The
crowns of the plants should be set out 1ft
(30cm) apart in each direction, with the tops of
the crowns scarcely beneath the soil's surface.
Planting is best undertaken during the late
autumn. Every few years, take the opportunity
of lifting and dividing the roots during the
dormant season and at the same time fortify
the soil with a fresh dressing of manure or
garden compost. Alternatively, one can supply
top dressing and mulch annually.
   Where a warm greenhouse is available,
established roots of *Convallaria* may be lifted
and gently forced to produce fragrant flowers
in the early spring time. When flowering has
finished they may be planted outside in the

garden once more to recover their strength.
Uses This small but elegant flower is a delight
to cut and bring indoors. Place them in a
simple glass vase or dish without artificial
support. In deep water they will last for at
least a week. The leaves of *Convallaria* are
glossy green and extremely tough, of
considerable use for concealing mechanics in
mixed flower arrangements.
Conditioning Where the flowers are to be
simply placed in deep water there is no need
to condition them. If water-retaining foam is
used, stand the cut flowers in a tumbler of
water for 2 hours.
Preserving To preserve them cut the stems
when the flowers are fully developed and bury
them in desiccant. The stem is quite thin and
will dry with very little distortion.

Cortaderia

Pampas Grass
Temperate South America
Gramineae

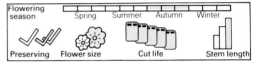

Cortaderia selloana 'Sunningdale Silver'

This is a very small genus of tall-growing
perennial grasses; their silky white plumes
form a spectacular focal point in isolation, or
in a mixed planting. They also make an
excellent contribution to a themed white or
green garden.
   The species most frequently grown is
Cortaderia selloana, syn. *C. argentea*, which in
autumn displays silvery plumes on stiff stems

above a dense tuft of long, narrow, arching leaves, height 9½ft (285cm).

There are several fine cultivars: *C.s.* 'Gold Band' is very similar to the species, height 6ft (180cm), and its leaves are striped green and gold; *C.s.* 'Silver Comet' has white-striped leaves. *C.s.* 'Sunningdale Silver', height 5-7ft (150-210cm) has silvery white plumes slightly larger than those of the species.

C.s. 'Pumila' is a dwarf form only 4ft (120cm) high, but nevertheless producing some very attractive shapely plumes on stiff stems.

For use in flower arrangements, the plumes are best cut as soon as they emerge as, if they are left very long, their general appearance begins to deteriorate.

Cultivation and propagation A deep sandy loam is the ideal for this plant, but it will grow satisfactorily upon a wide range of soils providing they are both deep and well drained. It needs a sunny sheltered site. *Cortaderia* could be planted in the lawn and would make a fine special feature in the garden if so positioned. Planting is best undertaken in the early spring, just when new growth is about to commence. Established clumps of this giant grass will multiply over the years if left undisturbed. The remains of the previous year's growth are trimmed back in the spring, each year. Propagation is by division of the clumps of grasses in the spring.

Uses Most people recognise *Cortaderia* by its more familiar name, Pampas grass. In the past it has been used in an unimaginative way often to merely fill up a quiet corner of the house or as something to stand at the bend of the stairs. Used in limited quantities it can be a very long lasting piece of outline material in pedestal or large-scale designs. I prefer to use it as fresh plant material when the plumes are a shining mixture of cream and green. It can be removed from the arrangement afterwards and dried.

Conditioning It requires very little conditioning, an hour or two in deep water.

Preserving Pampas will dry on the plant, but is prone to continuous seed dispersal. Preserve the stem in glycerine at the point of maturity. It should be reasonably fluffy and display a silvery sheen. Preserving in this way will hold the seed firm without reducing the bulk of the plume.

Gypsophila

Baby's Breath
S. Europe and Asia Minor
Caryophyllaceae

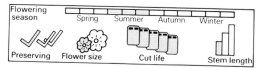

Gypsophila paniculata

Gypsophila brings a touch of delicacy to a border planting, its loose panicles of many tiny, star-like flowers creating a cloudy drift of highlighting in a colour themed or mixed colour bed. The white-flowered forms are particularly effective, but there are also cultivars that provide a range of pretty pinks. Gypsophila is much used in flower arrangements, both when it is freshly cut and when it is dried for winter decoration.

Gypsophila elegans is an annual species producing panicles of small, dainty flowers in white, rose or pink. This is very popular for cut flowers, and white is the colour most commonly grown. Recommended cultivars include *G.e.* 'Alba', with pure white flowers; *G.e.* 'Crimson', bright carmine; and *G.e.* 'Rosea', fine rose pink. All grow to 1½ft (45cm) in height.

The hardy perennial *G. paniculata* forms a mound of much-branched panicles bearing tiny white flowers throughout the summer. The small-scale leaves are an attractive grey-green. *G.p.* 'Bristol Fairy' is a superior form with a mist of double white flowers; *G.p.* 'Flamingo' produces a cloudy haze of tiny double pink flowers, and is slightly later flowering. All grow to a height of about 4ft (120cm). Also worthy of attention is *G.p.* 'Rosy Veil', height 18in (45cm), whose tiny double flowers gradually turn from white to pink.

Cultivation and propagation Any well drained soil is suitable providing that it is not deficient in lime. This can be remedied with a top dressing of hydrated lime. Choose a sunny position for the plants and loosen the soil deeply as *Gypsophila* push their long fleshy roots way down into the ground so that they can withstand any long summer drought. Planting takes place during spring, when the taller varieties are set out 3ft (90cm) apart in each direction and the short ones 20in (50cm) apart each way.

Seeds of *G. elegans* may be sown in the open in autumn for plants which will flower the following spring. A second sowing may be made in spring in the open ground to flower later in the summer. It is particularly important that the soil should not be too rich for the autumn sown plants, otherwise they will not survive the winter. Earlier flowering from the autumn sown *Gypsophila* can be produced if one is able to provide it with some protection from December onwards. When the seedlings are large enough to handle thin them out to 8in (20cm) apart in the row.

Gypsophila paniculata may be propagated either by seeds or by cuttings. Seeds are sown in the open ground, during early summer taking care to sow the seeds as thinly as possible. When the seedlings are large enough to handle, thin the plants out to 8in (20cm) apart in the row. The resulting plants are transferred to their permanent positions in the early autumn. *G. paniculata* is also easily propagated from root and shoot cuttings, inserted in sand in a closed coldframe, any time in summer. Shoots are most suitable for rooting when they begin to harden.

Uses This flower has a lightening effect wherever it is used. The small widely spread flowers break up the outline of more solidly formed or deeper coloured material used with it. It is not a flower to be used to excess. Treat it like thin clouds in a summer sky as too much can make an arrangement look fussy and distracting.

Conditioning It has an exceptionally long cut life and it requires only the simplest of conditioning, 4 to 6 hours in water.

Preserving The flowers can be pressed or desiccant dried, an exquisite form for those of you who enjoy creating arrangements in miniature. Air drying is the easiest method of preserving. Pick when most of the flowers are open, and tie them in loose bundles. Suspend them in a light airy room until they look and feel dry, and slightly crisp to the touch.

Helleborus

S. Europe and Western Asia
Ranunculaceae

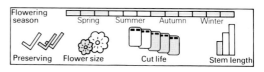

Helleborus niger

Helleborus is a herbaceous perennial of special value as it flowers outdoors at a time when other flowers are very scarce.

Helleborus niger (Christmas rose) produces delightful trusses of saucer-shaped white flowers, sometimes faintly tinted pink, in midwinter, height 1ft (30cm). *H. foetidus* produces trusses of creamy green flowers edged with maroon, in spring, height 2ft (60cm). *H. orientalis* (Lenten rose) is a very variable species with flowers from white to plum purple and spotted inside with crimson and maroon. It has a long flowering period, from autumn to spring, height 12-16in (30-40cm).

Cultivation and propagation Hellebores like a rich, moist, well-drained soil, in a shady location. If there is any doubt about the level of fertility give the soil a copious dressing of manure or well-rotted garden compost, at the time of cultivation. When once planted they resent being disturbed, so it is important that the soil conditions are correct from the start. Division of the roots should be infrequent, as this has a tendency to reduce flowering potential. Set the plants 1½ft (45cm) apart in each direction. The plants benefit from frequent watering during the spring and summer months, when they are in active growth. The application of a surface mulch of

Helleborus foetidus

Helleborus orientalis

Helleborus orientalis 'Bowles Yellow'

well decayed manure or garden compost is also useful.

Helleborus is best grown in a bed on its own, where it may be given some form of protection during the late autumn and winter. This produces earlier flowers with longer stems and will also prevent soil splashing upon the flowers in wet weather.

The normal method of propagation is by division as soon as flowering ceases. Great care should be taken not to damage any leaves for such injury weakens the buds and may result in no flowers being produced. The easiest way to divide the roots is with a sharp knife. They may be divided in two or three pieces each one of which must have one or more leaves attached to it together with some roots. These small sections are planted out in a shady coldframe, allowing 1ft (30cm) between these sections. Keep them cool and moist during the summer and plant them out into their permanent positions during the autumn.

Helleborus can be propagated from seed, but growth is slow and it takes some three years to get them to flower. The plants will be very variable. Seed sowing takes place in the autumn in a coldframe. Germination will take place during late spring. When the resulting seedlings are large enough to handle, they are pricked out 9in (22.5cm) each way in a nursery bed in a moist shady part of the garden. The plants are subsequently planted out in their permanent position the following spring.

Helleborus can also be forced in gentle heat, in the greenhouse. Choose plants that have been divided during the previous spring. When forcing has finished let the plants recover for two or three years in the garden before forcing again.

Uses *Helleborus* is a family of very showy flowers growing in the spring. Once the plant is established, it is very generous with flowers and foliage. *H. niger* flowers grow from the crown of the plant, separated from its foliage. Coming so early (or possibly late) in the season, it is a subject for landscape arrangements to herald the spring, or to group with snowdrops and crocus in a small basket. Hellebores with stem cluster flowers are unique in form and colour. Reserve them for something special, as a single fresh item in a modern design or as the focal area of a preserved foliage arrangement.

My fascination is with the colour forms, particularly seedlings of *H. orientalis*. The basic colour is cream overlaid with a freckle of crimson, but the seedlings will amaze you with their variations in colour. An added advantage is the stem length, anything up to 18in (45cm).

The leaves are just as important to the arranger as the flowers. *H. niger* has five leaves growing in a horseshoe design on a single stem, a fascinating inclusion for an all foliage arrangement. Equally attractive are the leaves of *H. foetidus*. The flowers are bell shaped, green with a margin of maroon. Its leaves grow from a single stem, deeply divided, like fingers, a deep black-green colour.

Conditioning *Helleborus* can be difficult to condition and it is advisable to cut the flowers only after they have set seed. Usually hellebores that flower on short stems are not temperamental, and will absorb moisture with the minimum of fuss. Thicker stemmed flowers are on the middle scale of reliability. If any wilting does occur they can generally be revived by floating or submerging them in water for about an hour.

H. orientalis is the most difficult, and must only be cut when the seed has set. I scar the flower stem with a pin from the cut end up to the level of the water that they are to stand in. Keep them cool at all times both during conditioning and when they have been arranged. Never put them in an over-heated atmosphere and at night move them to a cool area.

A number of rather odd recipes exist to help with the conditioning of hellebores. It is suggested that they are stood in a small amount of gin for a short period then transferred to water. Adding aspirin or sugar to the conditioning water is supposed to be as effective. If you follow the basic rules of conditioning you will not need to resort to the drinks or medicine cabinet. Cut the flowers at the coolest time of the day, preferably early morning when they have had time to recharge themselves. Float them on water for an hour making sure that the cut stem end is submerged, then stand them in water for at least 3 hours. Check them periodically and if any show signs of wilting re-cut the stem and repeat the process.

The leaves are much simpler and can be stood or floated in water until required.

Preserving Hellebore foliage will absorb glycerine greedily. The darker leaves of *niger* and *foetidus* adopt the brown/black colour of leather. They remain supple and once preserved last indefinitely. *H. orientalis* is particularly attractive when dried in dessicant. Remove the stem and place the flower in a depression of desiccant. Filter more preservative into the centre of the flower. The drying process is very rapid, but they can be left in the drying agent for a long period. Mount the flowers on to a short piece of *Corylus contorta* stem, with short pieces of *Garrya eliptica* catkins glued to the back of the hellebore flower. Arranged with delicacy and restraint this design has a truly oriental feel.

Iberis

Candytuft
Europe
Cruciferae

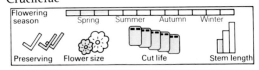

Iberis amara

The annual *Iberis amara* is a useful species for early spring, when the selection of flowering plants is restricted. *I.a.* 'Giant White' produces large, showy clusters of white flowers, height 1ft (30cm). A useful colour variation is *I.a.* 'Giant Pink', bright pink flowers, height 15in (37.5cm).

'Dwarf Fairy Mixed' is a short annual strain, growing to about 8in (20cm) in height. Although small, the plants are bushy and prolific, making attractive edging or container plants. The range of flower colours includes white, lilac, pink, carmine and maroon. The seed heads that follow are also attractive.

Cultivation and propagation Iberis grows very well on poor soils providing that it is given a sunny situation. When sowing the seeds in the autumn avoid over-rich soils, otherwise soft vegetative growth will be produced and the plants become susceptible to frost damage. Sow the seed in the place where flowering is to occur. Germination will take about 10 days. When the seedlings are large enough to handle, thin them out to stand 8in (20cm) apart. Protect the young plants with cloches during the winter to keep the plants dry. This protection will produce good plants and induce flowering in spring. The flowers will be of excellent quality and free from soil splashings in wet weather. Iberis which is grown without protection will flower later.

Uses *Iberis* flowers early in the season when there is a shortage of flowers in the colour range. They are a welcome addition to small groupings of short-stemmed flowers in a basket or posy bowl. They are extremely tolerant of town and city pollution.

Conditioning Conditioning is simple. A drink of water for at least 3 hours is sufficient.

Preserving The fresh flowers may be pressed, but I prefer to wait until the seedhead develops. It will dry naturally on the plant and provides interesting texture and form in a small dried arrangement.

Lunaria

Honesty
Sweden
Cruciferae

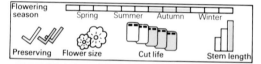

Lunaria

*L*unaria annua is treated as a biennial and thrives almost anywhere. While its purple and white flowers, height 2½ft (75cm), make a brave display during early summer, the real attraction of this plant is its moon-like seed cases. These are borne along branching stems and when dried turn silvery white.

Available forms include *L.a.* 'Alba' which has white flowers; *L.a.* 'Munstead Purple', which has rich purple flowers; and *L.a.*

'Variegata', a less commonly seen cultivar, which has purple-pink flowers and cream-edged foliage.

Cultivation and propagation *Lunaria* is shade tolerant and likes damp situations. Seed is sown in early summer where flowering is to take place. Germination usually takes 2 to 3 weeks. Once the plants are large enough to handle they should be thinned out to stand 9in (22.5cm) apart. These plants will flower the following year and, providing that one does not remove all the seed-heads, they will propagate themselves quite freely.

Uses As fresh plant material *Lunaria* may be considered quite dull, but as a dried component it is invaluable. The seed case will dry naturally on the plant. If you have no use for the entire stem, single seed cases can be removed with a pair of fine scissors. Check the plant daily for the right moment to harvest the seed, this must be done before the seed case splits and becomes brittle. Individual seed cases are useful for pictures or collages and their translucent quality can be utilized to advantage in making fantasy flowers by fixing them together on a false stem or gluing them on to a pine cone.

Polygonatum

Solomon's Seal
Northern temperate regions
Liliaceae

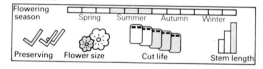

Polygonatum multiflorum

The hardy perennial species of Polygonatum described here have fleshy, rhizomatous roots which spread quickly, and because of this are best planted in an area where they are not likely to encroach on other plants. They have pointed oval leaves along the arching stems, which also bear clusters of green-tipped, creamy white, bell-shaped flowers during early summer.

Polygonatum japonicum is the larger species at 3ft (90cm) high. There is a variegated form, *P.j.* 'Variegatum', which has green leaves striped with white. *P. multiflorum*, a European native species, grows to a height of 2-2½ft (60-75cm).

Cultivation and propagation *Polygonatum* likes a moist soil and a shady position. Mulch annually. Plant in the winter. Propagation is by division of the roots during the dormant season.

Uses This is certainly a plant to recommend to the flower arranger. The arching stems are perfect for establishing the outline of any shaped design. The curving stems used in opposing directions create an 'S' shape, or used in the same plane they will establish a crescent shape. The leaves may be removed to reveal the hanging white bell flowers, which adds an unusual note to an arrangement.

Conditioning Allow the foliage to mature before cutting, then stand in water for 3 hours to condition.

Preserving The flowers can be carefully cut from the growing stem and preserved in desiccant. The ideal preserving material is the leaf. The time to preserve the leaves is once the flower has faded and the leaf is fully mature. Remove any lower leaves from the stem that are likely to come into contact with the glycerine solution. Stand the stem in the glycerine for about three days. The colour will change to a light biscuit brown. You should check them every day. Any that show signs of stem weakness should be given some support to allow the glycerine to reach the extreme tip.

ASSORTED COLOURS

Allium

Northern Hemisphere
Liliaceae

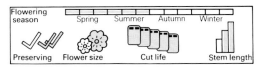

Allium siculum

Everyone is familiar with at least some of the edible Allium species, which include garlic, onion, leek and shallot. While the form of the garden flower is very similar to that produced by the onion, it appears in a wide range of colours, and most do not have an oniony scent unless the leaves are damaged; in fact, some are mildly fragrant.

Allium aflatense is a species originating from central China; it bears large umbels of rosy purple flowers in early summer, height 2½ft (75cm). *A. albopilosum* comes from Turkestan; its large flower heads appearing in early summer are deep purplish-mauve with a metallic sheen, up to 18in (45cm) in diameter, height 2ft (60cm). *A. coeruleum* is a species native to Siberia and Turkestan, with cornflower blue flower umbels in midsummer, height 2ft (60cm). The

Mediterranean species *A. pulchellum* has red-purple flowers in late summer, height 1½ft (45cm). The flowers of *A. sphaerocephalum* are dark purple, appearing in late summer, height 2ft (60cm).

White-flowered species contribute freshness to pale colour schemes early in the growing season. Among these are *A. cowanii*, which has pure white flowers in early summer, height 2ft (60cm); and *A. neapolitanum*, with umbels of star-shaped flowers in spring, height 1½ft (45cm).

An unusual but very attractive form is *A. siculum*, with pale greenish flowers in early summer, height 2ft (60cm).

Cultivation and propagation *Allium* will thrive in any sunny place in well-drained soil. Plant the bulbs in the late autumn, twice their own depth and some 6 to 9in (15 to 22.5cm) apart, according to height of growth. Leave the bulbs to multiply over the years until their crowded conditions indicate that it is time to lift and divide them. Take this opportunity to cultivate the site and introduce some peat or well rotted garden compost, before replanting the bulbs. Apply a surface mulch of peat in the spring.

Propagation is by seed. Sow in the dormant season and leave the young plants in their seedtrays till the following spring. Some species can be divided in autumn or spring.

Uses This family provides a most interesting range of flowers that are generally grown by the arranger for the resultant seed head. Once the bulb has established itself in the garden it will soon produce offsets so that you have enough flowers to use fresh. The globular shape of the seed head is quite striking and has a long stem that will help to create height in a design or a bold focal area.

Preserving Let the seed develop in the garden until the head changes from green to biscuit brown, then gently tug the stem from the bulb. Any resistance is an indication that it is not ready, so leave it for a day or two and try again. The dried head may be used in most styles of arrangements, it is often seen lightly gilded with preserved foliage and the pods of *Physalis franchetti* at Christmas.

Alstroemeria

Peruvian lily
Chile
Amaryllidaceae

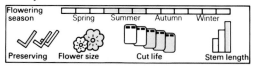

Alstroemeria ligtu

These elegant lily-like flowers on straight stems provide a rich colour range. *Alstroemeria aurantica* has loose umbels of deep orange flowers in summer, height 3ft (90cm). Once established the tuberous roots spread quite widely, so plant in a sunny, sheltered spot where the spread can be contained.

A. ligtu hybrids, height 2½ft (75cm), come in a variety of colours – pink, yellow, red, orange and white. These need moist root conditions, so careful watering is necessary during dry spells in summer.

Cultivation and propagation Most types of soil are suitable, provided they have been deeply cultivated and well supplied with manure or garden compost prior to planting. Plant the tubers in spring at least 6in (15cm) deep, so that they are not damaged by hard winter frosts. If you have space to spare in a greenhouse you can enjoy their flowers over an extended period, with a little heat to encourage them along. Their first flush of flowers will commence in spring and continue into summer. This will then be followed by a period of rest before a second and lighter flush of flowers are produced in the autumn.

Propagation of *A. aurantiaca* is best achieved by division of the tuberous roots in the spring.

A. *ligtu* cannot readily be propagated vegetatively and must be grown from seed sown in the early spring in seed-boxes containing a peat based compost, placed in a cool greenhouse. Prick the seedlings out in 3in (7.5cm) pots when large enough to handle and grow them on during the summer months in an open frame. Plant out the following spring. Young plants frequently succumb to winter damage.

Uses Given an adequate supply of water the *Alstroemeria* has a very long cut life, often up to a fortnight. It is like a lily in shape, with a cluster of flowers at the top of the stem and is generally used in massed traditional arrangements. *A. aurantiaca* is a vibrant orange, a startling companion to blue delphiniums arranged in a modern, upright container. The rainbow choice of colours of the *ligtu* hybrids has been expanded to include pink, flame, white, yellow and lilac, which provides a wide choice to use with flowers of pure hue or pastel shades. The large glowing white flower of *A. pelegrina 'alba'* is worth a special mention. Known as the Lily of the Incas, the flowers are large, often carried singly on a stem of about fifteen inches. If you can obtain this variety, do take advantage of it as it is excellent in an arrangement of white summer flowers.

Conditioning Condition the flowers in deep cold water for about 3 hours.

Preserving The thin flower petals will not absorb liquid preservative nor air dry properly. Individual blooms can be dried in desiccant.

Anemone 'St Brigid'

Anemone appenina

Anemone

Windflower
China
Ranunculaceae

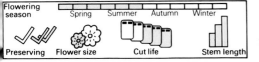

Flowering season		Spring	Summer	Autumn	Winter
Preserving	Flower size		Cut life		Stem length

SUMMER AND AUTUMN FLOWERING ANEMONES

The herbaceous perennial often referred to as *Anemone japonica*, more correctly listed as *A. hupehensis*, makes bushy plants with attractive saucer-shaped, mauve or carmine flowers which may be up to 2½in (6.2cm) across. It flowers in autumn, height 2-3ft (60-90cm). There is also a white form, *A.h. 'Alba'*, and many named hybrids flowering in late summer to autumn.

'Bressingham Glow' has pretty rosy red, semi-double flowers, height 1½ft (45cm); 'Lady Gilmour' carries large pink, almost double flowers, height 2ft (60cm); 'Louise Uhink' has semi-double white flowers, height 2½ft (75cm); 'Profusion' is deep pink, height 2½ft (75cm); and 'September Charm' has single soft pink flowers up to 4in (10cm) across, continuously through autumn.

The garden hybrid *A.* × *lesseri* flowers in early summer, with rosy purple, open-faced blooms, height 2ft (60cm).

All the above are fibrous-rooted, long-lived plants and the flowers, carried on sturdy stems, are freely produced.

Cultivation and propagation Once planted, *Anemone hupehensis* and the various hybrids are best left undisturbed for many years. Therefore good soil preparation is important. Heavy soils should have coarse sand or other suitable gritty material introduced to open up the soil. Granulated peat can be forked into the surface. These anemones thrust their roots deep down into the soil and are very long lived. Plant in the early spring. They flower little during their first year of planting, but settle down to flower well in subsequent years. They will grow equally well in sun or shade, providing there is some moisture around their roots while they are in active growth. Give them an annual mulch of peat in spring.

One method of propagating these anemones is by lifting and dividing the plants in the late autumn when flowering has ceased. The divided plants take some time to re-establish themselves with the loss of flowering during the first year. Root cuttings can also be used, taken in the dormant period by excavating round the parent plant so as not to disturb it. These are then potted-up and given the protection of a coldframe through the winter and the early spring. Once new growth from the pieces of root has developed sufficiently the various pieces are potted up individually, in the early summer and placed back in the coldframe with the top glass removed. Transfer to the flowering position in the early spring of the following year.

SPRING-FLOWERING ANEMONES

There are several species of tuberous-rooted anemones that flower in spring to early summer.

A. appenina **(common wood anemone) carries clear blue flowers on 6in (15cm) stems;** *A.a.* **'Alba' is white-flowered.** *A. blanda* **has small flowers which may be blue, pink, white or red, on 4-5in (10-12.5cm) stems.**

A. fulgens **flowers slightly later, in early summer, producing large, yellow-centred scarlet flowers, some 2½in (6.25cm) across, on 12in (30cm) stems. 'St Bavo' is a related strain, flowering in late spring, with a fine colour**

range and stems 12in (30cm) or more in length.

A. coronaria **provides two very popular strains: the single-flowered 'De Caen', with flowers up to 3in (7.5cm) across on 9in (22.5cm) stems; and 'St Brigid', with semi-double flowers of similar height. Both are available in brilliant colours – white, red and blue – and flower from late spring to early summer.**

Cultivation and propagation None are particularly difficult about soil, providing that it is well supplied with organic matter, so that it holds moisture well, and is in a sunny, sheltered situation. Fresh tubers must be planted each year to give good quality flowers, but otherwise need little attention.

Early flowering may be induced by giving plants the protection of a cool greenhouse, with a minimum night temperature of 42°F (6°C). Plant the tubers in early autumn. Soak them in water for 12 hours before potting them up in 6in (15cm) pots. Place them on the greenhouse bench and water just sufficiently to keep the compost slightly moist. When growth is in evidence begin to water more freely and apply a dose of a liquid fertiliser every 10 to 14 days.

Even anemones to be planted in the open ground should be soaked in water for 12 hours first, as this encourages the early development of roots. The tubers are irregular in shape and referred to as claws; it is particularly important that they are planted no more than 2in (5cm) deep. Upon close inspection one will see small buds surrounded with scales and these must be planted facing upwards. The rows of anemones should be some 6 to 8in (15 to 18cm) apart. Plant successionally through the winter to give an extended flowering period. Mulch in late spring.

Uses The short-stemmed spring flowering species look most attractive simply arranged in a small glass vase or grouped with other flowers in a basket. Plants grown in pots are an advantage to the busy arranger, as they can be positioned in a suitable dish and the pots concealed with a little moss. The only maintenance they need is a little water every day. The more widely recognized pink *Anemone japonica* is a delightful flower for the late summer and early autumn. The stems are long and willowy, making them an ideal component as outline material. The foliage is carried on erect stems arranged in whorls of three. Once it has matured it is a long-lasting cut leaf.

Conditioning Condition the flowers when they are about to open. Some of the hybrids shed their petals so handle them carefully. Stand them in water for up to 4 hours. The spring anemones are prone to wilting. If this occurs score the stem with a pin from the cut end to the flower and recondition.

Preserving Individual flowers will dry

Anemone blanda

successfully in desiccant; single flowers are particularly useful for pressing.

Antirrhinum

Snapdragon
Europe
Scrophulariaceae

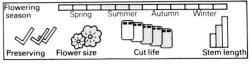

Antirrhinum

Although the antirrhinums grown in our gardens are treated as annuals, those commonly used for summer bedding displays are named cultivars of the perennial species *Antirrhinum majus*. The range of heights provides plants suitable for borders, edgings or container-growing. The introduction of modern F1 hybrids has provided larger flowers with longer stems, in the usual brilliant colours – bronze, orange, crimson, pink, rose, yellow and white. These have a vibrant effect planted en masse, and make excellent cut flowers.

Particularly fine examples of these hybrid forms are 'Bright Butterfly', bearing clustered spikes of open-mouthed penstemon-like flowers, height 2½ft (75cm); and 'Madame Butterfly', a double-petalled form, height 2½-3ft (75-90cm).

Cultivation and propagation *Antirrhinum* is fairly tolerant but prefers light, rich soils, in full sun. Seed should be sown in slight heat during early March. When the seedlings germinate give them plenty of light to keep them compact as they develop, thus producing

nice sturdy material for pricking out into seedboxes when they are large enough to handle. Grow on under a coldframe or cloche until they are planted out in early summer, spacing them 16 to 18in (40 to 45cm) apart. Flowering is continuous from midsummer to the first frosts.

Uses With their extensive colour range, long stems and pointed flower heads these are indispensable as outline material. Those with strong clean colours, crimson, yellow and orange, are ideal for modern and free-form arranging, where vivid and contrasting colour is needed. The lighter pastel shades of lemon, apricot and pink blend well in a scheme of mixed flowers adding a distinctive form and flowing line to delicate, less regimented styles. When cutting the first flush of flowers leave a number of leaves on the plant to encourage the side shoots to develop.

Conditioning Cut in the morning or afternoon. Remove the lower leaves and lightly crush the semi-woody stem. Stand the stems in water in a cool place for at least 4 hours.

Preserving Sadly this elegant flower is awkward to preserve. Pressing distorts the shape, and its form does not accommodate desiccant.

Aquilegia

Columbine
Temperate regions of the Northern Hemisphere
Ranunculaceae

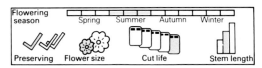

Some of the species Aquilegia have been hybridized to produce excellent named cultivars that have brightly coloured flowers with long spurs. All are summer-flowering plants.

'McKana's Giant' hybrids have large flowers up to 4in (10cm) wide, and spurs that are not much shorter. They are available in a mixed blend of colours which embraces blue, pink, maroon, purple, red, deep yellow, light yellow, cream and white, with many bicolours. They flower in late summer, height 2½-3ft (75-90cm).

'Coerulea F1 Hybrid Heterosis Olympia Red and Gold' is perhaps the best colour combination so far produced in aquilegias, and while the seed is fairly expensive, it is well worth the price. For a dwarfer type, try

Aquilegia 'McKana's Giant'

Aquilegia 'Nora Barlow'

'Dragonfly' hybrids, long spurred flowers in a fine range of colours, height 1½ft (45cm). Other good named cultivars include 'Crimson Star', with masses of crimson and white flowers, height 20in (50cm), and 'Nora Barlow', with fully double flowers quaintly tinted red, pink and green, height 28in (70cm).

Cultivation and propagation *Aquilegia* thrive in any cool, well-drained soil and can be grown in full light or partial shade. Although a perennial, it is not long-lived, so for top-quality flowers it is best to propagate annually from rootstocks purchased at nurseries, or by seed bought from a reputable seed merchant. Although *Aquilegia* sets seed very readily, it results in inferior plants in muddy colours not worth growing.

Sow seed in spring, preferably under glass. The aim is to give the plants the longest possible growing season, as all the development of these plants takes place in the first year. Germination is slow and irregular, so be patient. With the protection of cloches it takes about three weeks, but in the open ground it will take at least five weeks. When the seedlings are large enough to handle they are thinned out to 12in (30cm) apart. Under cloches ventilate the plants on warm sunny days in late spring. The plants are then hardened off ready for planting out in a nursery bed for the summer. In the autumn the plants are transferred to their flowering situation. None of these plants require any type of support.

Uses These flowers provide us with an almost unique distinctive form with graceful nodding flowers and long spurs, valued for their shape and interesting range of colour blends. They have long been associated with country cottage gardens and for this reason are often used in re-creating period styles of arrangements seen in the Dutch/Flemish flower paintings. While historically this is not accurate, as the majority of species were not introduced to Europe until the mid 19th century, they have that old-fashioned look and assist in establishing the period atmosphere which is so desirable.

Conditioning They will condition very easily. Stand them in deep water for about 4 hours.

Preserving Some of the smaller flowers and buds will dry in desiccant. If you are able to resist cutting all the flowers, you will be rewarded with an interesting cluster of seed heads, which may be lightly gilded for a fantasy style arrangement at Christmas.

Aster

Michaelmas Daisy
Eastern USA
Compositae

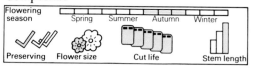

*A*ster *novi-belgii* has daisy-like blue flowers and slender, pointed green leaves, and reaches a height of 4ft (120cm). Many hybrids are available in a great range of colours, and heights varying from 9in (22.5cm) to 4ft (120cm). These are among the most popular of border plants, giving an unrivalled display of autumn colour. The taller types make good background planting, with smaller forms used as border edging.

The flowers are daisy-like with yellow centres, unless otherwise stated: 'Audrey', violet flowers, height 1ft (30cm); 'Blandie', pure white, height 3½ft (105cm); 'Coombe Margaret', light pink, height 3½ft (105cm); 'Countess of Dudley', deep pink, height 9in (22.5cm); 'Crimson Brocade', cyclamen purple double flowers, height 3ft (90cm); 'Little Pink Beauty', deep pink semi-double flowers, height 15in (37.5cm); 'Marie Ballard', powder blue double flowers, height 3ft (90cm); 'Mistress Quickly', deep blue, height 4ft (120cm); 'Raspberry Ripple', carmine-red double flowers, height 2½ft (75cm); 'Rev. Vincent Dale', deep purple, height 4ft (120cm); 'Royal Ruby', deep red, height 18in (45cm); 'Royal Velvet', deep violet, height 4ft (120cm); 'Sailor Boy', bright, rich blue, height 3½ft (105cm); 'Snowsprite', white, height 1ft (30cm); 'The Cardinal', rosy red semi-double flowers, height 3½ft (105cm); 'Winston Churchill', reddish-purple, height 2ft (60cm).

Aster 'Audrey'

Cultivation and propagation Any reasonable well-drained soil will do, provided it contains plenty of humus and is in full sun. Dwarf forms make neat compact growth, while taller ones will need some form of support to prevent them looking untidy. A few stakes with stout strings running between the plants provides the necessary support. This type of arrangement could also serve to support a sheet of clear polythene over the plants when they come into flower, preventing the autumn rains spoiling the appearance of the flowers, and thus extending their period of availability for cutting. Dwarf cultivars might also be given the protection of cloches or a portable cold-frame to extend the flowering period. *Aster novi-belgii* provides its best flowers from the young plants so they should be lifted and divided up every second year. In the autumn after they have ceased flowering cut down the dead stems to just above ground level and then lift and divide the clumps of roots. Discard the worn-out central portions and replant only the young vigorous outer portions (stolons), about 1 to 3ft (30-40cm) apart, depending on the height of the cultivar. At this time introduce some well-rotted garden compost and dig this into the soil as the work proceeds, supplementing this in the early spring with a surface mulch of peat or leaf mould between the plants.

Uses These flowers are an asset as intermediary flowers in traditional designs, large or small. The wealth of colour and ease with which they grow will allow you to use them in profusion. They have a distinctly rural atmosphere; though generally reserved for the traditional style of arranging *novi-belgii* 'Crimson brocade' used as a block of colour is an exciting flower for modern arranging.

Conditioning The flower stem can become woody. Lightly crush the end before standing them in water for 3 hours.

Aster 'Marie Ballard'

Aster 'The Cardinal'

Preserving Aster flowers with few petals will dry in desiccant. It is necessary to be selective when pressing the flower, a frill of petal that is too thick will bruise and discolour during the process.

Callistephus chinensis

China Aster
China
Compositae

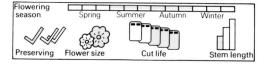

Callistephus chinensis 'Ostrich plume'

Among the most spectacular china asters are 'Ostrich Plume' and 'Bouquet Powder Puffs', both having large double flowers in the colour range pink, red, purple and white. They flower from late summer to autumn and grow to 18in (45cm) high.

'Duchesse' is a medium to late-flowering, vigorous strain growing to a height of 2ft (60cm). This has strong stems and produces large flowers with incurved petals, 5in (12cm) in diameter, resembling chrysanthemums, in a splendid range of colours.

'New Giants of California', late-flowering, has flowers up to 6in (15cm) in diameter, height 2½ft (75cm).

'Madeleine' is possibly the finest single-flowered aster, producing its blooms in mid-season. It is available in a good mixture of colours and grows to 2ft (60cm) high.

'Pompon Mixed' is a medium to late-flowering strain, bearing small, rounded

flowers, height 1½ft (45cm).

Cultivation and propagation *Callistephus* flourishes on a wide range of soils, providing that some lime is present, and this is the key to success with this plant. The aster is a half hardy annual and the seed may be sown directly under a coldframe or cloche in spring. If sown thinly the plants will need no attention until they are transferred to their flowering places in early summer. Plant 12 to 16in (30 to 40cm) apart, according to height.

Uses These flowers are most welcome in their season of late summer and autumn when there is less alternative material in their colouring of pinks and blue. The single-flowered cultivars are best suited to informal designs, whereas the double and ostrich plume could find a place in the more sophisticated arrangement. The regular rounded forms of 'Powder Puff' are both unusual and striking in modern or free-form designs.

Conditioning Remove any excess stem foliage and condition them in cold water for up to 6 hours.

Preserving The single flowers may be pressed or dried in desiccant. Their bold colours introduce an eye-catching note to a picture of preserved material.

Centaurea

Europe including Britain
Compositae

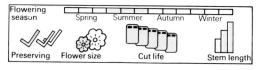

Centaurea 'Polka Dot'

These attractively informal flowers are associated with the cottage garden style of planting, and they provide a beautiful range of gentle and rich colours.

Centaurea cyanus (cornflower), which in its wild form is just a weed, has been much improved to produce larger flowers in other colours than the original cornflower blue. A mixed blend of colours is sold as *C.c.* 'Mixed', with flowers of mauve, blue, red, pink and white for summer flowering, height 2½ft (75cm).

C.c. 'Blue Diadem' has intense deep blue, powder-puff type flowers, height 2ft (60cm); 'Red Ball' has unusual scarlet to pink flowers 2in (5cm) across, appearing early in the season, height 3ft (90cm).

The dwarfer 'Polka Dot Mixed' has fully double flowers in shades of pink, carmine, blue and white, height 15in (37.5cm). *C.c.* 'Nana Jubilee Gem' has large double, dark blue flowers, height 12in (30cm).

C. moschata (sweet sultan) has fragrant vanilla-scented flowers in white, crimson, pinkish-purple, rose or yellow, height 1½-2ft (45-60cm). It is generally offered for sale in mixed colours, although the yellow is sold separately as 'Moschata Yellow'. A native of the eastern Mediterranean region, this plant is not fully hardy.

Cultivation and propagation *Centaurea* likes an open sunny situation and will grow in any well-drained soil. *C. cyanus* is quite hardy. Seed may be sown in autumn to give an early crop of flowers for cutting in the spring. It will grow quite happily in the open ground throughout the winter but for good quality early flowers it is well worth considering giving the plants some protection. A sowing of seeds in the open ground in spring will result in a crop of flowers being produced during the late summer. Seed should be sown in the flowering site, as seedlings do not transplant well.

Sow seed of *C. moschata* in spring where flowering is to occur. Germination will take 7 to 10 days. Thin out the resulting plants to stand 10in (25cm) apart. Flowering starts about 8 weeks after seed has been sown.

Uses In its season *Centaurea* provides a supply of intermediate or filler material and has a special use in wedding arrangements where 'something blue' is needed. For such an occasion they look especially attractive arranged in a basket with grey foliage carried by child bridesmaids. The length of stem will allow their use as outline material for large arrangements, but you may find that the stems are a little brittle and need support.

Conditioning Conditioning is simple. A drink of water for about 4 hours is sufficient. Remove any foliage that is likely to be submerged as it decays very rapidly.

Preserving Some attempt should always be made to dry the flowers in desiccant as there are few flowers of this colour for using in flower pictures or collages.

Cheiranthus

Wallflower
Europe
Cruciferae

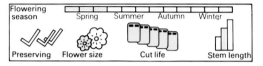

Cheiranthus 'Blood Red'

Cheiranthus 'Orange Bedder'

The vivid, densely packed flower spikes of Cheiranthus bring brilliant, fiery colour to the garden through spring. Two species are commonly grown: *Cheiranthus allionii* (Siberian wallflower) is a hybrid biennial plant which flowers over a longer period than the perennial species *C. cheiri*. Indeed, *C. allionii* flowers appear for up to two months in late spring; the plants grow to a height of 12-15in (30-37.5cm). *C.a.* 'Orange Queen' has bright orange flowers, while *C.a.* 'Golden Queen' is golden yellow.

C. cheiri (the true wallflower) is grown widely as a bedding plant for both the colour and fragrance of its sweet-scented flowers. Although perennial, it is treated as biennial. There are many named cultivars available, providing a strong colour range. The following recommended forms all flower in late spring.

'Blood Red', very fragrant dark red flowers, height 15in (37.5cm); 'Cranford Beauty', syn. 'Cloth of Gold', golden yellow flowers, height 18in (45cm); 'Fire King', vivid scarlet flowers, height 15in (37.5cm); 'Golden Bedder', clear golden yellow flowers, height 12in (30cm); 'Ivory White', creamy white flowers, height 12in (30cm); 'Orange Bedder', rich orange flowers shaded with apricot yellow, height 12in (30cm); 'Vulcan', rich crimson flowers, height 14in (35cm).

'Fair Lady Mixed' is an assorted strain including some attractive pastel colours, height 15-18in (37.5-45cm).

Cultivation and propagation Wallflowers will grow quite happily on a wide range of soils if they are well drained. However, they are subject to a disease commonly referred to as 'Club Root'. This is a fungus which attacks all members of the brassica family, causing swellings on the roots or stem base. This fungus thrives in poorly drained acid soils and it is important that one provides the plants with a well-limed soil and that they do not follow a previous crop of brassicas. So move them from place to place each year and treat any infected plants with 'Calomel Dust' both when setting the plants out in the nursery bed for the summer and when transferring them to their flowering site in the autumn. It is also worth while dusting calomel down the seed drill. Earlier flowering can be induced if the plants are protected through the winter with cloches.

Seed is sown in the open ground during late spring. Germination takes 7 to 14 days. When the seedlings are large enough to handle they are planted out in a nursery bed allowing 6in (15cm) between the plants. In the autumn the plants are transferred to their flowering sites, setting them out 12in (30cm) apart. Both species are treated as biennials.

Uses As an added bonus to any arrangement, wallflowers have an exquisite perfume which seems to become more intense after the flowers have been in a warmer indoor atmosphere. The relatively short length of stem somewhat limits their use to outline and filler material in smaller designs. The colour range has been much extended by the hybridist and now includes a number of unusual shades including reds/browns and greys/purples much prized by the arranger seeking the unusual in pursuit of recreating a period atmosphere.

Conditioning It is essential to crush the bottom of the woody stem before standing them in water for up to 6 hours. The crushed section should be cut away before arranging.

Preserving As the wallflower is so free flowering any difficulties in pressing the individual flowers can be overlooked.

Chrysanthemum

Widely distributed in the Northern Hemisphere
Compositae

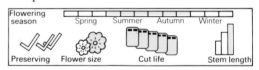

Chrysanthemum maximum 'Esther Read'

There is a vast range of chrysanthemums providing a great array of shapes and colours for summer and autumn flowering. The following are recommended forms representative of the range.

Chrysanthemum maximum (shasta daisy) has large white daisy-like flowers. By careful selection, you can have white-flowered cultivars that bloom from early summer to autumn.

C.m. 'Esther Read' has double flowers in

Chrysanthemum maximum 'H Seibert'

Chrysanthemum Korean hybrid 'Columbine'

Chrysanthemum rubellum

Chrysanthemum Korean hybrid 'Rosalie'

Chrysanthemum Korean hybrid 'Belle'

Chrysanthemum Korean hybrid 'Ruby Mound'

Chrysanthemum Korean hybrid 'Wedding Sunshine'

Chrysanthemum Korean hybrid 'Lorna'

Chrysanthemum Korean hybrid 'Betty'

summer, height 2½ft (75cm); *C.m.* 'Everest', also summer-flowering, has single flowers, height 3ft (90cm); *C.m.* 'H. Seibert' is a large-flowered single form, height 2½ft (75cm). The single flowers of *C.m.* 'Silver Princess' appear in early summer, height 1ft (30cm); this subject is ideal for covering with cloches or a coldframe in early spring, which encourages flowering to commence some four to five weeks earlier than in open ground. *C.m.* 'Thomas Killin' is a semi-double white form, height 2½ft (75cm), as is *C.m.* 'Wirral Pride', height 3ft (90cm). *C.m.* 'Wirral Supreme' produces double white flowers with anemone-like centres in autumn, height 3ft (90cm).

Following on from these summer-flowering kinds are the hardy autumn-flowering types, which are fairly resistant to early frosts. *C. rubellum*, a Japanese species growing to about 3ft (90cm) in height has produced a number of desirable cultivars. Among these are *C.r.* 'Clara Curtis', single clear pink flowers; *C.r.* 'Duchess of Edinburgh', clear red, semi-double flowers; and *C.r.* 'Mary Stoker', soft yellow.

The Korean hybrid spray chrysanthemums are a valuable source of colour late in the season, with a wide range of hues. With the aid of a little protection from the rain, the flowers of the following hybrids may last into early winter: 'Apollo', salmon bronze; 'Bright Eye', golden yellow; 'Ember', bronze; 'Orange Wonder', coppery orange. All grow to a height of 2ft (60cm) and need no disbudding.

The pretty little Japanese pompon 'Mei-kyo', with its double pink flowers, is one of the very last hardy chrysanthemums to flower in late autumn, height 2ft (60cm). 'Bronze Elegance' is a browny-yellow form of 'Mei-kyo', which flowers at the same time.

The popular florists' chrysanthemum *C. morifolium*, syn. *C. sinense*, comes originally from China and Japan. The wide range of cultivars provides flowers that are very long-lasting when cut, in the colour range white, yellow, pink, red, bronze and purple. The flowers are of various types, classified as follows:

Incurved Incurving petals that form a firm globe.

Incurving Incurving petals that do not form a globe, resulting in flowers with a less definite shape.

Reflexed Petals are of two types, as the outer ones are reflexed while the inner ones are incurving.

Anemone-flowered Single-flowered cultivars with several rows of outer petals but with a central cushion of tubular florets.

Singles Outer petals surrounding a central daisy-like disc.

Pompons **Small globular flowers of tightly packed, incurving petals.**

Cultivation *Early-flowering cultivars and species* Chrysanthemums can be grown successfully on any ordinary garden soil which is well drained and of reasonable depth. Heavy soils can have added grit or sharp sand. Choose an open sunny position for them. Give the ground a generous dressing of farmyard manure or well rotted garden compost prior to autumn digging. In spring break down the soil's surface to a fine tilth with the aid of a garden rake, then dress the surface with a good general fertilizer such as National Growmore at the rate of 4oz per sq yard (135.6gm per sq metre) and work this into the soil's surface with the garden rake.

If the weather is suitable early flowering chrysanthemums may be planted in the open ground in late spring. When growing them in a bed the plants should be set out 14in (35cm) apart each way with three rows of plants together with a gap of 30in (75cm) between each block of three rows of plants. This serves as a path for access. In exposed places one would be well advised to erect a hessian screen to afford some protection on the windward side. Tall growing cultivars may require support at an early stage either with individual canes or by 2in (5cm) mesh wire-netting stretched out over the chrysanthemum bed and held in place by a horizontal framework attached firmly to strong corner posts about 5ft (150cm) high. As the chrysanthemums grow taller the wire-netting can be raised up the posts while still remaining taut and giving suitable support to the plants. Shorter cultivars will not require any form of support until later.

Young chrysanthemums generally produce a single stem some 12-18in (30-45cm) long before they develop flower buds at the tips. Side shoots then develop from the leaf axils below, giving the plants a branched structure. The terminal bud on each plant is referred to as the *break bud* as it causes the plants to produce these side shoots. Subsequently these side shoots develop until they in turn produce flower buds at the tips of their stems and these are referred to as crown buds. In this particular instance they are *first crown buds*. In general early flowering chrysanthemums produce their best flowers from first crown buds, as do many of the mid-season cultivars too. However, some cultivars particularly of late flowering chrysanthemums such as the American Beauty Family produce their best flowers when stopped a second time and grown on to *second crown buds*. Once the crown buds can be seen developing, the process of *disbudding* should commence. The aim is to remove unwanted flower buds from a cluster, leaving just the one flower bud selected. All leafy side-shoots from the leaf axils below should also be removed. All the energies of the plant should be directed to the task of producing top-quality flowers from the selected flower buds and disbudding should not be delayed. Indeed, even if sprays are grown, the side shoots should still be removed without delay. When growing chrysanthemums as sprays, remove the crown bud and leave all the other buds in the cluster, as this bud is inclined to open in advance of the other flower buds.

Some cultivars break into side shoots in early summer, while others are shy at doing so and may be left some two or three weeks longer in order to develop enough sideshoots. If they fail to do this naturally, stop the leading shoot and, as the side shoots develop, select two or three of the topmost side shoots and stop these again when they have developed their first pair of leaves. In this way each of these will produce a couple of extra side shoots which will furnish additional flowers in due season.

Chrysanthemums like some moisture about their roots and while the soil must never be over wet it pays to water the plants regularly if the weather is dry. The provision of a dilute liquid feed occasionally is also beneficial, particularly after periods of very heavy rain.

Choose varieties that are doing well, and are healthy plants to propagate from in future years. Stout labels should be placed against these so that they may be readily identified. later. Once flowering has finished cut back the main stem of each plant to 6in (15cm) above ground level on those plants which have been selected to be retained. (Lift and destroy all the unwanted plants and their debris at the same time.) Then, with the aid of a garden fork, lift the stools, with as little soil as possible to enable the stools (roots) to be packed more closely together either on the floor of a greenhouse or in a garden frame. Some fine dry soil/compost is then spread over the roots to the original soil level to prevent them from becoming shrivelled during the winter dormancy period. This should then be given a light watering to settle it about the roots.

Ventilation of the greenhouse or garden frame should be given during mild weather to keep the temperature down. When garden frames are used the tops can be removed during the day, if the weather is dry and mild. When fresh growth commences the garden frame must be given additional protection on frosty nights and the covering removed each day if the weather permits.

Mid-Season Flowering Chrysanthemums Cultivation is as for early flowering chrysanthemums, but you need to erect a temporary structure clad with strong clear polythene to cover the plants from the beginning of October onwards. This is to prevent rain damage rather than frost.

Knock strong posts into the ground adjacent to the ends of the chrysanthemum bed, with intermediate posts along the sides of the bed if necessary too, of sufficient height to allow a gap of 1ft (30cm) above the top of the chrysanthemums when they are fully grown. Strong straining wire is then run down the sides of the chrysanthemum bed, from the top of each post and across the ends and between the intermediate posts. Galvanized staples are suitable for attaching the wire to the posts. The clear plastic is then rolled out over the top of this temporary structure, of sufficient width to enable it to hang down either side for a distance of approximately 2-3ft (60 to 90cm) and held securely in position by a number of 3in (7.5cm) long 'Bulldog' clips along the side wires and at the ends.

The alternative solution is to grow the chrysanthemums in 9 or 10in (22.5 or 25cm) pots in the open in the summer and move them into an unheated greenhouse in the autumn. This will necessitate several repottings during the course of cultivation. They will grow quite happily either in the traditional John Innes Potting Compost No. 2 or one of the peat-based potting composts. Spacing them out 18in (45cm) apart in the row. Each pot will require a cane to support the plant. The canes too will need to be tied to a straining wire stretched out along each row of pot plants and secured to a stout post at each end of the row to prevent the plants from being blown over and injured in strong winds. The plants grown in pots will need watering every few days. Once the chrysanthemums have become established in the final pots they should be given an application of dilute liquid feed every second week and this should continue until the flowers are showing colour. Move the plants into the greenhouse before the weather deteriorates and give as much ventilation as possible to keep the temperature down and prevent soft growth.

Once flowering has ceased and one has selected which plants are to be retained these should have the main stem cut back to 6in (15cm) above the top of the pot. The stools of these plants may be left in their pots and they can be given the protection either of a cold greenhouse or a garden frame during the winter months. If space is limited follow the procedure recommended for the early flowering cultivars.

Propagation C. *maximum* is propagated by root division in spring, either annually or biennially. C. *rubellum* is propagated either by root division in spring or by stem cuttings secured in spring and rooted in sandy soil in a garden frame.

In early spring, rising temperatures in the greenhouse or frame will stimulate the chrysanthemum stools into growth and some soft-wood cuttings can be taken from these. The cuttings should be some 2 to 2½in (5 to 6.25cm) long and cut just beneath a leaf joint. Remove the lower leaf. They should all be of a uniform size. So if there is a shortage of suitable shoots to secure as cuttings, it is better to wait a week or two before starting any propagation work. If the soil/compost is at all dry provide a light watering to encourage some root activity and shoot development. The ideal rooting medium consists of two parts by bulk of finely divided moist peat and one part sharp sand. When putting this compost in boxes or pots it is important to ensure that it is pressed down firmly. The cuttings are inserted into the compost to the depth of 1in (2.5cm) and spaced out 2in (5cm) apart, when rooted in boxes. If one is using pots for this purpose insert the cuttings around the rim. For speedy rooting the minimum night temperature should be 50°F (10°C). At lower temperatures rooting will take longer but sturdy plants can be produced. On bright sunny days it is important to shade the cuttings from the sun otherwise they may wilt. Once rooting has taken place no time should be lost in potting up the plants either in John Innes Potting Compost or one of the peat-based universal composts. The rooted plants should be grown on cold and merely be given the protection of a garden frame with extra protection given on frosty nights.

Once established in the pots ventilation should be given whenever possible and the plants hardened off prior to planting in the open ground.

Uses Unlike its sophisticated cousin the exhibition chrysanthemum, the Shasta daisy has an air of informality about it. The flower is round, white or creamy white and may be used almost to excess in a massed arrangement using the larger more perfect blooms as the focal area. Like so many simple flowers, they can look attractive placed in a deep vase. They are the perfect accompaniment to a foliage arrangement, but do not use many or you will lose the cool tranquil effect that green and white generates.

Conditioning Autumn-flowering chrysanthemums mix well with preserved foliage, and the warm colouring looks well in brass or copper containers. Given plenty of water they can last up to 10 days. Cut the flowers as they develop. The central disc should look fresh and not be discoloured. Stand them in deep water in a shaded position for 2 to 3 hours. If the stem is woody, this should be lightly crushed before conditioning.

Preserving Consider well what you would use a preserved flower for. I find them rather coarse for pictures or collage and much prefer to use them as fresh flowers. Simple flowers are best pressed, while double blooms need to be preserved in desiccant.

Cosmos

Mexico
Compositae

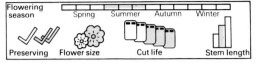

| Flowering season | Spring | Summer | Autumn | Winter |

Preserving | Flower size | Cut life | Stem length

Cosmos sulphureus 'Bright Lights'

Cosmos bipinnatus

Cultivars of the annual species of Cosmos (Cosmea) are attractive free-flowering plants suitable for planting in open ground or growing in containers.

Cosmos bipinnatus, a pink-flowered species, provides a number of vividly coloured cultivars. A particularly fine example is *C.b.* 'Candy Stripe', with ice white flowers edged and striped with brilliant crimson. It is early flowering and grows to 2½ft (75cm) high. *C.b.*

'Klondyke Goldcrest', also early to flower, has double flowers of an exquisite golden orange, height 2ft (60cm); *C.b.* 'Klondyke Diablo' is a fiery red form.

C. sulphureus is another desirable species, generally sold in a mixed blend of superb bright colours as *C.s.* 'Bright Lights Mixed', height 2-2½ft (60-75cm). *C.s.* 'Sulphureus Sunset' has brilliant red, semi-double flowers, height 2½ft (75cm). Both forms bloom freely throughout summer and continue flowering until early autumn frosts.

Cultivation and propagation Cosmos likes a dry, poor soil and does best in hot years. Dead head regularly. Sow seed either in a coldframe or under cloches in early spring, in boxes containing a peat based compost. When the seedlings are large enough to handle prick them out and grow them on under the coldframe. Harden them off for planting in their flowering positions in late spring. Where no protection can be provided delay sowing until late spring and sow where flowering is to take place. When the seedlings are large enough to handle thin them out to stand 1½ft (45cm) apart.

Uses This is a very showy flower that delights in the summer sunshine. The colours are extremely bright and the flower size can be up to 4in (10cm) across. This puts it in the range of the larger flower arrangement. Its rather flat face suits the focal area position, whilst any of the smaller blooms can be sprinkled through the design to continue the colour scheme.

Conditioning The flowers should be cut during the cool of the day as they flag slightly during conditioning if they are not charged with moisture. Stand them in deep water for 3 hours in a shaded area.

Preserving The finest flowers are the single varieties and these press extremely well. The colours are quite startling and make a fine centre for a pressed flower design.

Dahlia

Mexico
Compositae

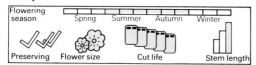

Dahlia 'Bellamour'

Dahlia 'Gerrie Hoek'

Dahlia 'Beechy'

Dahlia 'Doris Day'

Dahlia is a half-hardy tuberous perennial with a variety of flower forms and colours. The following are excellent garden cultivars for summer and autumn flowering, and all are suitable material for cutting, as the flowers are closely petalled, appear prolifically and have long stems that take up water easily.

Dahlia 'Amelisweert'

DECORATIVE DAHLIAS

These are fully double flowers with broad ray florets. Cultivars include: 'Arabian Night', dark red flowers, height 3½ft (105cm); 'Duet', white flowers tipped with blood red, height 4ft (120cm); 'Gerrie Hoek', yellow-tinted pink flowers, height 4½ft (135cm); 'Glory of Heemstede', sulphur yellow, early flowering, height 4ft (120cm); 'House of Orange', glowing orange flowers, height 4ft (120cm); 'Lavender Perfection', deep lavender flowers, height 5ft (150cm); 'Peter', deep pink flowers shading to light pink at the centre, height 3½ft (105cm).

POMPON AND BALL DAHLIAS

These are fully rounded forms, the pompon dahlias typically smaller than the ball types: 'Amusing' (ball), yellow edged with orange, height 3½ft (105cm); 'Brilliant Eye' (ball), brilliant scarlet, height 3ft (90cm); 'Doxy' (pom), ivory white, height 3ft (90cm); 'Potgeiter' (pom), bright yellow, height 3ft (90cm); 'Pride of Berlin' (pom), lilac-pink, height 3½ft (105cm).

CACTUS DAHLIAS

The characteristic of the cactus type is the pointed florets giving a spiky outer contour to the flower. Cultivars include: 'Cheerio', purple-red tipped with white, height 4ft (120cm); 'Doris Day', cardinal red, height 4ft (120cm); 'Hit Parade', signal red, height 4½ft (135cm); 'My Love', creamy white, height 3½ft (105cm); 'Preference', coral pink, height 3½ft (105cm); 'Promise', pure yellow, height 4ft (120cm); 'Purple Gem', glowing cyclamen purple, height 2½ft (75cm).

Cultivation and propagation Dahlias like a sunny position. They are gross feeders, so the plot should be well cultivated, and a generous amount of farmyard manure or well-rotted garden compost incorporated, in the autumn. A dressing of a good general fertilizer should be sprinkled on the soil just prior to planting in early summer. Over-wintered or divided tubers may be planted in late spring as the buds will not be very developed and a covering of soil will protect them from frost. Rooted cuttings must not be planted until all danger of frost is over. Plant dahlias carefully, taking out enough soil in the planting hole to accommodate the plant's rootball. Lightly firm the soil. At the same time carefully insert stakes of a length to match the final height of the variety. Tie the plant to the stake as it develops. Mulch between the plants and water in dry weather.

The tips of the young plants should be pinched out about three weeks after planting, to encourage lateral growth. The aim should be 6 to 8 shoots per plant, for prime quality flowers. The stems should also be disbudded regularly to give single flowers on long stems for cutting. Dead head as the blooms fade.

After flowering leave the dahlias until frost has blackened the stems. Lift carefully with a fork and shake the soil from the roots. Cut the stems back to 6in (15cm) and store the tubers for about a week in a frost-proof shed to dry. Shake any loose soil from the tubers and then pack in dry peat or straw in boxes. It helps to prevent fungus attack if the tubers are dusted with flowers of sulphur. Examine the tubers regularly and discard any that are showing signs of disease.

Dahlias may be propagated from seed, by division of the plants and by cuttings. Producing dahlias from seed is the method used for many of the bedding type dahlias each year but is not to be recommended for the other dahlias, as these do not come true to type from seed.

The easiest way of increasing plant stocks is by division of the dahlia tubers. This is best undertaken when the new buds begin to appear. Close examination will indicate that these new buds are usually situated at the base of the old stem and not on the tubers. Pieces of tuber which are to be used for planting must have attached to them some of the old stem, carrying one or more new buds, otherwise they will not grow. The division of the dahlia tubers is best undertaken with a sharp knife.

Start the tubers into growth in gentle heat 50°F (10°C) in early spring. If a greenhouse is not available perhaps one could start them into growth in a warm shed or some other suitable place. Light is not important at this early stage. Small numbers of dahlia tubers should be placed in boxes containing a layer of seed compost or peat. The plants need spraying with water once each day, in the first instance, more frequently as the buds begin to appear.

Dahlia cuttings may be obtained in one of two ways. When they are about 4in (10cm) long the cuttings may be taken, together with a piece of the old tuber, though this procedure limits the total numbers of cuttings which may be obtained from each tuber.

For a greater increase in numbers of plants it is far better to sever each cutting, with a sharp knife, about ½in (1.25cm) above the tuber. If you do this there is every likelihood that fresh buds will develop from the stump for further cuttings. Trim the cuttings by making a second cut just beneath a node (leaf-joint), as this is the place on the stem where rooting is best achieved. Dip into hormone rooting powder and insert several cuttings into seed trays or plant-pots containing a mixture of two parts peat to one part sand. This compost should be well watered prior to the cuttings being inserted and no further water should be given until the plants show some signs of growth. Place in a warm, light situation to encourage early rooting. The minimum air temperature should be about 55°F (12.5°C). Unrooted cuttings may wilt if not given some protection from the sun, such as a sheet or paper spread over the top of them. When the cuttings are well-rooted, pot up individually and keep in a frost free place until planting out.

Uses The petal shape of this generous flower often influences where it is to be used. The dramatic shape of the cactus dahlia adds considerable impact to a bold free form or a modern design. Decorative dahlias have more rounded petals and lend themselves more to the sophisticated traditional style of arrangement. They can be used at various stages of development allowing you to spread them throughout the design without losing continuity of form and colour.

Conditioning Cut the flower stem just above the leaf axil; remove any foliage that will come into contact with water and condition them for 3 hours in a shaded room. Aftercare is most important as they are gross drinkers, so top up the arrangement at least once a day.

Preserving A light spray with water will extend the cut life of the flowers. Dahlias are not easy to preserve. Small-flowered varieties can be dried in desiccant.

Digitalis

Foxglove
Europe, North Africa and Western Asia
Scrophulariaceae

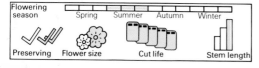

Digitalis purpurea 'Excelsior'

*D*igitalis purpurea **is the hardy biennial foxglove native to Europe and Great Britain. For garden planting, the original species has been replaced by 'Excelsior' hybrids which have tall spikes of tubular flowers in a colour range of white, cream, primrose yellow, pink and purple. These impressive flowers appear in midsummer and grow to a height of about 5ft (150cm).**

Cultivation and propagation *Digitalis* grows best in damp shady places under trees. However, it can grow successfully in a sunny situation providing that one keeps the soil about the roots moist at all times. The seeds are very small. Sow them very thinly in the flowering position, in early summer. Rake the soil to a fine tilth so that the seeds fall into the soil crumbs. They do not require covering with soil. Germination will occur within 2 to 3 weeks. When the plants are large enough to handle they should be thinned out to stand 6in (15cm) apart in each direction. Flowering will commence in midsummer the following year.

Uses The foxglove is a statuesque flower with a decided rural flavour. Used in limited numbers it will form a perfect foil for other unsophisticated flowers and foliages in a simple landscape arrangement. Because of its columnar growing habit it is often used to establish the height in a more formal design. As the flowers tend to clothe most of the stem it is particularly suitable for continuing the flower colour from the extremes of the design to the centre.

Conditioning The lower foliage should be removed before conditioning in water for at least 2 hours.

Preserving Always let a number of flowering stems set seed. These may be collected during the autumn and used almost immediately as dried material. Individual flowers can be removed from the flower stem and dried in desiccant, the tubular shape of the flower increases the three-dimensional quality of a dried flower picture.

Eremurus

Foxtail Lily
Asia
Liliaceae

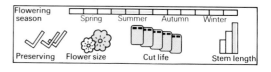

*E*remurus **provides some of the most stately spikes of flowers of all the herbaceous perennials. It is tolerant and easy to grow, well**

Eremurus bungei

Uses An extremely elegant flower to grow and arrange, the upright growth demands that it is used as height material in the large opulent designs of summer flowers and foliages. It is particularly useful in church arrangements when pastel shades are used. The height of the flower makes it very easy to be seen at a distance.

Conditioning Cut the stem when the lower flowers are open, it will continue to develop in a limited way once it is arranged. Stand the stems in deep water in a cool room for at least 3 hours to condition.

Preserving I have not been successful at preserving the entire flowering stem using any of the recognized methods. The small star flowers can be cut from the growing stem and dried in desiccant.

Eremurus robustus

suited to a position in the border or as a featured plant in island beds. **The flowers appear in early summer and are individually long lasting. The tall spikes need shelter from strong winds, as they can attain a height of 10ft (300cm).**

Eremurus bungei, **a native of Iran, produces large spikes of bright yellow star-shaped flowers, height 3ft (90cm).** *E. elwesii* **has fragrant pink flower spikes, height 7-9ft (210-270cm).** *E.* **'Highdown Hybrids' have a colour range of pink, orange, yellow and copper, height 5-6ft (150-180cm).** *E. robustus*, **native to Turkestan, produces flower spikes of soft pink or white, height 8-10ft (240-300cm).**

Cultivation and propagation *Eremurus* will grow in any well-drained soil in sun. Propagation is by division of the roots during the dormant season.

Gladiolus

Sword Lily
S. Africa, Asia Minor, S. Europe
Iridaceae

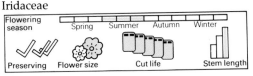

Gladiolus 'The Bride'

Gladiolus is a genus of herbaceous perennial flowering plants which in summer produce large flower spikes on stiff, erect stems. The leaves are sword-shaped, forming a fan-like arrangement. The showy flowers provide a wide range of bright colours, some interestingly bicoloured. They are popular for mixed border plantings and are excellent as cut flowers. Gladioli can also be

Gladiolus 'Red Cascade'

Gladiolus 'Blue Conqueror'

Gladiolus 'Sweepstake'

grown in large pots or tubs for patio planting.

During their resting period in winter gladioli survive in the form of corms (swollen stem bases). These are usually lifted in autumn and replanted in spring each year.

The following selection represents some of the best named hybrids currently available.

GLADIOLUS NANUS
Early summer flowering, height 18-24in (45-60cm): 'Amanda Mahy', deep pink; 'Albus', white; 'Charm', magenta rose; 'The Bride', white veined with greenish-yellow; 'Guernsey Glory', coral red with creamy blotch; 'Peach Blossom', rose pink with a white eye.

LARGE-FLOWERED GLADIOLI
Summer flowering in early, mid or late season, height 36-60in (90-150cm). The following recommended hybrids are grouped according to flower colour:

Red 'Aristocrat', carmine-red shaded with crimson-orange, late; 'Carmen', brilliant scarlet blotched white, early; 'Oscar', blood red, mid-season.

Orange 'Nicole', deep orange blotched red, early; 'Queen of Holland', pure orange, mid-season; 'Tiger Flame', bright orange with yellow marks, mid-season.

White and cream 'Classic', ivory white with rose stripes, mid-season; 'Mary Housley', creamy white with scarlet blotch, mid-season; 'Snow Princess', creamy white, mid-season; 'Tequendama', pure white, early; 'White Friendship', white with pale yellow blotch, mid-season.

Pink and salmon 'Albanberg', salmon rose, mid-season; 'Deciso', shell pink with scarlet blotch, early; 'Frosty Pink', lilac pink, early; 'Wine and Roses', rose pink blotched purple, mid-season; 'Sweepstake', shell pink and carmine, late.

Blue and purple 'Blue Conqueror', deep blue, early; 'Fidelio', cyclamen purple, mid-season; 'Mr W.E. Cobley', lavender blue with white blotch, mid-season.

Yellow 'Aldebaran', yellow with blood red blotch, early; 'Green Woodpecker', lime yellow with purple blotch, mid-season; 'Nova Lux', rich yellow, mid-season.

GLADIOLUS PRIMULINUS HYBRIDS
Late summer flowering, height 30-36in (75-90cm): 'Carioca', brilliant orange; 'Columbine, carmine-rose with creamy white centre; 'Leonore', pale yellow; 'Piquant', deep purple; 'White City', pure white.

DUTCH BUTTERLY GLADIOLI
Late summer flowering, height 36in (90cm):
'Eastbourne', violet; 'Green Bird', uranium
green; 'Ivanhoe', yellow with red blotch;
'Merry', coral pink.

Cultivation and propagation *Gladiolus* will
grow in any ordinary well-drained garden soil
providing it is in sun. Planting should take
place in the open garden as soon as the first
leaves on the trees begin to appear. If one
plants small batches of corms at 14 day
intervals from then to early summer, steady
supplies of flowers can be had over a long
period. If one has a garden frame, then
gladioli can be started into growth a month
earlier, in pots, and planted out in the open
ground when all fear of frost has past. The
time from planting to flowering is about 90
days for the early flowering gladioli; 100 days
for the mid-season ones and 120 days for the
late-flowering types. Corms planted in the
open ground should be 4in (10cm) deep and
6in (15cm) apart. Once flowering has ceased
and the stems have become brown, the
gladioli are forked from the ground. Upon
close inspection, it will be seen that the old
corm has withered and a new one has been
produced to replace it. There are usually small
cormlets attached. The large corms are stored
in a cool, frost-free place until the following
year, when they are planted and produce a
fresh crop of flowers. The small cormlets are
also planted, but in a nursery bed in an out-of-
the-way place, as they will need several years'
more growth before reaching flowering size.
Uses The list of *Gladiolus* in the text will enable
you to grow tall spiky flowers to suit any
occasion. It is a flower that will fit into all
categories of design. As outline material in a
formal design I prefer to use it to establish the
height of an arrangement. Used at the lower,
outer edges it tends to look stiff and
unyielding. In more modern, even abstract,
work it may be used for its form, texture or as
blocks of colour.
Conditioning Cut the stem when the lower
flowers are beginning to develop. It will
continue to open once it has been arranged.
Stand the cut stems in water until you need to
arrange them. The flowers can be advanced or
retarded depending on the amount of heat
they are subjected to, during the conditioning
process.
Preserving The form of the flower precludes
its preserving in the flower press. Some of the
smaller flowers may be preserved in desiccant.

Godetia

North West America
Onagraceae

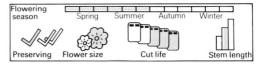

Godetia 'Sybil Sherwood'

Godetia 'Azalea flowered'

The two annual species of Godetia
commonly grown are *Godetia amoena*,
which attains a height of 2ft (60cm) and *G.
grandiflora*, which grows to only about 1ft
(30cm). Single and double or azalea-flowered
forms are available and they are all extremely
showy. The colour range includes various
shades of pink, red and mauve, with some
bicoloured forms. Seed catalogues tend to

offer strains of mixed colours, but you can usually find some straight colours in the form of named cultivars.

'Kelvedon Glory' has salmon orange flowers, height 1ft (30cm); 'Orange Glory' is scarlet-orange, height 1ft (30cm); 'Sybil Sherwood' has flowers of brilliant pink edged with white, height 1½ft (45cm); 'Whitnevi Duchess of Albany' has white flowers, height 1ft (30cm); 'Vivid' is shiny cherry rose, height 1ft (30cm).

Among the mixed strains of Godetia there is 'Grandiflora Double-Flowered Mixed', with flowers in various shades of pink, mauve, carmine, crimson and white. 'Grandiflora Azalea Flowered Mixed' has semi-double azalea-type flowers with wavy-edged petals, height 15in (37.5cm). These are available in an exotic range of colours and provide a breathtaking display when planted en masse.

Cultivation and propagation *Godetia* needs a sunny position and not too rich a soil. Seed of both species may be sown in the open ground either in the spring or the early autumn. After germination the plants are thinned out to stand 1ft (30cm) apart. Flowering commences in late spring from early autumn-sown seed and continues throughout summer with the aid of spring sowing. Autumn-raised plants may need protection in cold areas.
Uses Both the single and double flowered kinds are spiky, ideal for creating an outline. Their flexible stems allow them to flow in a downward direction. The taller cultivars are perhaps the most useful, as the flowers are more widely placed on the stems giving a lighter appearance. The dwarf varieties tend to form a solid clump, discordant as outline material but very useful as an intermediate flower.
Conditioning Remove the lower foliage and crush the stems before conditioning them for 4 hours.
Preserving The brightness of the flower colour is well worth preserving. Do this by pressing when the flower is fully open.

Helichrysum

Straw Flower
Australia
Compositae

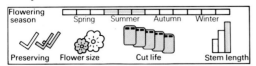

*H*elichrysum bracteatum is a half-hardy annual species also known as the everlasting flower, because the large daisy-like

Helichrysum bracteatum mixed

Helichrysum bracteatum 'Sulphur Light'

flowers dry easily and keep their colour well. For garden use there are both dwarf and tall-growing forms, bearing flowers in a wide array of colours.

H.b. 'Swiss Giants' has flowers of copper, red, orange, rose, scarlet, white, wine red and yellow. It forms tall plants, height 3ft (90cm). It can be obtained as separate colours or mixed seed.

The cultivar *H.b.* 'Monstrosum' has large double flowers and there is a fascinating dwarf form, 'Dwarf Hot Bikini', which bears a mass of glistening scarlet flowers, height 1ft (30cm).

'Bright Bikini', another dwarf form, is available in a blend of mixed colours and in straight colours – bright yellow, salmon rose, terracotta and white – height 1ft (30cm). These form neat, compact plants which create a fine effect when in full flower. When the flowers are preserved for use in dried arrangements, they retain the same bright colour throughout winter.

'Sulphur Light' has silver-grey leaves and clusters of small sulphur yellow, fluffy flowers which become bright orange, height 15in (37.5cm).

Cultivation and propagation The most suitable soil for these plants is a light sandy one, but they will grow equally well on heavier soils providing some sharp sand is introduced to improve drainage. Choose a sunny situation and sow the seeds in the open, where flowering is to occur. Germination takes about two weeks. When the seedlings are large enough to handle they should be thinned out to stand 1ft (30cm) apart. Dwarf strains will not need any support but in the case of the 'Swiss Giants' it is advisable to use canes and string or twiggy branches to keep the stems straight.

Uses *Helichrysum* is probably the most well-known flower for preserving, but because of this it is seldom used in its fresh state. The flowers will dry naturally on the plant, but when fully developed expose a large yellow daisy centre which makes the flower look very flat and is often at odds with the petal colour. When the flower is younger, the undeveloped petals form a cone in the centre making a much more attractive shape. Sometimes the colour on the reverse side of the petal is a different shade, which adds to the interest. It is in this cone stage that they should be gathered for drying. It is a continuous process, so you may have to collect them daily. Pick the flower heads only and immediately mount them on to stub wires. Bend a small hook shape in the wire and insert it in the top of the flower concealing the hook in the petals. The residual sap in the fresh flower will slightly rust the wire and create a strong bond. Once the head is wired, hang them upside down or push them into a block of oasis to complete the drying process which will take up to three weeks in a warm but dry atmosphere.

Iris pumila

Iris germanica 'Jane Phillips'

Iris

North Hemisphere
Iridaceae

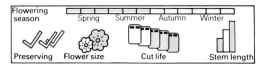

Iris unguicularis

Iris is a large genus of some 200 different species of plants. These are among the classic plants for spring and early summer flowering, with a wide range of fresh colours, notably white, yellow and shades of mauve and blue, but including some unusual brown and bronze tints and some very rich, dark colours. The grouping of two sets of petals creates the characteristic iris flower shape.

Cultivation requirements vary widely, so it is possible to choose a suitable form for specific conditions. The fan-like sprays of sword-shaped leaves provide a striking textural element for mixed plantings. The smaller-growing species and cultivars are well suited to informal plantings, and moisture-loving types can be included in water gardens.

Irises have two quite distinct types of root system. In one type there is a bulb, or bulb-like structure, as in the early-flowering species *Iris reticulata*. In the other type there is an underground stem or rhizome, which stores food through the dormant season and sends up shoots annually which terminate in flowers. The following are all rhizomatous types, listed in order of their flowering period.

The very earliest to flower is *I. unguicularis*, syn. *I. stylosa*. This is a native of Algeria which bears large, scented, lavender-blue flowers on short stems, in winter and early spring. It likes poor, limy soil and flowers best in full sun, which provides hot, dry conditions for the rhizomes during summer months. Heavy soils will need the addition of sharp sand and other gritty material. *I.u.* 'Mrs Barnard' is an improved cultivar with larger flowers which are more freely produced. Both grow to a height of 1ft (30cm).

I. pumila 'Aurea', originating from south-eastern Europe, has delightful pale yellow flowers in spring and grows 10in (25cm) high. This miniature iris should be planted in a sunny position in a rock garden or at the front of a herbaceous border.

I. warlsind is a delightful hybrid with deep blue and yellow flowers during spring, height 1ft (30cm).

I. wilmottiana comes from east Turkestan and has a very pretty cultivar in *I.w.* 'Alba', with pure white flowers blotched orange appearing during late spring, height 10in (25cm).

I. pallida dalmatica is an old favourite, one of the few bearded iris to have magnificent foliage. It bears clear lavender-blue and golden flowers in early summer, height 2½ft (75cm). *I.p.* 'Argentes-Variegata' has cream and glaucous foliage and blue flowers, height 2ft (60cm).

I. germanica (bearded iris) is the 'common iris' which grows some 2½ft (75cm) high and bears fragrant purple and yellow flowers during summer. It has been very long in cultivation and its origin is uncertain. There are many hybrid forms, all useful as cut material because they are of stiff habit and available in an extensive range of colours. The following selection is an indication of the range: all are readily available from garden centres and nurseries and all flower in early summer.

'Arabi Pasha', cornflower blue, height 40in (100cm); 'Berkeley Gold', bright yellow, height 3ft (90cm); 'Black Hills', excellent very dark blue, almost black flowers, height 40in (100cm); 'Butterscotch Kiss', glistening caramel, height 3ft (90cm); 'Golden Alps', ivory white and greenish-yellow, height 3ft (90cm); 'East Indies', light bronze, mauve and yellow, height 4ft (120cm); 'Edward of Windsor', pastel pink, height 40in (100cm); 'Jane Phillips', an outstanding iris with large, ruffled, intense blue flowers, height 3½ft (105cm); 'Ola Kala', rich orange-yellow, height 40in (120cm); 'Pearly Dawn', exquisite pearly pink, height 3ft (90cm).

Bearded iris succeed on a wide range of soils provided that they are well-drained and limy. If there is any doubt about the lime content it is wise to provide a dressing of carbonate of lime in late winter. The main source of sustenance is an annual top dressing of bonemeal, which is applied during late spring. The only other requirement is a sunny siuation. Once established, the plants should be lifted and divided every three years, immediately after flowering ceases.

I. acutiloba is native to Transcaucasia and has creamy white flowers in midsummer, height 6-8in (15-20cm).

I. foetidissima is a native British and European species which prefers a dry, shady, limy soil, even pure chalk. It has yellowish-green and lilac flowers during early summer, height 2ft (60cm). Large orange seeds are produced in autumn which make a marvellous feature for winter flower decorations.

I. sibirica is a native of central Europe and Russia. This is a moisture-loving plant which can be planted near the edge of a pond, or in some other moisture-retentive spot in the garden. When preparing the soil for planting, improve dry soils by the incorporation of lots of peat and well-decayed garden compost. Choose an open, sunny position if possible, although *I. sibirica* will tolerate partial shade.

This species forms bushy clumps of foliage and wiry stems which bear flowers during midsummer. The flowers are among the longest lasting for cut-flower arrangement. They also produce ornamental seed pods which can be dried for winter use.

There are several good cultivars: *I.s.* 'Blue King', deep blue flowers, height 3ft (90cm); *I.s.* 'Ottawa', clear blue flowers, height 3ft (90cm); *I.s.* 'Snow Queen', pure white flowers, height

Iris reticulata 'Harmony'

Iris kaempferi

Iris germanica 'Golden Alps'

32in (80cm); *I.s.* 'Tropic Night', dark violet blue flowers, height 3ft (90cm).

I. kaempferi is a native of Japan and flowers in high summer. It likes moist, lime-free soil. The flowers are orchid-like and quite large in the cultivars, but not so long-lasting as those of *I. sibirica*. It has mauve-purple flowers, height 2½ft (75cm). *I.k.* 'Snowdrift' has pure white flowers, height 3ft (90cm); *I.k.* 'Rose Queen' has soft pink flowers and may be grown in very moist soil or even shallow water, and still remains hardy, height 2ft (60cm).

Propagation Propagation of rhizomatous iris is by division of the rhizomes into smaller pieces after flowering ceases during the summer months. Growth buds may also be removed from the sides of the rhizomes when about as big as a garden pea. A sharp knife is needed for their removal and they are then inserted as cuttings, and given the benefit of a closed shaded coldframe or cloche to encourage rooting. One can also propagate irises from seed in order to obtain additional plants. This is particularly useful for obtaining *I. k.* hybrids and *I. s.* hybrids. Soak the seeds in water for 24 hours and then sow in a well-drained compost, in a closed coldframe, in the early summer. Propagation from seed is slow as the plants take 2 or 3 years to reach flowering size.
Uses The form of this flower is both dignified and individual. It is at home in a massed traditional design or as a focal flower in a stark modern arrangement. Those that flower in the early spring add a welcome touch of blue to a basket of mixed spring flowers. The soft stems can be put into small plastic phials then placed in the water-retaining foam. The larger bearded iris with its strong upward movement is a handsome flower to use in a vertical design where little plant material is needed.
Conditioning The flowers can be cut as the bud is about to open, as they will continue to develop after they have been arranged. Condition them in deep water for 3 hours.
Preserving Sadly the flower does not preserve well, but some seed pods are worth collecting. The best of these is *I. foetidissima*. The seeds are bright orange and revealed once the pod has burst, making an exciting complement to preserved *Choisya ternata* and *Mahonia* foliage.

Lathyrus

Leguminosae

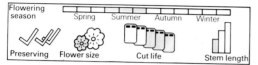

Lathyrus odoratus

This is a large genus of climbing plants. *Lathyrus odoratus* (sweet pea) comes from Italy and Sicily. There is a huge variety of different cultivars – the Spencer range is widely used, plants which are free-flowering throughout summer and grow 6-10ft (180-300cm) high.

The following vigorous cultivars can be recommended for fine colour and prolific blooms: 'Cream Delight', rich cream; 'Firebrand', deep scarlet; 'Gigantic', very large, pure white flowers; 'Hunter's Moon', creamy primrose, frilled flowers; 'Leamington', frilly lilac flowers; 'Monty', deep creamy pink; 'Noel Sutton', rich blue; 'Olympia', deep purple; 'Rosy Frills', large frilled white flowers edged with deep rose; 'Southbourne', almond-blossom pink with white base; 'Winston Churchill', brilliant crimson, frilled and fluted flowers.

Cultivation and propagation The sweet pea, unlike other annual flowering plants, is a gross feeder. While it will grow quite happily in a wide range of soils it will only do so if they are deep, well-drained and well supplied with bulky organic matter in the form of manure or well rotted garden compost. Deep cultivation is essential if good results are to be obtained. Ideally the ground should be double dug in 2ft (60cm) trenches. If this is not possible, liquid feed will be necessary every 14 days through the flowering season.

Towards early spring, when soil conditions will permit, a good dressing of bone meal should be forked into the soil's surface along the line of the trench. Each of these trenches will accommodate two rows of sweet peas and where more than one trench is to be dug they should be some 4ft (120cm) apart. Round holes about 4ft (120cm) in diameter are better than trenches on heavy soils.

Sweet peas may be sown at three distinct times of the year. They may be sown during late spring outdoors in their flowering positions to flower in late summer and autumn. They may also be sown in the autumn in a coldframe or under cloches. Once the seeds have germinated they are grown on cold, with ventilation, but sheltered from rain. Once the plants have developed their second pair of leaves, they are transplanted 3in (7.5cm) apart into other boxes or singly into 3½in (8.75cm) pots containing potting compost. Once the plants have recovered from this move they should have their shoots removed, as this induces the development of basal growths which are much stronger than the original shoots. The plants are grown throughout the winter without any heat, with ventilation being given whenever the weather will permit, keeping the compost on the dry-side. The resulting plants may be transferred to their flowering positions in early spring to flowering in early summer. It is also possible to sow seeds in a warm greenhouse in early spring, following the general advice on pricking out and shoot removal just given. Growth will be fairly rapid under these conducive conditions and by late spring the resulting plants can be hardened off in a coldframe or cloches before planting in their flowering positions. These plants will then flower during midsummer.

Sweet peas need the support of netting or stakes. Canes will prove the most economical as they last for years. The aim is to produce good quality flowers on long stems and the best way of achieving this is by growing the sweet peas on the cordon system, though it reduces the quantity of blooms. For this the plants are set out 8in (20cm) apart in the row. Each one of these plants is then trained up a single cane or string as the case may be. All side growths and tendrils are removed so that all the energies of the plant are devoted into the development of larger flowers and longer stems than normal. No flowers should be permitted to develop until the plants are about 3ft (90cm) high or it is clear that the flower stems have at least four flower buds on them. When the sweet pea plants reach the top of their canes or other supports, they are untied and laid along the ground for some distance down the row before being trained up another support. This encourages the strong growth of the terminal shoot.

Sweet peas grown in a less intensive way are still useful for cut flowers. Just give them something to climb up and allow to grow naturally.

Uses Surely here we have the most feminine of flowers. The slender stems, soft texture, sensitive perfume and delicate colour is sufficient to justify its claim as queen of the annuals. The flowers are well spaced on the stem, giving it a light, airy appearance for outlining a medium-size arrangement or as an adjunct to the focal flowers in a large design. The flowers are elegant and sophisticated and on occasions deserve to be arranged by themselves in an equally elegant container, crystal or silver. They need no added foliage, though a little light grey *Artemisia* or *Senecio* will enhance the pink shades. It is essential to cut sweet peas at least twice per week to encourage further flowering. At the same time any seed pods should be removed, for if left on the plant they make the plant give up producing flowers.

Conditioning Cut the flowers when the top two buds are displaying colour and are beginning to unfurl, as this will prolong the flower's cut life.

Sweet peas have the most amenable habit of going to sleep after cutting, resuming development when placed in water. They can therefore be cut and left in a cool place for a day until you need them. Re-cut the stem and stand them in deep water; they will fully recover within 3 hours.

Lilium henryi

Lilium regale

Lilium

Lily
Northern Hemisphere
Liliaceae

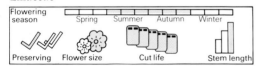

Flowering season	Spring	Summer	Autumn	Winter
Preserving	Flower size		Cut life	Stem length

Lilies all have beautiful flowers and some are of considerable fragrance. While they are popular garden plants for inclusion in mixed beds and borders, their elegant shapes and clear colours are also seen to advantage planted singly or in small groups in large containers. The following recommended are:

Lilium auratum (lily of Japan) has large, very fragrant white flowers, each petal banded with gold and speckled crimson. It is autumn-flowering, height 5ft (150cm).

L. candidum (Madonna lily) is one of the most beautiful and best-loved lilies, with its ivory white flowers and yellow anthers, height

Lilium speciosum hybrid

Lilium auratum

Lilium candidum

Lilium hansonii

4ft (120cm). A native of the eastern Mediterranean region, it requires a warm, sunny situation and likes some lime in the soil.

L. hansonii has bright golden yellow flowers speckled with maroon, which appear in early autumn, height 3ft (90cm). This is a vigorous plant and its clumps of bulbs will need dividing every three to five years. Ideally, this should be grown in a slightly shady situation, such as on the edge of a shrub planting or where it is in the shadow of a building during the hottest part of the day, as it likes to keep its roots shaded and cool.

L. henryi bears bright orange flowers in early autumn, height 5-6ft (150-180cm).

L. longiflorum has very fragrant, glistening white flowers in midsummer, height 2ft (60cm). This species can also be forced into flower in spring, in a cool greenhouse. Plant in the open in a sunny, sheltered place and if possible provide the protection of a cloche to prevent shoots being damaged by late frosts.

L. regale carries large white flowers flushed yellow, with the backs of the petals flushed maroon, in midsummer, height 4-5ft (120-150cm). It should be planted in a sheltered sunny place and given some protection from late frosts.

L. speciosum is very easy to grow and is recommended for the beginner growing lilies for the first time. It bears brilliant white flowers, which are speckled pink or crimson, in early autumn, height 3ft (90cm). It prefers a lightly shaded situation in a lime-free soil and it can be forced in spring, if grown in a cool greenhouse.

There are some very good hybrid lilies with an interesting colour range. 'Black Dragon' has fragrant, creamy white flowers with the outsides of the petals dark purple; it flowers in midsummer, height 4ft (120cm). 'Fiesta Hybrids' vary in colour from pale yellow to bright red and orange; these are summer-flowering, height 3-5ft (90-150cm). 'Golden Clarion Strain' bears excellent golden yellow flowers in summer, height 3-5ft (90-150cm). 'Moonlight' also produces its blooms in summer and these are an unusual greenish colour, height 5ft (150cm). 'Pink Perfection' has clear, deep pink flowers in summer, height 5ft (150cm). 'Stargazer' flowers in late summer and the blooms are red with a white border, height 3ft (90cm). 'Yellow Blaze' has yellow flowers in late autumn, height 3ft (90cm).

Cultivation and propagation Many *Liliums* are stem-rooting, that is to say they grow roots on that section of the stem immediately above the bulb, in addition to the roots which grow from the base of the bulb in the customary manner. *L. candidum* is of this type and should be planted so that the tip of the bulb is just 1in (2.5cm) below the soil surface. All the other species are stem-rooting and require planting 8in (20cm) deep in the soil, so that there is at least 4in (10cm) of soil above the tip of the bulb. They are planted some 6 to 12in (15 to 30cm) apart according to the height of growth of the species concerned, in the late autumn.

The ground in which *Liliums* are to be grown needs to be well drained and not too rich in organic matter, as this causes losses from fungoid diseases and encourages pests which attack and destroy the bulbs. The ideal soil is a light sandy soil. However, heavy soils can be made suitable providing that sand or other suitable gritty material is incorporated. Poor soils can be enriched with either leafmould or peat. Do not use fresh manure. A surface mulch of peat should be applied each spring and forked in each autumn. Some watering will be required during the summer.

Support the taller growing *Liliums* with canes to prevent wind damage.

Lilium species may be increased by seed, but the time it takes for them to germinate varies amazingly as some remain dormant for many months and a great deal depends on the species involved. *L. regale* seed germinates in a matter of weeks, sown in a garden frame or greenhouse, and the resulting seedlings develop into bulbous plants which will flower during the second year. Some other species will take several years more before flowering. Hybrids do not come true from seed and it is necessary to wait for them to multiply naturally, which can be a slow business. It is possible to speed this up by pulling the scales off mature bulbs in the autumn and planting these, with their tips just visible, in sandy soil within a garden frame. These scales will, given time, develop into new flowering bulbs. Bulbils are another means of propagation. Bulbils may be found on the stem of a plant either above or below ground level depending upon the species concerned. These can be removed when they are mature enough to drop off when touched. They should be sown just like one would sow seed, immediately they are collected. They vary in the length of time it takes to reach flowering size.

Uses I hope that I can do sufficient justice to the beauty of this flower in such a short space. Always plan an arrangement around the lily flower. The foliage is stem borne and some must be left to feed and strengthen the bulb. Cutting the flower to the correct length will enable you to enjoy it in an arrangement and ensure a future supply. There are many ways to arrange lily flowers. The splendid form sets it apart as a flower for the centre of a formal design. Those that grow on very long stems can be placed at the sides of a large arrangement to emphasize the bell shape of the flower. They are equally at home in a modern design.

Conditioning Cut the stems when most of the flowers have opened. Remove the stamens to prevent the inner surface being marked by disturbed pollen. Condition them in water in a cool place for up to 4 hours. Once the conditioning process is underway, resist any temptation to handle them as they bruise and discolour very easily.

Preserving It is possible to dry the smaller flowers in desiccant. Some of the larger-flowered types display an exciting arrangement of seed pods that resemble a candelabra. If you are not saving the seed these should be collected as the pod changes to a brown colour and allowed to continue to dry suspended from a line in a light, dry atmosphere.

Limonium

Sea Lavender syn.*Statice*
S. Europe, N. Africa
Plumbaginaceae

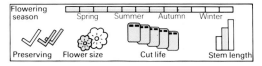

Limonium sinuatum

Limonium species provide bright colour for garden beds or containers. They are particularly valued for providing dried flower material and are often grown mainly for this purpose.

Limonium bonduellii is a perennial species with yellow flowers, height 18in (45cm). *L. sinuatum* bears blue flowers, height 18in (45cm) and has cultivars providing flower colours of light and dark pink or blue, yellow or white. This too is a perennial species, but both *L. bonduellii* and *L. sinuatum* are treated as annuals.

L. suworowii is an annual with long, narrow, slightly curving spikes of rosy pink flowers, height 18in (45cm). By making timed sowings, you can achieve a continuous display of flowers from late spring through summer to autumn.

Cultivation and propagation All these species do well in an open sunny place in any ordinary well drained garden soil.

The earliest flowers are obtained from seeds sown under coldframes and cloches during early spring for transplanting to the open ground during early summer. In late spring further sowings are made in the open to produce later flowers for cutting. Germination takes 14 to 21 days. When the seedlings are large enough to handle they are pricked out into seed boxes containing seed compost and the young plants are hardened off for transferring to the open. Plant out 10in (20cm) apart. Seed may also be sown directly where flowering is to occur.

Uses *Limonium suworowii* and to a lesser extent *L. sinuatum* may be used fresh as outline material for any arrangement. It is as material for drying that these have a much greater value. The stems are strong enough to support the flower head after drying and the flower colour is retained with little or no fading. A favourite area for arranging these flowers is in a seascape. They have an association with the shoreline and certainly add authenticity to a maritime theme. The stems should be cut when the flowers are fully developed, showing maximum colour. Collect them when they are dry and tie them into very loose bundles. Suspend them in a warm room for 2 to 3 weeks. Once they are dry, they can be stored in a box for later use.

Lupinus polyphyllus

Lupinus polyphyllus 'Lulu' strain

Lupinus

Lupin
North America
Leguminosae

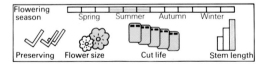

*L*upinus polyphyllus is the commonest and best-known of the lupin species, a rather unpretentious herbaceous perennial with blue flowers. The Russell strains are stronger plants bearing flower spikes in a wide range of colours. The following selection contains some of the best modern cultivars: all flower in midsummer unless otherwise indicated and are readily obtainable.

Lupinus polyphyllus 'Lulu Mixed'

'Chandelier', golden yellow flowers, height 40in (100cm); 'Fireglow', orange-flame flowers, height 3ft (90cm); 'Harlequin', a striking bicolour of bright pink and yellow, height 3ft (90cm); 'Lady Fayre', a dwarfer cultivar, height 2½ft (75cm), with delightful pink and white flowers in late summer; 'Noble Maiden', exquisite ivory white flowers, height 40in (100cm); 'The Governor', blue and white flowers, height 40in (100cm); 'The Pages', carmine-red flowers, height 40in (100cm); 'Thundercloud', violet-purple flowers in early summer, height 3ft (90cm).

'Lulu Mixed' is a good dwarf strain, height about 2ft (60cm), with an impressive range of richly varied flower colours, including bicolours.

Cultivation and propagation Lupins grow best in a light, lime-free soil, which is given a dressing of peat at the time of cultivation. Choose a sunny position for these plants and set them out 15in (38cm) apart in each direction. Established lupins require an application of bonemeal in spring. Mulch with well rotted garden compost or peat in late spring. Lupins are not long lived plants and will need to be lifted and divided every 3 years early in the spring. Stake early in the season before much growth has developed. A second, light crop of flowers can be encouraged by deadheading regularly.

Propagation of named cultivars is always by division of the roots in spring or by root cuttings. Basal cuttings may also be taken in late spring. Lupins can also be propagated from seeds e.g. 'Russell Dwarf Lulu Mixed', height 2ft (60cm) and 'Russell Hybrid Mixed', height 3ft (90cm). These are sown in the open deep, in late spring and when the plants are large enough to handle they are pricked out 6in (15cm) apart and transferred to their flowering positions in the autumn to flower the following year.

Uses This elegant flower is most evocative of cottage gardens and is often simply arranged in a vase without accompanying flowers or foliage. It is not reliable as a cut flower, though this is not to say that you should not try.

Conditioning The stems are hollow and should be filled with water and plugged with a tiny amount of wet oasis and immediately placed in deep water for 3 hours. They can then be arranged in water-retaining foam with confidence, removing the plug before arranging. If they are placed directly into a vase they should still be filled with water and, with your finger covering the end, stood in the vase to prevent an airlock forming.

Preserving It is distressing that a plant as generous in its colour forms will not preserve to any degree. With a little care individual flowers can be removed and dried in desiccant. If the seed head is left, it will prove useful for a limited time as a component for both fresh and dried designs before it finally sheds its pods.

Matthiola

Stocks
Europe and West Asia
Cruciferae

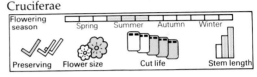

Matthiola 'Ten-week Stocks'

Most of the garden stocks derive from *Matthiola incana*, a species native to southern Europe. The colours range from white and creamy yellow to pink, lilac and deep red, and all are fragrant.

For summer flowering, the 'Ten Week' and column-type stocks are chosen, and are treated as annuals. These are available both in straight colours and mixed blends. 'Trysomatic Giant Imperial Mixed' is a good form, height 1½ft (45cm). It contains about 80 per cent double and 20 per cent single-flowered plants: select them as seedlings – the doubles are stronger-growing.

'Giant Rocket Mixed' is a vigorous column-type stock with a good range of colours, height 2ft (60cm). Another good, taller-growing strain is 'Pacific Column Mixed', height 2½-3ft (75-90cm). At least 65 per cent of the flowers will be double.

Cultivation and propagation Any ordinary garden soil will do providing it contains some lime and is well drained. Choose an open sunny position. Where a warm greenhouse is available, seed may be sown very early in spring and subsequently pricked out into seed boxes which are placed in a coldframe or cloches to harden off before planting. A second method is to sow the seeds thinly where they are to flower in spring, and provide protection with cloches. Seed may also be sown in the open ground where flowering is to occur in late spring. Germination takes 10 to 14 days and the resulting plants should be thinned to stand 10 to 12in (25 to 30cm) apart. They flower throughout the summer.

Uses In their season these are standard material for the arranger. *M. incana* channels its energy into producing a single imposing flower spike. The form is most impressive and the colour range sufficiently wide to warrant a considerable space in the garden. Their bold form makes them highly suitable for the largest of arrangements, flowering at a time when the garden is at its most bountiful and allowing you to compose an arrangement that will be both opulent and heavily perfumed.

Conditioning The stems are woody and should be lightly crushed before conditioning them for up to 6 hours. If it is possible remove the whole plant, wash the soil from the roots and condition the complete plant as usual. The plant can then be arranged in a cone of water. I use both methods and find that the cut life of the flower is not affected by either.

Preserving *M. bicornis* will press. The dull lilac colour is an exciting foil to preserved materials in darker colours.

Nicotiana

Tobacco Plant
Tropical America
Solanaceae

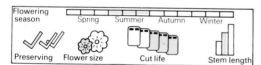

Nicotiana F1 hybrid 'Nicki'

greenhouse. In early summer transfer the plants to a garden frame and harden them off for planting 12in (30cm) apart in the open ground in midsummer.

Uses This is an annual flower that comes in a wide range of colours including that much-sought-after green. It is not sophisticated in appearance, though it is more suited to the full traditional styles of arrangement. The medium size allows its use throughout the design.

Conditioning The leaves are slightly sticky and should be removed before conditioning to prevent them sticking to each other. Stand the stems in water for up to 3 hours.

Preserving *Nicotiana* can be dried in desiccant. To do this, collect the individual flowers just as they open. Any that develop a short tubular back to the flower may be pressed in the usual way.

Papaver

Poppy
Northern sub-Arctic
Papaveraceae

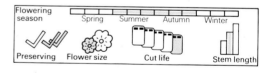

The half-hardy annual species *Nicotiana affinis* bears tube-shaped, highly fragrant flowers in a wide range of colours. The F1 hybrid 'Nicki Mixed' provides a good selection of all the available colours, which include various shades of pink, purple, rose red, pale yellow-green and white, height 16in (45cm).

Cultivation and propagation *Nicotiana* can be grown successfully either in full sun or partial shade. Sow the seeds in spring in a greenhouse with a temperature of 60°F (16°C). Germination will occur in 2 to 3 weeks. Once the seedlings are large enough to handle, prick them off 2in (5cm) apart into seedboxes and grow them on in the first instance in the

Papaver nudicaule (Iceland poppy) is a perennial plant which is best grown as a biennial. From early summer to autumn the long, leafless stems bear large, fragile, paper-thin flowers in the colour range red, pink, yellow and white. They are particularly well suited to informal planting styles, such as mixed border or cottage garden effect.

Papaver nudicaule

P.n. 'Champagne Bubbles' is an F1 hybrid which has large flowers in shades of apricot, bronze, orange, scarlet and yellow, height 1½ft (45cm). **P.n. 'Garden Gnome'** has a tidy habit and bears bright scarlet, salmon, orange, yellow and white flowers on sturdy stems, height 1ft (30cm). **P.n. 'Goodwins'** is another large-flowered strain, in a range of attractive pastel shades, height 2ft (60cm). **P.n. 'Matador'** has large scarlet flowers, height 2ft (60cm). **P.n. 'Tasman Strain'** provides a fine mixture of bright colours, height 15in (37.5cm).

Cultivation and propagation These plants like a sheltered sunny situation in any well drained fertile soils. They need plenty of water in hot dry weather.

Iceland poppies are raised from seed sown during late spring in the place where they are to flower. Sow in the open ground. Germination will take some 10 to 14 days. Once the plants are large enough to handle thin out in two stages. In the first thinning, leave the plants spaced 6in (15cm) apart and about four weeks later go back and make a second thinning choosing the strongest of the remaining plants and discarding the remainder so that they are spaced out 12in (30cm) apart in each direction. In cold areas it may be better to sow earlier in individual pots in the greenhouse to transplant after the last frost.

Uses These flowers, with their interesting cup-shaped bloom and long stems, provide us with useful material for all but the smallest of arrangements. The colours are solid and clear; flowers from a mixed packet of seeds will give an exciting wide range to blend with most other garden colours. The pastel shades of apricot and pink are ideal for delicate designs that are based on flowing lines. The bright yellows and oranges are a striking note when used in modern work or when associated with driftwood. For me, the most attractive arrangement is a simple collection of harmonious colours in an earthenware jug.

Conditioning It is essential to cut the flowers as the buds are about to open. This will prolong the cut life as they continue to develop once they have been cut. At the same time, remove any seed heads that are developing on the plant as this weakens the flower production. As they exude a milky sap, the end of the stem must be sealed. Do this over a naked flame until the tip has turned to charcoal, then stand them immediately in water for up to 4 hours. Alternatively stand the bottom 1in (2.5cm) of stem in boiling water for 20 seconds.

Preserving Allow a number of the flowers to go to seed. The head will dry on the plant and should be collected before it is damaged by adverse weather. Individual petals can be carefully removed from the flower and pressed.

Phlox

E. North America
Polemoniaceae

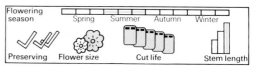

Phlox paniculata 'Sandringham'

The herbaceous Phlox provides bright panicles of fragrant flowers all summer long. They are plants of medium height suitable for planting in borders and mixed beds. By careful selection of cultivars you can create a themed effect of harmonious colours or a brilliant array of multicoloured blooms. The following is a selection of popular cultivars.

Phlox maculata **'Alpha' has fine tapering**

Phlox paniculata 'Starfire'

spires of pink flowers, height 3ft (90cm), and is early-flowering. *P.m.* 'Omega' has white flowers with red-violet centres, freely produced, height 2½ft (75cm).

**   *P. paniculata* 'Border Gem' has flowers of deep violet-blue, height 3ft (90cm). *P.p.* 'Brigadier', one of the most popular cultivars, is brilliant orange-red, height 3ft (90cm). *P.p.* 'Cherry Pink' has exquisite bright carmine-rose flowers, height 3ft (90cm). *P.p.* 'Fujuyama' is outstanding for its pure white flowers, height 2½ft (75cm). *P.p.* 'Harlequin' has red-purple flowers and variegated cream and green foliages, height 3ft (90cm). *P.p.* 'Mother of Pearl' has white flowers suffused pink, height 2½ft (75cm); this is a weather-resistant cultivar which flowers over a long period. *P.p.* 'Pinafore Pink' has light pink flowers, height 2ft (60cm). *P.p.* 'Prince of Orange' is a beautiful, brilliant orange, height 3ft (90cm). *P.p.* 'Sandringham', a popular and well-established cultivar, has striking cyclamen pink flowers with darker centres, height 2½ft (75cm). *P.p.* 'Starfire' is by far the best deep red form, height 2½ft (75cm).**

Cultivation and Propagation *Phlox* likes to grow in a rich loam and is most long flowering in a shady situation. Soils which are lacking in humus should be given a generous dressing of bulky organic matter in the form of farmyard manure, if obtainable. If this is not available well-rotted lawn mowings are the next best material. The secret to obtaining a long flowering season is plenty of humus in the soil and plenty of moisture around the roots during the growing season. A mulch is also beneficial.

   Flowers cut from plants grown in a sunny situation generally have a shorter vase life than those grown in the shade with their roots enjoying a moist cool root run. Planting may take place at any time while the plants are dormant, and the plants should be spaced out 15 to 18in (38 to 45cm) apart in each direction according to the vigour of growth.

   Established beds of *Phlox* should be lifted and replanted every third year, as beds left undisturbed longer than this very quickly deteriorate in vigour. If possible choose a new site each time they are lifted. Divide the plants in the late winter, just before new growth is due to commence. Choose young fibrous roots as free as possible of the older woody bases of the stems. Do not replant too deeply. If eelworm is a problem it is better to propagate by root cultures in the dormant season. For the best flowers, thin out the weaker shoots in spring when they are a couple of inches (a few centimetres) high.

Uses These are flowers for opulent arrangements of mixed summer flowers. *P. maculata*, with its fine tapering flower spike, is a good flower for establishing the height of a massed design. *P. paniculata* has a domed head, carrying multiple flowers on one stem. If the sizes of the heads can be graded they can be used as transitional material or for the focal area. They are very thirsty flowers and should never be without a constant supply of water. ·

Conditioning To condition them remove a good quantity of foliage and stand the stems in water for at least 4 hours.

Preserving Pressing the individual flowers is the most effective way of preserving them. The petals reflex from a small but significant tube formation, which prevents them from lying flat. Place the flower face down on the paper and crease the tube with a pair of tweezers to fold it out of the way.

Primula

Primulaceae

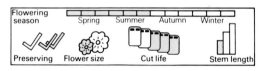

Primula is a large genus of well over five hundred species of herbaceous perennials and monocarpic herbs, which are to be found very widely distributed throughout the world. *Primula polyanthus* is a hybrid which has resulted from crosses between the cowslips and the primroses, and it is known to have been grown since as early as the sixteenth century. Originally all the flowers were yellow, but about the mid-seventeenth century other coloured forms appeared. Modern strains are very brightly coloured.

   'Pacific Giants' is an excellent strain with long stems and large flowers in a wide range of delightful colours – shades of blue, red, pink, white, yellow, height 10in (25cm). There is also another winter hardy F1 hybrid of the

Primula hybrids

Pacific type which is very free-flowering; this is 'Crescendo Hybrid Mixed' and it is particularly useful for growing in cold frames and cloches for early flowering. It has the same large flowers and delightful colours as the 'Pacific Giants', height 12in (30cm). When given protection both these hybrids may be in flower from early spring onwards, and when grown in the open, flower in spring and early summer.

Cultivation and propagation Any reasonably fertile soil will be suitable, and the *polyanthus* prefer sun or partial shade. While these plants are perennials they are generally treated as biennials, with the seed sown one year resulting in plants that flower the following year. The seed is sown on the surface of seed-boxes containing seed compost, in spring, and these are then given the protection of a coldframe or cloche, which during bright sunny days is provided with some temporary shading. A second sowing may also be made in the open in summer, in a moist shady part of the garden. The resulting seedlings are planted out in a nursery bed, in a cool moist place, 6in (15cm) apart in each direction. The nursery bed will need frequent watering in summer. The plants are transferred to their flowering places in the autumn, and should be set out 9in (22.5cm) apart each way. When the planting has been completed dust some bone meal between the plants. Where used, cloches should be placed in position in late autumn.
Uses Here are flowers that have been improved out of all recognition in the last few years. The hybridists have increased the vigour of the plants, giving us flower trusses of up to 9in (22.5cm) across. Perhaps of greater importance is the colour range. Apart from black, all shades can be obtained. The clear colours of red, orange and yellow are a

striking inclusion in a modern design, while the softer shades add charm to traditional styles. Small plants can be lifted from the garden and used wrapped in polythene in a landscape design or added to a basket arrangement.
Conditioning Cut the flower head when most have opened and stand them in deep water for 3 hours. Where it is possible, arrange them directly in water as they sometimes react badly to oasis. Some people like to burn the lower end of the cut stem before conditioning.
Preserving Individual flowers are ideal for pressing and drying in desiccant, providing an exquisite source of delicate flowers in bright or subtle colours for dried flower pictures.

Ranunculus

Asia Minor
Ranunculaceae

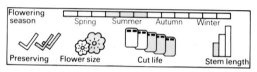

Ranunculus

*R**anunculus asiaticus* has been cultivated from very ancient times and has been the subject of much selection and hybridization, with the result that four distinct types are now available. All are in the colour range white, yellow, orange, red and pink.
  The 'French' ranunculus is best planted in early spring. It produces large double flowers of red, pink, yellow and white with a distinct black central blotch, appearing in early summer, height 10-12in (25-30cm).
  The 'peony-flowered' ranunculus has large double or semi-double flowers in early

summer, but is not so free-flowering as the previous type. In mild districts or under cloches, planting may take place in early winter. This form is available in a varied range of colours.

The 'Persian' ranunculus is far more tender and susceptible to weather damage, even in the mildest districts, and should not be planted until spring. Flowers may be double, semi-double or single and they have a wider range of colouring than the French ranunculus. Flowering begins in midsummer, height 12-16in (30-40cm).

The 'Turban' ranunculus is somewhat hardier than other types and may be planted in autumn or spring. It bears large double or semi-double flowers in midsummer, in a brilliant range of colours, height 9-12in (22.5-30cm).

Cultivation and propagation If possible choose a site in the garden in an open sunny situation. Good drainage is essential, so raised beds may be best. Coarse sand and gritty material should be introduced at the time of cultivation. The peculiar claw-like tubers are planted claws down, 1½in (3.75cm) deep and some 6in (15cm) apart in the row, with the rows set some 6 to 8in (15 to 20cm) apart. A mulch of peat between the plants at the time they peep above the soil is very beneficial to them as this helps to maintain moist conditions around their roots without interfering with the general drainage.

Vary the time of flowering by making several separate plantings of *Ranunculus* in the open so that there is a steady supply available for cutting through the summer. With the aid of a cool greenhouse or perhaps a coldframe or cloches flowering may be induced even earlier. All the above *Ranunculus* last well as cut-flowers. Tubers are lifted for storage when the leaves turn yellow. Store in a dry, frost-free place until spring.

Propagation is by offsets from the old tubers when they are lifted for storage, or from seed germinated in a coldframe.

Uses The bulbous and creeping buttercups are a natural flower to include in a landscape arrangement with other flowers and grasses from the wild area of your garden. The cultivated *Ranunculus* is much taller, with a wider range of colours. Peony-flowered, double or semi-double, they look as though they are made from the finest silk. They grow on fine slender stems and are an elegant component in a formal arrangement. I prefer the arrangement to be small so that each flower is seen and appreciated clearly.

Conditioning Cut them at a cool time of the day and condition them for 2 hours in a cool position.

Preserving The double and semi-double flowers will be spoiled by pressing, so it is wiser to dry them in dessicant. Buttercups and buttercup types may be pressed successfully, to be used in a collage or picture of other wild flowers and grasses.

Rosa

Rose
Northern Hemisphere
Deciduous
Rosaceae

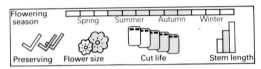

Rosa 'Blue Moon'

There are varying estimates as to the numbers of different roses that exist, but the genus is known to have at least 130 species, and a vast multitude of garden hybrids has been produced over the years. Roses are extremely popular garden flowers and cut flowers, as their range of colour is so wide and many are very fragrant. Ideally, you should see different varieties for yourself during the flowering season, in order to choose. The following is a selection of favourite hybrid tea (HT) and floribunda (FL) roses grouped according to colour. They flower from early summer to late autumn.

RED
'Alec's Red' (HT), large bright red flowers of considerable fragrance, sturdy growth, height 32in (80cm). 'City of Belfast' (FL), clusters of brilliant orange-scarlet flowers, height 2ft (60cm). 'Josephine Bruce' (HT), very large, richly fragrant, velvety deep crimson flowers, height 32in (80cm). 'Wendy Cussons' (HT),

Rosa 'Peace'

Rosa 'Iceberg'

Rosa 'Wendy Cussons'

large cherry red flowers with paler red reverse, vigorous growth, height 32in (80cm).

PINK

'Blessing' (HT), large, soft coral pink flowers in clusters; upright habit, height 32in (80cm). 'Congratulations' (HT), large deep pink flowers fading to soft pink, borne in clusters; sturdy, erect growth, height 40in (100cm). 'Elizabeth of Glamis' (FL), intense salmon, richly fragrant flowers in clusters, height 32in (80cm). 'Queen Elizabeth' (FL), large clear pink flowers borne singly and in clusters on sturdy, almost thornless stems, height 5ft (150cm).

YELLOW

'Arthur Bell' (FL), clusters of highly fragrant buttercup yellow flowers which age to pale yellow, height 32in (80cm). 'Grandpa Dickson' (HT), large lemon yellow flowers borne in great profusion on long, sturdy stems; erect growth, height 32in (80cm). 'Peace' (HT), very large, deep yellow flowers with a reddish flush, borne in great profusion; vigorous, erect growth, height 5ft (150cm). 'Troika' (HT), large orangey yellow, richly fragrant flowers; upright habit, height 32in (80cm).

LILAC

'Blue Moon' (HT), large, ice blue strongly fragrant flowers freely produced on long stems; erect habit, height 32in (80cm).

WHITE AND CREAM

'Iceberg' (FL), clusters of large, pure white, sweetly fragrant flowers, which have a tendency to become tinted pink in autumn; erect, vigorous habit, height 32in (80cm). 'Margaret Mevril' (FL), well-formed, very fragrant white flowers borne singly or in clusters, height 3ft (90cm). 'Pascali' (HT), medium-sized, creamy white flowers on long stems; free-flowering all season, height 32in (80cm).

BICOLOURS

'Chivalry' (HT), well shaped bright red and ivory white flowers on sturdy stems; vigorous, erect habit, height 40in (100cm) or more. 'Court Jester' (FL), finely shaped golden orange and yellow flowers borne singly and in clusters; upright habit, height 40in (100cm) or more. 'Matangi' (FL), clusters of orange-vermilion and silver flowers; moderate vigour, height 26in (65cm). 'Piccadilly' (HT), large scarlet and gold flowers produced steadily throughout the summer, beginning early in the season, height 32in (80cm). 'Pink Parfait', freely produced, pink and cream flowers in dense clusters on almost thornless stems, height 2½ft (75cm). 'Rose Gaujard' (HT), large magenta and silvery white flowers on stiff, erect stems, height 32in (80cm).

Cultivation and Propagation Roses can be grown successfully on a wide range of soils providing they are not subject to water-logging during the winter. Contrary to general belief roses do not like heavy clay soils. Choose an open sunny site. Light soils will require the incorporation of some bulky organic matter to improve their fertility and moisture retention. Clay soils will need the incorporation of coarse sand or other suitable gritty material to improve their drainage. Where the soil is shallow, raised rose beds can be constructed by the introduction of suitable soil from elsewhere to provide the appropriate depth. This is also a suitable solution when confronted with heavy wet clay soils. Planting is best undertaken during autumn or spring.

Pruning of newly planted roses should be fairly severe and this is best done in late spring. The weaker shoots are cut back to two buds while the strong shoots are cut back to four buds. Prune established roses in mid-spring, in a similar way. Dead and diseased shoots are also cut out at this time. The aim is to create an open vase-shaped bush and the pruner should endeavour to cut to an outward facing bud. Established roses of vigorous growth such as 'Peace' (HT) and 'Queen Elizabeth' (FL) should have their long stems shortened by up to half in late autumn, to prevent damage from wind-rock during the winter. Summer pruning consists of removing dead flowers by cutting back to a wood bud, and not simply cutting off the flower heads.

Hybrid Tea roses and Floribunda roses are increased in number by budding them on to rootstocks of wild species of roses such as *R. canina*, *R. laxa*, *R. rugosa* etc., during late summer and this is a job best left in the hands of the commercial nurseryman.

Uses No flower arranger would want to be without roses. They are not flowers to be arranged in the accepted fashion, and there will be times when the flowers will be best displayed in a simple glass or silver vase. As a feature in a design of mixed summer flowers arranged in a traditional style they are beyond compare. Roses that are of a particularly striking colour or size should be restricted to the focal area. Those that have not been disbudded and are on a slender stem can be used throughout the design. 'Peace' will grow to a considerable size and looks most effective arranged with wood in a simple modern container. One of the most traditional styles is the basket of roses. This need not contain masses of roses, as other flowers like *Alchimella mollis* or *Astrantia* may be included. The flowering period is often long, and sometimes roses flower twice a year which makes them useful in September for arranging with dahlias and chrysanthemums.

Conditioning Cut the flowers in bud, remove the lower thorns and leaves, and stand the stems in deep water in a cool area for at least 2 hours. Any that show signs of wilting should be removed. Recut the stem and stand the tip in boiling water for 10 seconds before returning the flower to the conditioning bucket.

Preserving The rose is an ideal flower to preserve. It can either be pressed or dried in desiccant. I favour the latter method to maintain the shape of the flower.

Tulipa

Tulip
Spain, the Mediterranean region, Asia Minor, Asia and Russia
Liliaceae

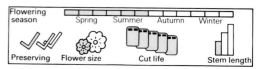

Tulipa 'Sorbet'

Tulip species have, for the most part, been superseded by hybrids. There are fifteen categories of tulip types, those below being selected to provide a good range across the flowering season; other popular types include the single-flowered Greigii and Kaufmannia hybrids. The flowering times listed are the natural ones; most can be forced into flower earlier in the year.

SINGLE EARLY TULIPS (SPRING)
'Bellona', deep golden yellow, fragrant flowers, height 16in (40cm). 'Christmas Marvel', cherry pink, height 14in (35cm). 'Ruby Red', scarlet, height 14in (35cm).

TRIUMPH TULIPS (LATE SPRING)
'Grevel', rose pink edged with ivory white, height 16in (40cm). 'Sorbet', exterior feathered

red with creamy white interior, height 2ft (60cm). 'Paul Richter', bright geranium red, height 20in (50cm). 'Prince Charles', purple-violet, height 18in (45cm).

DARWIN HYBRIDS (LATE SPRING)
'Ad Rem' (not for forcing), scarlet, height 24in (60cm). 'Gudoshnik', creamy yellow with red and rose, height 24in (60cm). 'Striped Apeldoorn', red striped yellow, height 24in (60cm).

LILY-FLOWERED TULIPS (EARLY SUMMER)
'Aladdin', rich crimson edged with yellow, height 20in (50cm). 'Lilac Time', violet-purple, height 22in (55cm). 'White Triumphator', large pure white flowers, height 28in (70cm).

PARROT TULIPS (EARLY SUMMER)
'Blue Parrot' (not for forcing), bluish-purple, height 24in (60cm). 'Orange Favourite'(not for forcing), fragrant orange flowers, height 22in (55cm). 'Red Champion', rich scarlet flowers, height 22in (55cm). 'Texas Gold', deep yellow flowers with narrow red edge to the petals, height 20in (50cm). 'Sunshine', golden yellow, height 18in (45cm). 'White Parrot' (not for forcing), large pure white flowers, height 20in (50cm).

Cultivation and propagation Tulips can be grown on any ordinary well-drained garden soil either in full sun or slight shade. Plant in the open garden in late autumn, 8½in (22.5cm) apart and 4in (10cm) deep.

Propagation is by the removal of the small bulblets which develop on the base of the mature tulip bulbs. These are removed when the bulbs are lifted after flowering. These are then stored until replanted in the late autumn. It takes several years to produce flowering bulbs of a suitable size.

Uses Choosing which tulips to grow in the garden can be as exciting as seeing them grow and subsequently arranging them. The colour range is vast and as the form of the flower is pleasing in itself there is no need to worry about what to associate them with. As a component in a massed design of spring flowers they can be used throughout the arrangement. One or two self-coloured flowers look very striking arranged with a bare branch in a modern container.

Conditioning The cut flower will last a considerable time. Cut the flower as it is showing colour, as it will continue to develop once it has been arranged. The main problem is that the stem continues to grow after cutting, which usually means that the stem becomes bent. To reduce this, wrap a small number of stems in newspaper, secure with an elastic band and condition them in deep water for at least 3 hours. Once the flower has been arranged it will still be attracted to the light

Tulipa Darwin hybrid

Tulipa 'Sunshine'

Tulipa greigii 'Marjoletti'

and those that have been arranged at a downward angle usually turn upwards like candelabra. It is best to accept this and leave room in the arrangement to compensate. **Preserving** Unfortunately they do not preserve easily. The best method is to press each petal separately and reassemble them on to a seed head.

Zinnia 'Dahlia Flowered'

Zinnia

Mexico
Compositae

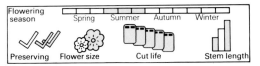

Flowering season	Spring	Summer	Autumn	Winter
Preserving	Flower size		Cut life	Stem length

Zinnia 'Red Sun'

Zinnia 'Ruffles' hybrid

Zinnia elegans **is a half-hardy annual suited to sheltered places. They make generous plants with lush green foliage and large, bright flowers. Frequent cutting encourages prolific flowering throughout the summer; if blooms are not taken for cut flowers, the plants should be deadheaded regularly.**

The 'dahlia-flowered' zinnias are a popular form, with very large, double flowers up to 5in (12.5cm) across, which may be white, yellow, gold, salmon or crimson, with a contrast of one of the other colours, height 2-2½ft (60-75cm). Generally these are available in mixed colours, but occasionally straight colours are offered in seed catalogues.

Modern F1 hybrids are in single colours: 'Golden Sun', golden yellow flowers 4in (10cm) across; 'Red Sun', flowers of similar

Zinnia 'Pacific Yellow'

Zinnia 'Golden Sun'

size which are brilliant scarlet; 'Pacific Yellow' is another F1 hybrid of the dahlia-flowered type, producing soft yellow flowers early in summer, and noted for its weather-resistant qualities. All grow to 2ft (60cm) in height.

The giant dahlia-flowered hybrid 'Envy' is a specially interesting form, with unusual pale apple green, double and semi-double flowers up to 4in (10cm) across, height 2ft (60cm).

For large cactus-flowered zinnias, choose the F1 hybrid 'Zenith All Colours Mixed'. The flowers are 5-6in (12.5-15cm) across and have a thick, ball-shaped form. They make excellent cut flowers and grow to a height of 2½ft (75cm). Flowers in a wide range of colours are found in 'Ruffles Mixed'. They are 2in (5cm) across and the plants grow 2ft (60cm) high. Some seed catalogues offer straight colours of rose or pale pink, deep yellow, deep scarlet and creamy white.

Cultivation and propagation *Zinnia* likes a deep fertile soil which has been well prepared. The soil must contain adequate humus and it is necessary for some manure or well rotted garden compost to be incorporated at planting time. Heavy soils will also benefit from the incorporation of sharp sand or other gritty material to improve their drainage. Choose an open, sunny, yet sheltered situation for these plants.

If good-quality flowers are to be produced it will be necessary to remove all side buds as they develop. Some watering of the plants may also be required during periods of dry weathery They flower in summer and autumn.

The seed is sown either in a cool greenhouse or in a coldframe, in spring, in seed boxes containing seed compost. Germination may take 9 to 16 days. When the seedlings are large enough to handle, they are pricked out into other seed boxes containing potting compost and grown on in the protection of a coldframe. Ventilation is given during the warmer spring days and the plants are hardened off in readiness for transferring to their flowering positions after the frosts. Seed may be sown later, where it is to flower. When the plants are large enough to handle they are thinned out to stand 12in (30cm) apart. Once established in their flowering positions, in the open, Zinnias should have a mulch of peat spread about their roots to help conserve soil moisture.

Uses If any flower adds distinction to an arrangement it must surely be the *Zinnia*. The multi-petalled round form comes in such a variety of sizes, that it is possible to grow sufficient to meet the needs of any scale of arrangement. The texture is slightly coarse without affecting the beauty of the colour so it can be used in both traditional and modern styles of design. The smaller blooms can be used as intermediate flowers to establish a framework of colour and form. While the larger blooms may be used to create a focal area. One exciting colour form for this position is 'Envy', a clear green colour which darkens slightly as it ages. Never cut many to use with mixed flowers, but reserve one or two as a highlight for an all-foliage arrangement – the effect is quite breathtaking.

Conditioning The flowers have thin, tough petals, so little wilting takes place after cutting and about 3 hours in water is all they need to condition them. Occasionally the stem will kink just below the flower head as it conditions, but a small length of wire inserted through the top of the flower down into the stem will correct this with no detrimental result to its cut flower life.

Preserving The layered effect of the petals reduces their suitability as pressed flowers, though it can be done. I much prefer to dry them in desiccant, as the colour remains sharp and the exquisite form is not affected. They are very easy to mount on to false stems or wires. If wire is used a spray effect can be achieved by binding several flowers together. Arrange them with preserved foliage and seed heads, where the Zinnias will introduce a change of colour without the need to use any other flowers either fresh or dried.

SHRUBS AND TREES

Acer

Maple
Northern Hemisphere
Deciduous
Aceraceae

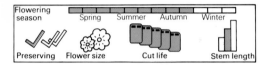

Acer palmatum 'Dissectum'

Acers are popular ornamental shrubs and trees for their interesting leaf shapes and, in some cases, very spectacular colouring. Smaller forms can be grown in containers.

Acer *japonicum*, a species native to Japan, forms a large bush of soft green, lobed leaves with good red autumn tints before leaf fall. It has some even more attractive cultivars: *A.j.* 'Aconitifolium' has deeply lobed green leaves that turn brilliant crimson in autumn; it is also a rounded shrub, height 6ft (180cm). *A.j.* 'Aureum' is a golden form that makes a delightful round, slow-growing bush, height 3-4ft (90-120cm). It benefits from being in slight shade so that its leaves are not scorched by the sun, and sheltered from cold winds, which can delay development of new leaves in spring.

A. palmatum (Japanese maple) forms a

beautiful ornamental tree, growing to a height of 12-14ft (360-420cm). It has large palmate, deeply lobed, bright green leaves which turn orange-red in autumn prior to leaf-fall. It has quite a few cultivars which vary in habit and leaf form.

A.p. 'Dissectum' forms a low, rounded bush of slow growth. It has finely divided leaves consisting of five to eleven pointed lobes, fresh green becoming bronzy yellow in the autumn, height 2½-4ft (75-120cm).

A.p. 'Dissectum Atropurpureum' has rich purple leaves during the summer, which turn crimson before leaf-fall. *A.p.* 'Dissectum Garnet' has the same finely divided leaves and these are deep crimson all summer. It is of more vigorous growth, height 4½ft (135cm).

A. pseudoplatanus 'Brilliantissimum' is a cultivar of the native European sycamore. This is a small, slow-growing tree of mop-headed habit, which in time reaches 12ft (360cm). The young leaves are coral pink, later turning to yellow-green before finally becoming green.

Cultivation Acer will grow in any fertile moist soil in sun or partial shade.
Uses A striking leaf to use in a foliage arrangement. The autumn colour that the foliage adopts late in the season is particularly attractive when used with dried seed pods and chrysanthemums.
Conditioning Immature foliage must be floated in water for 1 hour, then allowed to stand for a further 2 hours in cold water.
Preserving Sprays of leaves do not absorb glycerine, so the best method of preserving is to press the individual leaf. This can be done at any stage of development.

Artemisia

Deciduous
Compositae

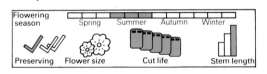

Artemisia *arborescens* is a sub-shrub native to southern Europe which has provided the attractive garden cultivar *A.a.* 'Powis Castle'. This has finely divided, silver-grey leaves and is of compact, rounded habit, height 2-3ft (60-90cm).

A. ludoviciana is a herbaceous perennial that forms a dense clump of pale grey foliage: the cultivar *A.l.* 'Silver Queen' has downy stems and silvery-green, divided leaves, height 2-3ft (60-90cm).

Cultivation and Propagation Artemisia

Artemisia ludoviciana

Aucuba japonica

requires a poor, not rich, well-drained soil. It is particularly suited to growing on the rock garden or a dry sunny bank. Plant in spring. Propagation is by stem cuttings secured in summer and rooted in a sandy soil in a closed and shaded garden frame or cloche. Roots may also be divided during spring.

Uses This is a valuable grey foliage for arranging with pink and blue flowers. The leaves clothe the entire stem and are light and delicate in appearance. The plant produces sufficient material to make a complete outline of foliage for a traditional design.

Conditioning As the stems are woody they will need to be lightly crushed before conditioning in water for 2 hours. Remove any leaves that are likely to be submerged as they deteriorate quickly.

Preserving Sadly, as with most grey foliages, *Artemisia* does not preserve well. Individual leaves may be pressed. These will increase the textural quality of a collage or picture.

Aucuba

Spotted Laurel
China and Japan
Evergreen
Cornaceae

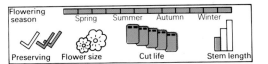

Flowering season		Spring	Summer	Autumn	Winter
Preserving	Flower size		Cut life		Stem length

*A*ucuba japonica forms a rounded bush, height 5-6ft (150-180cm), and has narrow oval, pointed, slightly toothed, leathery, shiny green leaves about 2-3in (5-7.5cm) wide and 4-7in (10-17.5cm) long. There are both male and female shrubs. After flowering (the flowers are of no significance) suitably pollinated female plants produce bright scarlet berries, which retain their colour late into autumn. Some of the cultivars provide attractively variegated leaves.

A.j. 'Crotonifolia' has large leaves generously blotched and spotted bright yellow. This is a male form and has no berries. The leaves of *A.j.* 'Fructoluteo' are variously marked with pale green and yellow and the berries are yellow-white. *A.j.* 'Gold Dust' is a red-berried female form with leaves boldly speckled and blotched with golden yellow. In *A.j.* 'Picturata' the leaf centres are generously splashed with pure gold and the leaf margins are rich green; this is a male form with no fruits.

Cultivation and Propagation No regular pruning is required. Any shaping which may be necessary can be achieved when cutting material for use, over the course of the year.

Propagation is by hardwood cuttings 8in (20cm) long taken in the late autumn. These may be rooted in a nursery bed in the open ground or given the protection of a frame.

Uses This is an all-purpose foliage, useful in concealing mechanics or as a focal area in a foliage arrangement. As the bush matures the leaves get bigger, an asset for large arrangements in the winter when little else is available. The flowers are insignificant, but the resulting fruit is an interesting addition to an autumn arrangement of berries and foliage.

Conditioning Stand them in deep water for up to 3 hours.

Preserving The leaves will absorb glycerine, though the variegation will be lost.

Ballota

Mediteranean Region
Evergreen
Labiatae

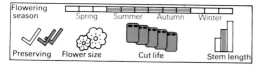

Ballota pseudodamnictus

Only one species is of any real importance as a garden plant, and that is *Ballota pseudodamnictus*. This is a small sub-shrub that grows only about 2ft (60cm) high; it is sometimes listed in catalogues as a herbaceous perennial. It has arching stems which are woody at the base, and obovate, greyish-white, woolly leaves about 1in (2.5cm) long. Whorls of lilac-pink flowers appear in summer.

Cultivation and Propagation Cultivation is quite easy, as it will grow in any ordinary well-drained soil, providing it is given a sunny situation. The best time to plant it is in spring. Established shrubs should be pruned in spring to encourage the production of new stems.
   Propagation can be achieved by either division of the roots in the spring or by stem cuttings which are taken during the summer and rooted in a shaded garden frame. Rooted cuttings are planted out in the open ground the following spring.
Uses This green/grey plant can be arranged in so many ways. The arching growth is a useful outline material. As the plant matures, the colour is a more distinct grey with a soft texture. It relates perfectly with pastel colours especially pale pink.
Conditioning Use only the mature stems. Burn

the stem ends over a flame and stand them in water for up to 2 hours.
Preserving It is the stem and bract that preserve; the flower is small and quickly shrivels. Remove the stem foliage, leaving the bracts intact; stand the stems in glycerine. The colour will change to a soft beige.

Berberis

Barberry
Wide distribution
Evergreen and deciduous
Berberidaceae

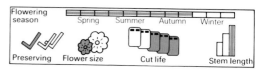

Berberis thunbergii 'Atropurpurea'

These hardy and adaptable shrubs provide a range of attractive colours in their foliage, flowers and berries.
   Berberis aggregata is a deciduous species, native to western China, which forms a dense bush 4ft (120cm) high. It has the spiny stems characteristic of the barberries. It bears clusters of small, pointed green leaves that take on orange-red tints in autumn. This shrub is covered in pale yellow flower clusters in summer and these are followed by red berries, which last into late autumn. Among the many hybrids available is *B.a.* 'Barbarossa', which has so many autumn berries that their weight causes the branches to arch under the burden. This is a vigorous shrub attaining 6ft (180cm).
   B. candidula is an evergreen species of dwarf habit, also originating from China. This is an excellent ground cover subject of slow growth,

height 2ft (60cm). It has shiny, arching
branches clothed in small oblong-elliptic, dark
green leaves with silvery blue undersides. In
spring its branches are studded with single
bright yellow flowers, and these are followed
by small oval, purple berries. *B.c.*
'Armstelveen' is of similar habit but the upper
surfaces of its leaves are fresh green and it is
faster growing.

B. thunbergii is native to Japan and is a
deciduous shrub of compact, erect growth,
height 4ft (120cm). Its spiny stems bear small
obovate green leaves which turn brilliant
orange-red in autumn. Small pale yellow
flowers appear in the spring, and these are
followd by red autumn berries. *B. thunbergii*
has a number of cultivars with richly varied
foliage colours.

B.t. 'Atropurpurea' is of similar height to the
parent and has rich red-purple leaves. *B.t.*
'Atropurpurea Nana' is a beautiful purple-
leaved dwarf form which has few, if any,
spines and is slow growing, height 2ft (60cm).
B.t. 'Aurea' is a very striking small shrub,
height 3ft (90cm), with golden yellow leaves
becoming pale green in autumn. *B.t.*
'Helmond Pillar' is of stiff, erect habit and has
large, reddish-bronze leaves. It grows about
5ft (150cm) high by 1½ft (45cm) wide and
makes a fine ornamental boundary hedge.

B. wilsonea is a beautiful low, densely
branched, semi-recumbent shrub, height 2-3ft
(60-90cm), with tiny soft, grey-green leaves. It
bears clusters of small yellow flowers in
spring, followed in autumn by quantities of
coral-red berries. The leaves also take on red
and orange autumn hues.

Cultivation and Propagation *Berberis* grows on a
wide range of soils, provided they are well-
drained, in sun or partial shade. No regular
pruning is required and the removal of material
for floral arrangements over the year will serve
to keep individual shrubs in shape. Hedges are
best trimmed in the winter after fruiting in the
case of deciduous species. Evergreen species are
best trimmed in the early spring.

Propagation is by half-ripe cuttings secured in
the summer and rooted in a closed and shaded
garden frame.

Uses A splendid range of shrubs that offer
exquisite leaf colour during the growing season
with an abundant crop of berries to use in the
autumn. The fruiting branches can be arranged
with the ripening pods of *Physalis* and dahlias to
excellent effect.

Conditioning Avoid using immature foliage as
it tends to wilt. Mature stems should be lightly
crushed and stood in water for 2 to 3 hours.

Preserving Preserve very early foliage in
desiccant. The process is rapid and the brilliant
colour is retained.

Buddleia

Butterfly Bush
Asia, South Africa and South America
Evergreen and deciduous
Loganiaceae

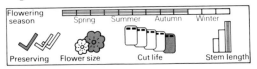

Buddleia fallowiana

Buddleias are vigorous growers with soft
foliage and large, fragrant flower heads.

Buddleia alternifolia can be grown either as
a large shrub or a small tree. It has a weeping,
willow-like habit and small lanceolate, dark
green, deciduous leaves, the lower surfaces
bluish-grey. In summer its branches are
abundantly covered in clusters of bright
purple flowers which have the frgrance of
heliotrope. The cultivar *B.a.* 'Argentea' has
leaves covered in silvery down, height 8ft
(240cm). Prune by removing the branches
bearing old, faded flowers as soon as flowering
ceases.

B. fallowiana is another deciduous species
of more vigorous growth which, given the
protection of a sunny wall, can attain a height
of 10ft (300cm) or more. When grown as a
shrub in an open position it will achieve about
5-6ft (150-180cm) in height. It has long
pointed, silvery leaves which are covered
with white felt on the lower surfaces; leaves
vary in length from 4in (10cm) to 8in (20cm).
Terminal panicles of mauve, fragrant flowers,
up to 12in (30cm) long, appear during late
summer.

B.f. 'Alba' has the same silvery grey leaves
but it has fragrant white flowers with orange
eyes. It is somewhat less vigorous, height 4-5ft

(120-150cm). This flowers on the current year's growth and should be pruned in early spring as renewed growth commences.

B. globosa is a semi-evergreen species with long, pointed leaves which are dark green on the upper surfaces and have tan-coloured felt on the undersides. This species is commonly referred to as the 'orange ball tree', due to its bright tangerine balls of flowers which appear in early summer and have a sweet fragrance like honey. The flowers are borne both on the old wood of the previous year and on new shoots of the current year's growth, therefore any pruning to shape the shrub should be done as soon as flowering ceases.

Cultivation and Propagation *Buddleia* is easy to grow in any fertile soil in sun. Propagation is possible in either of two ways. The one is by seed sown in the open ground in the spring, and the other is by cuttings taken in the late summer. Cuttings root quite easily at this season of the year but need protecting with a garden frame until the following spring.

Uses A firm favourite with arrangers is *B. alternifolia*, as its weeping habit makes it a suitable outline material. Most of the varieties may be used in the same way for both large and small designs.

Conditioning The flowers are long lasting, so pick them when most are open. Remove any excess foliage and stand the stems in water for 3 hours.

Preserving The flowering branches will not absorb preserving liquid. *B. globosa* may be dried in desiccant, when the majority of flowers are open. The brilliant orange colour will associate well with the pressed leaves of *Acer*.

Buxus

Box
North Africa, Asia and Central America
Evergreen
Buxaceae

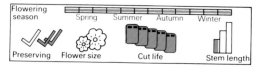

***B**uxus sempervirens* is a native European species with a mass of small, glossy, dark green leaves, height up to 10ft (300cm). *B.s.* 'Aurea Marginata' is an attractive variegated cultivar with leaves margined and splashed with yellow, height 6ft (180cm). These are upright shrubs that respond well to cutting and are used as hedges or low edging for flower borders and beds.

Buxus sempervirens

Cultivation and Propagation Box is not particularly fussy about the soil in which it may have to grow, providing it is reasonably well drained, and it is a useful shrub for growing on chalky soils. It will even flourish on exposed sites or in the shade of trees. No regular pruning is necessary other than for the removal of dead or diseased branches. However, one should keep a watch out for variegated branches which may revert to the common dark green of *Buxus sempervirens* and remove these as soon as they appear, otherwise the whole shrub may revert in due course!

Propagation is by cuttings of mature shoots, during autumn and these are rooted in a shaded garden frame and planted out in the open ground the following spring.

Uses The virtue of this foliage is its longevity. It is both a background foliage and medium for concealing small areas of mechanics. The shiny surface is an excellent complement to dried foliage with a matt finish.

Conditioning Stand the cut sprays in water for up to 2 hours.

Preserving On occasions the foliage will dry in the arrangement if it is left that long. Preserving it in glycerine will give it a longer dried life. The time will vary for the process to be completed, but the colour will change to beige.

Camellia

sia

vergreen

heaceae

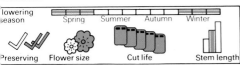

lowering
season

Spring   Summer   Autumn   Winter

Preserving   Flower size   Cut life   Stem length

Camellia japonica 'Mathotiana Rosea'

Camellias are among the finest late winter and early spring flowering shrubs. *Camellia japonica* (common camellia), native to China and Japan, together with its many cultivars, provides some of the most scintillating flowers and foliage.

C. japonica is quite hardy and forms a large shrub or small tree, up to 10ft (300cm) in height. It has glossy olive green, leathery, elliptic, pointed, slightly toothed leaves, the lower surfaces shiny and fresh green in colour. The wild species bears red five-petalled flowers and from this parent shrub a large number of cultivars has been evolved. The following selection is a general indication of the rich range of these plants.

Red-flowered forms include *C.j.* 'Adolphe Audusson', of vigorous yet compact growth, bearing large blood red, semi-double flowers with prominent yellow stamens; *C.j.* 'Alexander Hunter', of more erect habit, with medium-sized single, crimson flowers; *C.j.* 'Apollo', of open, vigorous habit, with medium-sized rose red, semi-double flowers.

Good white camellias are *C.j.* 'Lady Vansittart White', a shrub of slow growth and bushy, compact habit with medium-sized white, semi-double flowers which have wavy-edged petals; *C.j.* 'Mathotiana Alba', open

vigorous growth and large white, double flowers; *C.j.* 'Nobilissima', one of the earliest to come into flower, a shrub of vigorous, compact habit with medium-sized creamy white, peony-form, semi-double flowers.

Pinks are represented by *C.j.* 'Mathotiana Rosea', large clear pink double flowers; *C.j.* 'Nagasaki, vigorous growth and spreading habit with large rose pink, white-marbled, semi-double flowers; *C.j.* 'Pink Perfection', of vigorous, erect habit with small shell pink double flowers; *C.j.* 'Tricolor' (sometimes listed as 'Sieboldii'), of erect, compact habit with medium-sized, blush pink streaked with red, semi-double flowers.

Cultivation and Propagation Camellias are not fond of limey or chalky soils but prefer acid, peaty soils. Nevertheless, they can flourish in loamy soils if a good dressing of peat or leafmould is added when preparing the ground. Once established the camellias should have a peat mulch spread about them each spring to keep roots cool and retain moisture. *Camellia japonica* is quite hardy providing it is grown in a reasonably well-drained soil which is not liable to flooding during the winter. Flowering is encouraged in an open sunny situation but plants need shelter from cold north-east winds. Partial shade offers flowers a little protection from the spring frosts. *Camellia* is a particularly good subject for growing in a large tub where space is strictly limited or ground conditions are not satisfactory. Try growing them in a cool greenhouse and ventilate well on sunny days to prevent the temperature rising above 65°F (18°C). Keep the atmosphere from drying out by damping the greenhouse floor as necessary. Flowering will then commence in late autumn and continue until well into the spring of the following year, providing the roots of the camellias in the tubs are not allowed to become dry. Once all flowering has ceased the tubs may be placed outside in a shaded spot during the summer before bringing back into the greenhouse the following autumn again. Give tub-grown plants a weak solution of a liquid fertilizer once every two weeks, during the growing season. Provide a peat mulch each spring. The best time to plant young camellias, either in the open ground or in tubs or large pots, is in the autumn just when growth has ceased and before the flower buds have developed very much, otherwise bud drop may result. No regular pruning is required, other than the removal of damaged or unwanted branches, during the dormant season.

Propagation is by half-ripe cuttings secured in summer. These are inserted 4 per 3in (7.5cm) pot containing equal parts of peat and sand. The cuttings are set out around the sides of the pot and then placed in a closed propagation case in the greenhouse to root. If this has

bottom heat set it at 60°F (16°C). Alternatively branches could be layered during late summer.
Uses This must be the most elegant flower the arranger can grow. The texture of the petal is soft and delicate, which gives the flower a classical beauty. The shrub is slow growing so you may have to limit the number of flowers picked per year. Choose an elegant container and arrange the branch with a limited quantity of suitable foliage that will enhance the design without overpowering the flower.
Conditioning Crush the woody stem and stand in deep water for 2–3 hours.
Preserving The beauty of the flower fades very quickly and the tragedy is compounded with its inability to preserve. However the leaf will absorb glycerine. To prevent damaging the shape of the shrub, remove individual mature leaves and float them in a dish of glycerine. The leaf will change to an olive green and feel quite pliable, in up to 3 weeks. The foliage can then be mounted on to wires and wired into a spray.

Carpinus

Hornbeam
Temperate regions of the Northern Hemisphere
Deciduous
Carpinaceae

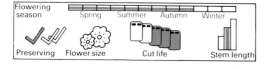

Carpinus betulus 'Fastigiata'

Carpinus is similar in appearance to beech and is often mistaken for it, but this tree grows to more modest proportions. However, like the beech, it can be used as a hedging

subject and retains its attractively coloured dead foliage through winter in like manner. *Carpinus betulus* (common hornbeam) generally grows too large for inclusion in a town garden. It is better to plant either of its cultivars *C.b.* 'Columnaris' or *C.b.* 'Fastigiata'.

'Columnaris' is of slow growth and compact spire-like habit, which later becomes columnar, height 15ft (450cm). 'Fastigiata' grows larger and while it is fastigiate (erect and close-branched) when young, it becomes broader when mature, height 21ft (630cm).

Through spring and summer the oval, pointed, toothed leaves are green, and in autumn take on rich orange and yellow hues. These trees bear green catkins in spring, which are followed in autumn by the fruiting clusters, or keys, as they are commonly called. The keys generally remain on the branches well into winter.

Cultivation and Propagation *Carpinus* thrives on poor wet clays and on chalky soils too, either in a sunny or partially shaded situation.

Propagation is by seeds sown in the spring either in the open ground or in a garden frame in the case of *C. betulus*. Propagation of the named cultivars is best left in the hands of the skilled nurseryman as these are grafted on to other wild species.
Uses The Hornbeam can be used for arranging at most times of the year. The spring growth is a delightful pale green. Small branches are most useful for landscape arrangements. The mature leaves during the summer form the outline for traditional styles of mixed garden flowers. It is in the autumn that it really comes into its own, when the leaf colour changes to a bronzed yellow, with clusters of keys, to arrange with other autumn fruits and flowers.
Conditioning The spring foliage should be submerged in water for at least 1 hour then allowed to condition in deep water for a further 2 hours. Mature foliage requires only a deep drink for about 2 hours.
Preserving The leaves can be preserved in glycerine, when they are fully developed. It is possible to preserve the keys in the same way, though the autumn leaves may fall.

Chamaecyparis

Cypress
North America, Japan and Formosa
Evergreen
Cupressaceae

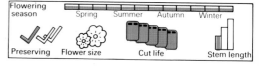

Chamaecyparis lawsoniana 'Pembury Blue'

The distinguishing characteristics of these elegant conifers are flattened branches and small cones. The following cultivars of *Chamaecyparis lawsoniana*, a species native to Oregon and California, provide some of the best foliage colours.

C.l. 'Elegantissima' is clothed in silvery grey foliage and has a broadly conical habit. It is of moderate growth, height 15ft (450cm). *C.l.* 'Kilmacurragh' is a narrow columnar tree of dense habit with dark green foliage, height 15-20ft (450-600cm). *C.l.* 'Pembury Blue' is an outstanding cultivar, also conical in shape, with rich silvery blue foliage, height 10ft (300cm). *C.l.* 'Stewartia Erecta' is a compact conical tree, height 10-14ft (300-420cm); its foliage colour changes with the seasons, being bright yellow in spring and summer, turning yellow-green in late autumn and winter.

Cultivation and Propagation *Chamaecyparis* flourishes on loamy moist soils and does not grow so vigorously on dry soils. Choose a site not exposed to strong winds. They may be planted either in a sunny or shady place. Purchase container-grown stock. Planting is best undertaken during autumn or spring. No regular pruning is required.

Propagation is by cuttings secured in the autumn and inserted in a heated propagation case in a greenhouse.

Uses This has useful foliage for creating a background for flowers. The foliage is arranged in a flat spray which you will find indispensable for concealing mechanics and for creating a foil for focal area flowers. 'Stewartii Erecta' is a light foliage to use with summer flowers; it will provide sufficient visual weight without causing the design to look dark and heavy.

Conditioning Cut branches should be stood in water for at least 2 hours.

Preserving The shrub will provide lots of fresh cut material so it is not worth preserving it, though pieces can be pressed between sheets of newspaper under the carpet.

Choisya

Mexican Orange Blossom
Mexico
Evergreen
Rutaceae

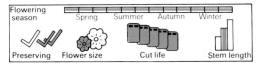

Choisya ternata

Choisya ternata is of rounded bushy habit growing up to 6ft (180cm) in height and bears glossy bright green, trifoliate leaves. The leaflets are lance-shaped, some 1½-3in (4-8cm) long, fanning out from the leaf stalks. Choisya's white fragrant flowers are borne in clusters at the ends of the shoots, mainly during late spring, but spasmodically through to winter. The individual flowers are about 1in (2.5cm) across, composed of five rounded petals.

Cultivation and Propagation This shrub does well in any ordinary garden soil which is freely drained. While it is suggested that this shrub is not entirely hardy this is usually when it is grown in over-rich damp conditions. It prefers a sunny situation which is sheltered from the cold north-eastern winter winds, but can be grown in partial shade at the risk of reduced flowering. The best time to plant it out is during autumn or spring. No annual pruning is necessary except for the removal of the occasional damaged branch.

Propagation is by stem cuttings taken during summer rooted in a closed and shaded frame.

Uses A very valuable foliage. Long sprays can be used to outline a design, while terminal rosettes can make alternative focal areas or they may be used to conceal the mechanics. The white flowers look most effective in a design of early summer pastel flowers.

Conditioning Stand the cut stems in cool water for 2 hours in a shaded area.

Preserving The special quality of *Choisya* is that in preserving, the leaves turn an exquisite shade of beige. The process takes a variable length of time, so check them each day. A lighter shade can be attained by standing them in direct light.

Cornus

Dogwood
Northern Hemisphere
Deciduous
Cornaceae

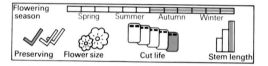

Cornus kousa

Cornus alba** is commonly known as the red-barked dogwood, as stems of the current year's growth turn deep red in winter. This is a useful feature at a time when colour in the garden is limited. The shrub is of very vigorous growth and succeeds on all types of soils.

C.a. 'Sibirica' is less vigorous and has thinner shoots than the parent plant, but these are brilliant crimson in colour and make a rich contribution to the winter display. Both plants have mid-green leaves with grey undersides that may become tinted red or orange in autumn. Height depends on frequency of pruning, which may be done either annually or biennially. To maximize production of the coloured winter stems, the shrubs should be cut back close to the ground in spring each year. Established shrubs pruned in this way will make about 5ft (150cm) of growth each year.

C. stolonifera is a far more vigorous species native to North America. The true species has dark purplish-red shoots and its cultivar *C.s.* 'Flaviramea' has attractive yellow stems. Leaves turn pale yellow in autumn before leaf-fall. It can easily attain 7ft (210cm) in height when it is pruned in spring each year. Selective pruning can also take place throughout the winter if stems are being used as cut material for arrangements.

C. kousa is a large shrub of slow growth and bushy habit, height 6-9ft (180-270cm). It has ovate, pointed, green leaves 2-3in (5-7.5cm) long and 1-1½in (2.5-4cm) wide, which turn bronze and crimson in the autumn prior to leaf-fall. It is noted for its beautiful white bracts (modified leaves) which surround the inconspicuous flowers in summer. These are followed by strawberry-like fruits which hang from the branches.

C.k. 'Chinensis' is a larger-growing shrub of more open habit, and the white bracts and green leaves are also slightly larger; foliage turns to brilliant crimson in autumn.

C. mas (cornelian cherry) is a deciduous shrub or small tree native to Europe. It is valued for the masses of tiny yellow flowers clustered along naked stems in spring each year. These are followed by small red fruits, which unfortunately are not borne in any quantity. The ovate dark green leaves are similar in size to those of *C. kousa* and turn red-purple in autumn.

Cultivation and Propagation The species of *Cornus* which are recommended for flowering prefer a rich fertile, well-drained soil of some depth, and are not suitable for growing on shallow chalky soils. They will flourish equally well either in a sunny or partially shady situation and do not need any regular pruning.

Propagation of *C. alba* and *C. stolonifera* is by hard-wood cuttings taken in autumn and rooted in the open ground. *C. kousa* and *C. mas* are best propagated from half-ripe cuttings secured in summer and inserted in a closed shaded garden frame.

Uses For winter arranging there is nothing finer than the bare brilliant red stems of *C. Alba*. They can be used in both traditional and modern styles. If the container will allow, many intricate and interesting geometric patterns can

e created. The bracts of *C. kousa* are utstanding if used in a large traditional rrangement, as the long arching sprays hang own in a most graceful manner.
Conditioning The young foliage needs to be submerged for an hour then transferred to deep water for a further 2 hours. Once the plant is mature, the bracts and leaves can be stood in deep water for about an hour. Stems cut in winter can be arranged without conditioning.
Preserving As the plant produces so much new growth, this compensates for its lack of preserving ability.

Corylus

Hazel
Northern Hemisphere
Deciduous
Corylaceae

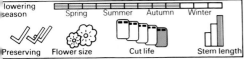

Flowering season	Spring	Summer	Autumn	Winter
Preserving	Flower size		Cut life	Stem length

Corylus maxima 'Purpurea'

Two shrubby forms of Corylus are of special interest for their foliage colour and charming spring catkins.
    Corylus avellana, a species native to Europe, western Asia and North Africa, has produced the cultivar *C.a.* 'Contorta' (corkscrew hazel), with curiously twisted stems and attractive yellow male catkins, about 2in (5cm) long, in early spring. Its leaves are broadly heart-shaped and toothed, green with downy lower surfaces. In autumn they take on a soft yellowish hue.
    C. maxima 'Purpurea', a cultivar of the southern European species *C. maxima*, has dark purple rounded leaves and purplish-red catkins in early spring. This attains a height of 8ft (240cm).

Cultivation and Propagation Both may be grown quite successfully on any well-drained soil either in full sun or partial shade and they are particularly useful for planting in windswept situations where little else will succeed. Dead and diseased branches, together with branches which are more than 4 years old, should be pruned from these shrubs in spring, thus stimulating new more vigorous growth to be produced.
    Propagation is by layering shoots in summer.
Uses The twisted stem of the *Corylus*, dripping with golden yellow catkins, is a traditional representational tree in a landscape design. Stripped of its leaves, it may be painted and gilded for Christmas designs or used for linear balance in a modern arrangement. The leaf tends to crowd the stem giving it a rather heavy appearance, one reason why it should be used for its contorted effect only.
Conditioning Split the stem end and stand it in water for up to 2 hours.
Preserving The branch, once cut, continues to dry and should last a number of years.

Cotinus

Smoke Free
Temperate regions
Deciduous
Anacardiaceae

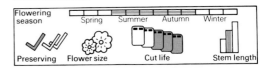

Flowering season	Spring	Summer	Autumn	Winter
Preserving	Flower size		Cut life	Stem length

Cotinus coggyria 'Foliis Purpureis'

Cotinus coggygria (formerly *Rhus cotinus*) is a deciduous shrub well noted for its large panicles of pinky beige flowers and rounded green leaves some 2-3in (5-7.5cm) long. The flower panicles last a long time and finally turn a smoky grey, while the leaves fade to an attractive yellow in autumn. This plant forms a well-rounded bushy shrub which grows to about 9ft (270cm) high. *C.c.* 'Flame' has bright orange-red autumn foliage; *C.c.* 'Foliis Purpureis' is a purple-leaved cultivar with light red autumn tints.

Cultivation and Propagation *Cotinus* grows very well in any ordinary well-drained garden soil providing it is placed in a sunny situation. No special effort should be made to add manure or garden compost to the soil. The poorer the soil the more brilliant will be the autumn colouration of the leaves.

Propagation is by removal of rooted suckers during the dormant season or by half-ripe cuttings secured in summer and inserted in a closed shaded garden frame.

Uses Purple foliage can be most useful for arranging with certain pure colours. I always feel that reds and blues become vibrant when associated with foliage like *Cotinus*. The autumn colour of the leaf is a warm addition to designs of preserved leaves and dried grasses.

Conditioning Once the leaves are mature it conditions very easily; just stand the cut stems in water for a minimum of 2 hours.

Preserving Branches of foliage will absorb glycerine. Do this in the summer but do more than you need as it is notorious for objecting to the preserving process. Leaves that have adopted their autumn shades may be pressed with much more success.

Cupressus arizonica

foliage; *C. macrocarpa* 'Gold Crest' forms a narrower conical shape and can grow taller – up to 25ft (750cm). Its rich yellow foliage makes a striking feature in winter.

Cultivation and Propagation *Cupressus* needs a deep moist soil. Both these varieties need a sunny sheltered position. Plant container-grown stock in autumn or spring.

Propagation is by autumn cuttings inserted in a heated propagation case in a greenhouse.

Uses The foliage of the closely pressed almost fleshy scales is borne on longer branches than the *Chamaecyparis*. It is an outline material for traditional designs that can be used all year. The cones that are produced in the autumn are an interesting foil for preserved foliage and berries with one or two fresh flowers.

Conditioning Like most evergreen leaves they are easy to condition, just stand them in water until you need to arrange them. They have a very long cut life.

Preserving I have found that they will absorb glycerine, but it is not always successful.

Cupressus

True Cypress
Asia, Southern Europe and Central and North America
Evergreen
Cupressaceae

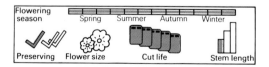

This genus of conifers is related to Chamaecyparis. These are trees for spacious gardens, growing to 20ft (600cm) in height, but they are a source of attractive evergreen colour. *C. arizonica* 'Conica' is of broadly conical habit and it has silvery blue

Cytisus

Broom
Europe, Asia Minor and North Africa
Deciduous and Evergreen
Leguminosae

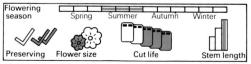

Cytisus 'Lord Lambourne'

Cytisus albus (white Portugal broom) is a deciduous shrub native to Portugal, Spain and North Africa. It bears masses of small white flowers on slender branches during early summer, height 6ft (180cm).

C. battandieri is a deciduous shrub of vigorous growth originating from Morocco. It is unlike the other brooms, being upright in habit with silky grey-green trifoliate leaves; the narrow leaflets are 2-3in (5-7.5cm) long. It displays terminal racemes of bright yellow, fragrant flowers in midsummer and can attain a height of about 9ft (270cm) if given a sheltered site against a warm, sunny wall.

C. nigricans is a native of central and south-eastern Europe. It is valued for its display of bright yellow, fragrant flowers which are borne on shoots of the current year's growth during late summer. Prune this species in the spring just before new growth commences. It makes a rounded shrub 3ft (90cm) high.

C. praecox (Warminster broom) is a shrub of rounded habit which bears masses of creamy yellow flowers in early summer, height 4ft (120cm). *C.p.* 'Allgold' has deep yellow flowers.

C. scoparius (common broom) is native to western Europe. It is a deciduous shrub which bears a great profusion of bright yellow flowers in early summer, height 5ft (150cm). This species has been subjected to a good deal of hybridization with excellent results, as the hybrids are equally free-flowering and are available in an array of striking colours.

'Andreanus', yellow and crimson; 'Cornish Cream', ivory white and pale yellow; 'Crimson King', large crimson flowers; 'Criterion', orange and apricot; 'Daisy Hill', crimson and cream; 'Dorothy Walpole', rich crimson; 'Dragonfly', deep yellow and crimson; 'Firefly', yellow stained with bronze; 'Killiney Salmon', salmon and bright orange; 'Lord Lambourne', crimson-scarlet and pale cream; 'Zeelandia', creamy pink.

Cultivation and Propagation Good drainage and ample sunshine are the only prerequisites to their successful cultivation. However, once they are planted in the selected site they resent having their roots disturbed. Buy containerized plants from garden centres or shrub nurseries, so as to avoid this problem when introducing them to the garden initially. They all have pea-shaped flowers and some are of considerable fragrance. *Cytisus* is best planted in late autumn. With the exception of *C. nigricans*, pruning should be undertaken by cutting back stems which have flowered by approximately half their length, immediately flowering ceases.

Propagation of the species is by seed which may be sown in a garden frame in early spring or in the open ground during late spring. Stem cuttings should be taken during late summer and inserted in a closed and shaded garden frame, containing sandy soil. The frame should remain in position until the following spring. *Cytisus* hybrids are propagated by cuttings.

Uses A truly lavish flower for the arranger. It is a late spring-early summer blossom that should be used in profusion in massed arrangements of flowers. The colour range is so wide that you can choose several to go with a predominant garden flower colour. I favour *C. battandieri* for its pineapple fragrant flowers and silky grey-green foliage. The pendulous habit of the flowers looks effective in a formal design.

Conditioning Cut when the flowers are just showing colour. Crush the woody stems and stand in deep water for 2 hours.

Preserving The small individual flowers can be removed and dried in desiccant. Once the flowers have faded, the multi-stemmed branches can be preserved in glycerine; they darken in colour as an indication of readiness. To give a curving shape to the fresh or dried stem, carefully wrap it around a bottle and submerge it in water. After 2 to 3 hours it can be removed and the curve will dry and straighten slightly, but still retain a graceful curving line.

Deutzia

Asia and America
Deciduous
Philadelphaceae

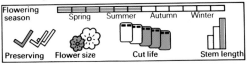

Deutzia × elegantissima

Deutzia is a genus of early-flowering shrubs which have eloquent clusters of star-like, fragrant flowers in summer.

Deutzia chunii is of Chinese origin and its arching branches present a fine array of fragrant white flowers, whose reflexed petals have pink interiors in summer. The foliage is grey-green and willow-like, height 4-5ft (120-150cm).

D. × elegantissima is of garden origin and it bears fragrant rose-tinted flowers in summer. It has dull green, pointed oval leaves, each about 3in (7.5cm) long, and forms a graceful shrub of bushy habit, height 5ft (150cm).

D. gracilis is a native of Japan, and has strongly fragrant white flowers in summer and lanceolate dark green leaves up to 3in (7.5cm) long, height 4ft (120cm). *D.g.* 'Rosea' is a cultivar with rose pink flowers.

D. monbeigii is native to China and bears glistening white, star-shaped flowers unusually late in the summer. It has small pointed oval leaves with white lower surfaces. It forms a compact shrub about 4-5ft (120-150cm) in height.

D. pulchra is a vigorous shrub which can grow 8ft (240cm) or more in height, but it responds well to pruning when it is necessary to contain its growth. It bears drooping racemes of white flowers in early summer and has lanceolate leaves 2-4in (5-10cm) long.

D. scabra is a very vigorous species of erect habit which can attain a height of 10ft (300cm). The summer flowers may be either pure white or suffused pink on the outside. *D.s.* 'Pride of Rochester' has double white, pink-tinted flowers and is less vigorous, height 6ft (180cm). *D.s.* 'Plena' has double rose-purple flowers tinted white on the outside.

Cultivation and Propagation Deutzias thrive on any ordinary, well-drained soil either in sun or in partial shade. They are pruned as soon as flowering ceases, as flowers are borne on shoots of the previous year's growth. This is the time too to remove some of the older wood to encourage new growth from the base of the shrubs. Planting of new shrubs may take place at any time during the dormant season.

Propagation of the species may be accomplished by seeds sown in a garden frame in spring or by cuttings of half-ripe shoots in summer which are rooted in a closed and shaded garden frame. They can also be rooted from hardwood cuttings taken outdoors in the autumn. The various cultivars mentioned are best rooted from cuttings as they do not necessarily come true from seed.

Uses *Deutzia* produces masses of delicate small flowers to enhance any traditional design of summer materials. The sprays are an asset used as outline material or as a grouping for a focal area. The fragrance is a bonus.

Conditioning It conditions remarkably easily. Lightly crush the end of the branch and stand it in water for about 2 hours.

Preserving Small sprays of flowers can be dried in desiccant.

Eleagnus

Europe, Asia and North America
Evergreen and Deciduous
Elaeagnaceae

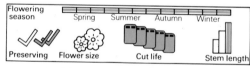

Eleagnus pungens 'Maculata'

Evergreen forms of Eleagnus provide a year-round display of glossy foliage, some plain green and some variegated.

Elaeagnus ebbingei is a fast-growing hybrid shrub with broadly elliptic, pointed, leathery leaves up to 5in (12.5cm) long. These are a glossy mid-green, with silvery undersides. Small, insignificant but fragrant flowers are borne on older wood in autumn, height up to 10ft (300cm).

E. pungens comes from Japan and has similarly textured elliptic, wavy-edged dark green leaves some 2-4in (5-10cm) long. This species has some attractive and popular variegated cultivars. *E.p.* 'Maculata' has glossy dark green leaves generously splashed with gold at the centres. It is a shrub of moderate growth, height 5ft (150cm). *E.p.* 'Dicksonii' is of erect habit and slow growth, eventually reaching a height of 5ft (150cm). Its shiny dark green leaves are irregularly margined with rich yellow.

E. 'Limelight' is a more vigorous cultivar, height 10ft (300cm). Its large leaves, up to 5in (12.5cm) long, are mid-green with central splashes of deep yellow and have silvery undersides.

Cultivation and Propagation *Elaeagnus* are very tough shrubs which will grow in a wide range of soils, either in full sun or partial shade. Any pruning which may be necessary to shape the shrubs can be done when removing foliage for display or in spring, when new growth commences. Planting of new shrubs should take place in autumn or spring.

Propagation is either by stem cuttings, in a closed shaded garden frame in late summer, or by rooted suckers removed during spring.

Uses *Eleagnus* is essential foliage for using with yellow and orange flowers, creating a light effect when used in massed arrangements. Most produce long sprays of leaves, which can be used to establish the outline of the design.

Conditioning When the leaves have matured the stems are easy to condition. Stand them in deep water for about 2 hours. Immature foliage should be floated in water prior to this.

Preserving *Elaeagnus* will preserve very well in glycerine, even the variegated types. The variegation will be lost, but the resultant colour compensates.

Enkianthus

North Eastern Asia
Deciduous
Ericaceae

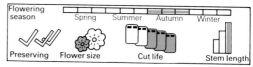

Enkianthus campanulatus

Enkianthus campanulatus is an erect-growing shrub with elliptic, pointed and finely toothed, dull green leaves, which in autumn turn bright yellow, and finally bright red. Pendulous racemes of tiny urn-shaped, creamy yellow and red-tipped flowers are borne during late spring. These make a splendid display lasting several weeks. Enkianthus is a beautiful garden shrub for summer and autumn colour, height 8ft (240cm).

Cultivation and Propagation This shrub likes moist, lime-free soil containing humus, in a lightly shaded situation. It is a good idea to apply a dressing of peat to the soil when preparing it for planting and to apply a mulch of peat around the roots of this shrub each spring. *Enkianthus* needs no regular pruning. The removal of autumn foliage for display will stimulate the production of new shoots. The flowers are produced on the previous year's growth, so any shaping of this shrub should be done as soon as the flowers begin to fade. Planting of new shrubs can be undertaken at any time during the dormant season.

Propagation is either by seed sown in a cool greenhouse or garden frame during early spring or by cuttings taken in summer and inserted in a closed and shaded garden frame.

Rooting cuttings is a slow process, as it takes about 18 months and propagation by seed is to be preferred.

Uses This interesting foliage plant carries its leaves on the upper side of the branch with the pendulous flowers slung underneath like bell-shaped earrings. Branches that show individual beauty in shape should be arranged by themselves in a low dish with sufficient extra foliage to conceal the mechanics. To prolong the cut life of the autumn foliage, cut the stem when the leaf is turning from yellow to red.

Conditioning Condition it in the ordinary way for about 2 hours.

Preserving The fresh foliage can be preserved in glycerine, but then you are denying yourself the magnificent autumn coloration.

Escallonia

South America
Evergreen
Escalloniaceae

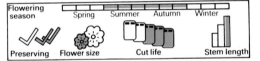

Escallonia 'Slieve Donard'

There are numerous cultivars of this tolerant flowering shrub, which make a pretty summer feature with their dense masses of small leaves and bright flowers. *Escallonia* 'Donard Brilliance' has arching stems of shiny foliage; through summer and autumn the large rosy red flowers are borne on mature wood of the previous year's growth. *E.* 'Slieve Donard' is a more compact plant of similar height, 5-6ft (150-180cm), bearing apple blossom pink flowers.

Cultivation and Propagation *Escallonia* will grow on any ordinary well-drained garden soil in either a sunny or partially shaded place. In cold districts it should be given the protection of a wall with a southern aspect. In milder districts and in proximity to the coast *Escallonia* makes a fine hedging subject. Any pruning should be undertaken in the autumn as flowering ceases. Plant in autumn or spring.

Propagation is by stem cuttings secured in midsummer and rooted in a sandy soil in a closed and shaded garden frame or cloche.

Uses The flowers extend along the full length of the branch which arches in a most attractive manner. Its obvious use is for outlining traditional styles of arrangements; it is a little too delicate to be used in a modern design. Once the flowers have faded it can still be used for its foliage, again as outline material.

Conditioning Cut the branches as the flowers are beginning to open, and stand them in water for 2 to 3 hours.

Preserving The flowers will preserve in desiccant or they may be pressed, *Escallonia's* real value is as preserved foliage. Select the stems when the flowers have dropped, crush the end of the stem lightly to allow the glycerine solution to be absorbed easily. The process will take from one to two weeks. The colour change will be variable depending on the variety used, but generally it is towards the dark brown shades.

Eucalyptus

Gum Tree
Australia and Tasmania
Evergreen
Mytaceae

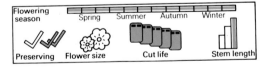

Eucalyptus species are a good source of grey foliage. **Eucalyptus gunnii has rounded silvery grey juvenile leaves up to 2½in (6.25cm) wide. E. parvifolia has ovate-lanceolate, greenish-grey juvenile leaves 1½in (4cm) long and is the hardier of the two, once established.**

While both are capable of making substantial trees, their leaf characteristics alter when they become adult and they are then less decorative. This change of leaf form can be prevented, however, by cutting the stems back annually in spring to create a stool-bed which will keep on producing strong stems with

attractive juvenile leaves. **This also maintains the plant as a shrub attaining a height of about 5-6ft (150-180cm).**

Eucalyptus gunnii

Cultivation and Propagation They will both grow quite happily on a wide range of soils providing the winter drainage is satisfactory. Plant in a very sunny spot. Water during the drier summer months to encourage fast growth. Purchase only pot grown plants as they resent having their roots disturbed when being planted out in the garden. These species have been found to be reliable in cooler climates, if provided with some shelter during the first few years until they become fully established. The shelter should be in the form of a section of wattle fencing or a screen made from stout hessian on a wood frame. This should be placed in position on the windward side of the *Eucalyptus*, before the onset of winter and it may be removed again in the spring each year. Better still, plant them in a sunny sheltered spot near a wall which will give them permanent protection.

The propagation of *Eucalyptus* is by seeds sown in a seed-tray containing a sandy soil in a greenhouse in spring. To obtain a fairly even germination the soil temperature should be 65°F (18°C), so a heated propagation case with temperature control is desirable but not essential. Seeds should be barely covered when sown. Germination will take some 21 to 28 days. Once the seedlings are large enough to handle, they should be pricked out individually in 3in (8cm) pots and grown on in the same manner as half-hardy annuals.

Uses This foliage can be cut frequently, for the bush will benefit, producing more cutting material and keeping it at a manageable height. Its silvery blue colour is a perfect foil for pink flowers. The long sprays almost demand a traditional setting.

Conditioning It is simple to condition; stand it in water for 2 hours.

Preserving Its finest quality is for preserving — it absorbs glycerine as though it had a thirst for it. There is very little colour change, sometimes it will go a shade darker, if stood in strong light. The preserved leaves last almost indefinitely, and look equally attractive arranged with fresh or dried flowers.

Euonymus

Spindle Tree
Widely distributed
Deciduous and Evergreen
Celastraceae

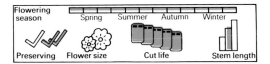

E **uonymus europaeus is a European species found growing naturally as a shrub or small tree in hedgerows or woodlands, particularly on chalky soils. It has pointed oval green leaves some 2-3in (5-7.5cm) long, which in the autumn, prior to leaf-fall, produce brilliant pink or red hues. It also carries an enormous crop of rosy red fruits. It grows to a height of between 10ft (300cm) and 20ft (600cm).**

E.e. **'Red Cascade' is a cultivar with arching branches, height 8-10ft (240-300cm). It has the same rosy red fruits in abundance, and brilliant autumn foliage colour.**

E. fortunei **is an extremely hardy evergreen species which will form a prostrate ground-covering shrub or climber. It has oval, slightly toothed, leathery, glossy green leaves, which in their juvenile state are about 1in (2.5cm) long. However, in maturity, when the shrub attains more bushy and erect growth, the leaves are more than twice that length. There are several cultivars useful for their variegated foliage colours.**

E.f. **'Colorata' has a climbing or trailing habit, with shiny green leaves through summer which in autumn and winter develop purplish tints.**

E.f. **'Emerald 'n' Gold' is a small shrub of open, erect habit, growing only about 18in (45cm) high. This has fine golden yellow variegated foliage which develops exquisite reddish tints in winter.**

E.f. **'Gold Tip' has somewhat larger leaves, dark green with yellow margins changing to a delightful creamy white later in the year.**

E.f. **'Silver Pillar' is rather less hardy than**

Euonymus europaeus 'Red Cascade'

Euonymus fortunei 'Emerald 'n' Gold'

Euonymus japonicus

the other cultivars and should be grown in the open ground only in milder districts. Elsewhere it is advisable to grow it as a pot plant and give it the protection of a greenhouse until all fear of frost has passed. It forms a compact, erect shrub with narrow dark green leaves broadly margined in white.

E.f. 'Silver Queen' is a compact shrub of slow growth which in time attains a height of 6ft (180cm), best in the shelter of a wall. Its young spring foliage is at first creamy yellow; during summer the leaves become green with generous creamy white margins, and later, as winter approaches, they develop pretty rose tints.

E. japonicus (evergreen spindle tree) will grow either as a shrub or small tree and is useful in coastal districts as a hedging subject. It has glossy dark green, oval leaves, but it is the variegated forms which are mostly required.

E.j. 'Aureopictus' has emerald green, broad leaves generously splashed with golden yellow at the centres. *E.j.* 'Ovatus Aureus' is of slow growth and its leaves are margined and suffused with yellow.

E. yedoensis is a deciduous shrub or small tree with leaves about 4-5in (10-12.5cm) long that develop brilliant red autumn tints. It also carries attractive pink fruits.

Cultivation and Propagation All the above species and named cultivars can be grown on any ordinary garden soil either in a sunny or partially shaded situation. Deciduous species can be planted at any time while they are dormant. Evergreen species are best planted either during autumn or spring.

Propagation of prostrate forms presents no difficulty as they usually root themselves quite freely. Bushy evergreens are best struck from cuttings taken in the summer and inserted in a closed and shaded garden frame, while deciduous ones are best struck from hardwood cuttings inserted in the open ground shortly after leaf-fall. No regular pruning is required. **Uses** *Euonymus* covers the spectrum of arranging needs. It will act as outline material or as a focal area in an all-foliage design. The smaller varieties will help to conceal the mechanics without darkening the centre of the arrangement. The fruits of *E. europaeus* look quite startling cascading from the centre of an arrangement of leaves or preserved material. **Conditioning** To condition *Euonymus*, simply stand it in water until you need it. **Preserving** I have had very little success with preserving the foliage or the fruits. As both are generously supplied I am not too disappointed.

Fagus

Beech
Asia, Europe and North America
Deciduous
Fagaceae

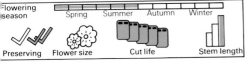

Flowering season | Preserving | Flower size | Cut life | Stem length

Remove any damaged leaves and trim away any that are crowded. Stand the branch in glycerine solution. The process is fairly rapid so check them each day. The colour varies slightly but generally it will turn to a delightful golden brown. Once the branch has been preserved it will last a long time. Any leaves that get squashed during storage can be revived and flattened in a jet of steam.

Fatsia

Eastern Asia
Evergreen
Araliaceae

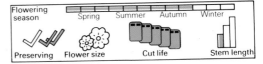

Flowering season | Preserving | Flower size | Cut life | Stem length

Fagus sylvatica 'Zlatia'

Two cultivars of the species Fagus sylvatica have specially attractive leaf colouring. F.s. 'Tricolor' has coppery leaves striped with rose and pinkish-white; the foliage of F.s. 'Zlatia' is at first bright yellow, bcoming green in late summer. These are trees for large gardens, but the size can be controlled to some extent by annual pruning.

Cultivation and Propagation Fagus may be grown in any ordinary well-drained garden soil. Choose a sunny position. Plant during the dormant season.
   Propagation is for the experts.
Uses Don't be put off by the ultimate size of this tree. I am sure that you will be able to keep it well trimmed by using the foliage as fresh cutting material and for preserving. The long sprays of leaves are an invaluable source of material to create the shape of any arrangement.
Conditioning Immature leaves should be floated in water before being conditioned in deep water for about 4 hours. Full mature leaves may be stood in deep water for 2 hours.
Preserving It is probably the most popular preserved piece of plant material used by the arranger. Select the branches carefully, making sure that you have the shape you want.

Fatsia japonica

Fatsia japonica, syn. Aralia japonica or A. sieboldii, is an exotic-looking subject originating from Japan. It grows 8-12ft (240-360cm) or more in height and has large, palmate, deeply lobed, leathery, glossy dark green leaves. These are 6-12in (15-30cm) or wide, borne on stiff stalks up to 10in (25cm) long. Large umbels of creamy white, globular flowers appear in late autumn.
   The lobed leaves of F.j. 'Variegatus' are elegantly tipped with creamy white. This cultivar produces only a few thick stems and forms a shrub of open, spreading habit.

Cultivation and Propagation This is an ideal evergreen for growing in coastal areas. It is quite hardy and can be grown successfully on a wide range of soils. However, it does prefer a sheltered, partially shaded situation. No annual pruning is necessary. Sometimes it must be cut back to more moderate proportions. Do this in spring as new growth is about to commence.

Propagation is by seed in a warm greenhouse in the spring or in a heated propagation case with the bottom heat set at 65°F (18°C). Alternatively half-ripe stem cuttings some 4 to 6in (10 to 15cm) long can be taken during late summer and rooted in a heated propagation case with the bottom heat set at 65°F (18°C).

Uses The *Fatsia* leaf is in the realm of sculptured foliage. It grows to quite a large size and is often seen as an element for modern and abstract designs. As part of the linking foliage in a pedestal or a large arrangement, it is beyond compare. To bring out the best in the plain and the variegated leaf, lightly wash them with a very mild vegetable oil.

Conditioning The immature leaf will not condition well, so select the leaves when they have fully developed and stand them in water for about 2 hours.

Preserving This leaf will preserve perfectly in glycerine, but the stem and leaf joint will need a little support. This can be achieved by taping a light wire up the stem and the back of the leaf. The process takes anything up to 3 weeks to complete. It turns a dark leathery brown.

Forsythia

Southern Europe and Eastern Asia
Deciduous
Oleaceae

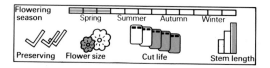

These popular shrubs produce some of the brightest flowers of the new growing season, typically emerging on bare woody stems before the young leaves have formed.

Forsythia ovata is one of the earliest-flowering species, with dainty primrose yellow flowers in early spring. It has a somewhat lax, spreading habit and the branches become clothed in large ovate leaves which later develop yellow autumn tints, height 4ft (120cm). It does well when grown against a wall receiving full sun.

F. suspensa is a shrub of rambling habit useful for clothing a wall or trellis. The stems are covered with masses of slender primrose yellow flowers in late spring. *F.s.* 'Fortunei' is

of similar habit but its branches tend to be arching and it grows more vigorously, height 8-10ft (240-300cm) or considerably more if trained on a wall.

F. **'Beatrix Farrand'** is a tall-growing hybrid of erect, dense habit and vigorous growth which, if left unpruned, can reach 10ft (300cm) in height. It produces large, canary yellow flowers in late spring.

F. **'Lynwood Gold'** bears a profusion of broad-petalled, deep yellow flowers in late spring. It is an erect shrub growing to a height of 6ft (180cm).

Forsythia 'Lynwood Gold'

Cultivation and Propagation Forsythias do well on any ordinary soil containing some humus. While they will tolerate some partial shade they are most floriferous and commence flowering earliest when planted in a sunny yet sheltered situation. No regular pruning is called for and should be strictly limited during the first few years after planting, to enable the shrubs to develop naturally. When shrubs are becoming too large for their location, pruning should take place immediately their flowering ceases. The flowers are borne on wood of the previous year's growth.

Propagation is by hardwood cuttings inserted in the open ground in the late autumn, once the leaves have fallen.

Uses *Forsythia* is one of the earliest spring blossoms. It can be brought indoors in its bud stage and encouraged to open with indoor heat. The long arching sprays of yellow flowers may be used in any traditional style. Small branches in full flower will dictate an attractive outline in a basket of spring material.

Conditioning Conditioning is simple; stand the cut stems in water until you need them.

Preserving Individual flowers may be pressed or dried in desiccant.

Garrya

Mexico and Western North America
Evergreen
Garryaceae

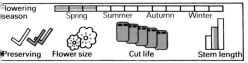

Flowering season	Spring	Summer	Autumn	Winter
Preserving	Flower size		Cut life	Stem length

Garrya elliptica

Most Garrya species are not frost-hardy, the exception being *Garrya elliptica*, a native of California and Oregon. This is a strong-growing shrub of rounded habit, height 10ft (300cm), with broadly oval, wavy-edged, dark green shiny leaves; the leaf undersides are grey and felty. It flowers in winter and displays clusters of beautiful silvery green, silky catkins. There is a cultivar with longer catkins which is worth seeking out, *G.e.* 'James Roof'.

Cultivation and Propagation This shrub grows quite happily even in the poorest of soils and is at home in either a sunny or partially shaded situation. It may need the shelter of a wall in cold districts. It does not transplant very easily and should only be purchased as container-grown stock. The best time to plant is in autumn or spring.
    Propagation is by layering of the stems in summer or by seeds sown in a warm greenhouse during early spring.
Uses As *Garrya* is a special feature shrub in the garden, it should also be in an arrangement. The tassels are elegant with a silky sheen to them. They suit both formal and informal styles of arranging, as a focal point in an all-foliage design, or cascading at the edge of a large formal arrangement.

Conditioning Allow the catkins to reach their maximum length before you cut stems and stand them in water for 2 hours.
Preserving The joy of this fascinating material is that it can be made to last. It will preserve in glycerine quite readily. Stand the branch in glycerine, removing only any foliage that is damaged. The time will vary for completion, but usually takes from one to two weeks. The leaves darken to an olive green and the catkins go a metallic grey.

Griselinia

New Zealand and the southern part of South America
Evergreen
Cornaceae

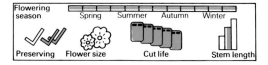

Flowering season	Spring	Summer	Autumn	Winter
Preserving	Flower size		Cut life	Stem length

Griselinia littoralis 'Dixon's Cream'

There are two cultivars of *Griselinia littoralis* that have fresh-looking, attractively variegated leaves. *G.l.* 'Dixon's Cream' has apple-green, oval leaves generously splashed and mottled creamy white. This is a sport taken from *G.l.* 'Variegata', which has white leaf markings. Both form compact, dense-leaved shrubs of erect habit, height 6ft (180cm).

Cultivation and Propagation *Griselinia* thrives in a well-drained soil in either a sunny or partially shaded place in milder parts and by the coast. Individual shrubs make useful special feature subjects in small gardens.

Griselinia may also be used to make an evergreen hedge near to the sea as it is tolerant of salt-laden air. In cold districts it should be grown in a warm sheltered place as it is slightly tender and is liable to damage by frost. No regular pruning is necessary. However some shortening of long branches may be considered necessary in order to maintain shapely shrubs and this work should be undertaken during late spring. The best time to plant new shrubs is during autumn or spring.

Propagation may be hardwood cuttings taken in autumn and inserted in a sandy soil in a closed garden frame or young shoots may be taken as half-ripe cuttings in midsummer and rooted under a mist propagator.

Uses This is truly a flower arranger's foliage. Both the plain green and variegated forms are an ideal foil for any colour scheme. The variegated leaves are especially attractive outline material in a foliage arrangement.

Conditioning Simply stand the cut mature branch in water for 2 hours.

Preserving Its ability to preserve without problems is an asset not to be ignored. This may be done at any time during the growing season. Select a well formed branch, discard any damaged leaves and stand it in a solution of glycerine and water. The process may take up to a fortnight to complete, and the leaves will change colour to almost black/brown.

Hamamelis

Witch Hazel
Eastern Asia, North America
Deciduous
Hamamelidaceae

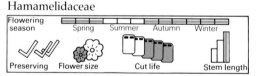

T his is a tiny genus of shrubs and small trees, with hazel-like leaves, which have good autumn leaf tints. Spidery petalled flowers appear on the leafless branches during late winter or early spring. A number of cultivars are worthy of note; both they and the species are frost-hardy plants.

Cultivars of *Hamamelis* × *intermedia* (a cross of *H. japonica* and *H. mollis*) are large shrubs growing about 9ft (270cm) high: 'Diana', which has large, deep coppery red flowers and yellow foliage tints in autumn; 'Jelena', with large yellow flowers suffused coppery orange, appearing very early, and orange, red and scarlet autumn foliage colours; 'Moonlight', with medium to large, sulphur yellow flowers tinged with red, and yellow

Hamamelis × *intermedia* 'Jelena'

autumn leaves.

H. japonica starts flowering early, sometimes in autumn, and continues to spring. It has deep yellow, medium-sized flowers and attains a height of 7-9ft (210-270cm). *H.j.* 'Zuccariniana' has small pale sulphur yellow flowers, sometimes scented, which appear in spring. Both *H. japonica* and the cultivar have glossy mid-green leaves turning to yellow in autumn.

H. mollis is one of the most popular witch hazels in cultivation, for its large, very fragrant, golden yellow flowers borne from winter to spring. It can grow to a height of 10ft (300cm) or more. Autumn foliage is brilliant yellow. *H.m.* 'Brevipetala' has short-petalled deep yellow flowers, while *H.m.* 'Pallida' displays very large sulphur yellow flowers.

H. virginiana is a native American species with yellow fragrant flowers which appear in autumn, but these are mainly hidden from sight by the yellow-tinted autumn leaves, height 12ft (360cm) or more.

Cultivation and Propagation *Hamamelis* prefers a lime-free, loamy, moist soil, which is well drained. Heavy soils should be improved by the addition of leafmould or peat. Plant during autumn in either a sunny or slightly shaded situation. No regular pruning is necessary.

Propagation of *Hamamelis* is by layering the ripened shoots which were produced in the previous year. This should be undertaken in spring just before new growth commences. Bury the layered shoots some 4in (10cm) into the soil and place canes close to the tips of the shoots appearing above the soil and secure them.

Uses The flowers that clothe the branches of this plant are light and spidery in appearance. It is the type of flower that requires very little extra material to make a fine arrangement. One or two stems with a little sculptural foliage in a

Hamamelis × intermedia 'Jelena' – flower

suitable container creates an arrangement that
will last for many days.
Conditioning The flowers can be encouraged to
open if they are cut in the bud stage. A short
time in deep water will condition them.
Preserving Sadly the flowers will not preserve
successfully but the autumn foliage is well
worth collecting and pressing.

Hedera

Evergreen
Araliaceae

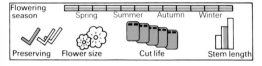

Hedera canariensis 'Variegata'

The many varieties of Hedera provide a
range of attractive leaf shapes and colours
which, being evergreen, feature year-round.
These are mainly climbing plants that will
gradually clothe a wall or fence, or can be
grown on a smaller scale in containers.

Hedera canariensis is a handsome plant with
lobed green leaves that take on a bronze tinge
in winter. In the cultivar *H.c.* 'Variegata' the
large, shiny, shield-like leaves are olive green
margined broadly in cream, carried on red leaf
stems; older leaves may become flecked with
red. This climber is not entirely hardy and
should be planted against a sunny, sheltered
wall. In mild districts it will attain a height of
12ft (360cm) and similar spread.

H. colchica has many sports, among them
H.c. 'Dentata Variegata' which has large,
broadly elliptic, glossy, emerald green leaves,
shading to grey-green with rich creamy yellow
margins. This is a hardy plant growing to 10ft
(300cm) high. The leaves of *H.c.* 'Sulphur
Heart', syn. 'Paddy's Pride', are boldly
splashed bright yellow, fading to light green
and margined with emerald. The intensity of
the yellow splash fades as the leaf ages, and
its extent on each leaf varies. This plant grows
to 10ft (300cm) high with a similar spread.

H. helix (common ivy) is a native of Europe
and is the source of a great many sports. *H.h.*
'Conglomerata' is a slow-growing form, of
creeping habit, best grown as a rock garden
plant or edging to paths and low walls. It has
small dark green, shiny leaves with wavy
margins and stiff stems.

H.h. 'Golden Heart' is a particularly
beautiful form with medium-sized, rich green
leaves generously splashed with golden
yellow at the centres. When first planted it
takes a couple of years to become established,
but ultimately attains a height of 10ft (300cm)
and about the same spread. *H.h.* 'Glacier' has
delectable small silvery grey leaves narrowly
margined with white. This is a plant of
moderate growth, height and spread 6ft
(180cm).

Cultivation and Propagation *Hedera* can be
grown quite successfully on a wide range of
soils, but a poor one is best suited to the
variegated forms as it brings out their leaf
colouring more clearly. The best time to plant is
in spring as new growth is commencing.

Propagation is by half-ripe cuttings taken
during late summer and inserted under a
closed and shaded garden frame. Another
method of propagation is by hardwood cuttings
taken during late autumn and inserted in an
open garden frame. This simply serves the
purpose of sheltering them from the wind.
Uses The arranger should grow at least one
variety of *Hedera*. The small-leaved varieties
will provide delicate arrow-shaped leaves to
emphasize the focal flowers. Any branches that

need pruning from the plant will prove invaluable for establishing an outline to a design. Those with much larger leaves (and I strongly recommend *H. c.* 'Sulphur Heart') act in the same way for much larger arrangements. Those of you that favour modern arranging will find them terribly useful for hiding mechanics as well as adding impact to the design.
Conditioning Stems should be cut when mature, as new growth will invariably let you down. Float or stand them in water for 2 hours.
Preserving To preserve them stand freshly cut stems or float individual leaves in glycerine. Any variegation is generally lost but the resulting range of preserved colours will compensate.

Hydrangea

Eastern Asia and North America
Deciduous
Hydrangeaceae

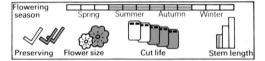

Hydrangea macrophylla

Hydrangeas make an impressive garden feature with their generous flower heads and large, soft green leaves. The following selection includes medium-sized to large shrubs and a tolerant, adaptable climber. These are useful plants for bringing fresh, bright colour to a partially shaded site, and shrubby types can be container-grown.
Hydrangea arborescens is a native of the eastern United States and has pointed leaves about 4-6in (10-15cm) long and 2-5in (5-12.5cm) wide. Its cultivar *H.a.* 'Grandiflora' is noted for its display of elegant globular, creamy white flower heads, about 8in (20cm) across, borne

Hydrangea paniculata 'Grandiflora'

on shoots of the current year's growth from summer to autumn. This should be pruned in the spring, height 4ft (120cm).

The familiar mop-headed hydrangea, *H. macrophylla*, syn. *H. hortensia*, is native to China and Japan. It flowers in late summer and autumn. It is available in a range of colours – white, pink, red and blue – however to produce blue flowers the plants need an acid soil. In alkaline soil blueing powder has to be added at about 10-day intervals prior to flowering. This method of controlling the colour is best achieved when the hydrangeas are grown in tubs.

Good white cultivars include 'Madame Emile Mouilliere' and 'Soeur Therese'. Recommended pink forms are 'Europa', dark pink; 'Gerda Steiniger', bright pink; 'Neidersachen', pale pink; and 'Wilhelmina' deep pink. Fine reds are 'Colonel Lindberg', light red; 'Hamburg', true red; and 'Sibilla', deep rosy red.

These cultivars need no regular pruning other than removal of the old flower heads in spring just before new growth commences. 'Europa', 'Neidersachen' and 'Hamburg' will produce good blue flowers provided they are treated with blueing powder during the growing season.

H. paniculata, originating from China, Formosa and Japan, provides the cultivar *H.p.* 'Grandiflora' a truly graceful shrub which produces great panicles of creamy white flowers in early autumn. The flower heads are up to 12in (30cm) long and fade to pink as they age. The shrub has pointed oval leaves some 4-6in (10-15cm) long and is of vigorous, erect habit, attaining a height of 6ft (180cm). Prune in spring just before new growth commences.

H. petiolaris is a climbing species from Japan, a particularly tough subject which will

adily clothe any wall, even in shade. It is
lf-clinging, needing no support. It has rich
een foliage and saucer-shaped clusters of
hite flowers, up to 9in (22.5cm) across,
uring midsummer. It attains a height of about
ft (300cm) and spread up to 14ft (420cm).

ultivation and propagation All the
ydrangeas like a fertile well-drained soil and
enefit from the introduction of some peat
hen the ground is being prepared. Planting
ay be undertaken at any time during the
ormant season, preferably in a lightly shaded
tuation.

Propagation is by cuttings, some 4in (10cm)
ng taken in the early summer and rooted in a
osed, shaded garden frame or a greenhouse.
alf-ripe cuttings may also be taken late
ummer and rooted in a closed, shaded garden
ame.

ses You will find both the flower and the leaf
f the *Hydrangea* of use. The range of sizes is
onsiderable in both leaf and flower so it will
dapt to any type of arranging style. Individual
eads with intense colour look most striking
rranged in a modern container with a piece of
riftwood or several *Fatsia* leaves. The
owering form of *petiolaris* is particularly
ffective in pedestal designs.

onditioning If the bract is used before it
as begun to dry naturally it should be floated
n water for 1 hour. Split the stem if it is woody
nd stand it in deep water for a further 2 hours.
reserving The foliage will, in some instances,
reserve in glycerine. The bracts preserve
etter. Cut them in the late summer as they are
hanging colour, remove any leaves and stand
hem in 1in (2.5cm) of water. Don't top up the
vater, allow them to drink it and continue to
ry. Let one or two heads remain on the bush
hroughout the autumn and winter. Often the
ract will naturally skeletonize.

Ilex

Holly
Europe, North Africa and Asia
Evergreen
Aquifoliceae

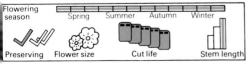

*I*lex aquifolium (common holly) is of fairly
wide distribution. Over the years it has been
the parent of a large number of cultivars,
including plain green and variegated forms.

I.a. 'Ferox' (hedgehog holly) not only has the
traditional spiny, toothed leaves, the small
dark green leaves are puckered and have pale

Ilex aquifolium 'Golden King'

spines on the upper surfaces as well. *I.a.* 'Ferox
Argentea' is similar but the leaf margins and
spines are creamy white, most effective against
the background of dark green. Both cultivars
are slow-growing and in time attain 8ft
(240cm).

The leaves of *I.a.* 'Golden King' have few if
any spines: they are pointed oval, rich green
margined with bright yellow. This grows to be
a large shrub exceeding 10ft (300cm) in height
and is one of the best gold-variegated forms,
with bright red berries.

I.a. 'Silver Queen' is a handsome subject
with dark green leaves marbled grey and
margined with creamy white. Its young shoots
are purplish-green. This is of slow growth and
reaches 6-8ft (180-240cm) in height.

Cultivation and propagation Ilex will grow on
any well-drained soil in either a sunny or
shaded situation. Putting a little peat into the
soil, when planting, helps them to get
established. Prune in the spring when new
growth commences or as one requires material
for display work. Plant in autumn or spring.

Propagate by layering in the spring or by
hardwood cuttings, in an open garden frame,
in the autumn.
Uses By tradition *Ilex* is a foliage for winter
arrangements. As cut material it will last for
many weeks, and this quality should be
exploited. Create an arrangement of sprays of
the holly foliage and add it to any late flowers
that appear in the garden. When they have
faded they can be replaced with flowers bought
from the florist. Carnations are an attractive
addition. If the *Ilex* is a dull green, red
carnations will introduce a note of brightness.
Conditioning As the foliage is usually cut late
in the year it is already mature. Often it needs
only the barest of conditioning times, though it
should be given at least 1 hour. Most of us

associate Holly with its red or sometimes yellow berries. Late in the year when there is virtually nothing else to arrange them with, make them a feature of the design. Carefully cut away extra leaves to expose the fruit.
Preserving It is not often seen as preserved foliage, but in fact it will absorb glycerine readily. This can be done from late spring onwards. Trim the cut branch of any crowded leaves and stand the stem in glycerine. It can take up to a fortnight to preserve fully, and the colour will vary depending on type, usually becoming a mid beige.

Ligustrum

Privet
Japan, China, the Philippines and Australia
Deciduous and Evergreen
Oleaceae

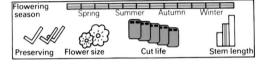

Ligustrum ovalifolium 'Aureum'

This is widely grown as a hedging plant and the species frequently used is *Ligustrum ovalifolium*, a native of Japan. This has dark green leaves which form a rich, dense backdrop for flower colours, but there is a brighter coloured cultivar that can be used for the same purpose. *L.o.* 'Aureum' (golden privet) has bright yellow leaves, occasionally with a splash of green in the centres but usually entirely yellow. Terminal panicles of white flowers are borne in late summer.

L. lucidum is an evergreen species of shrub or small tree. The form *L.l.* 'Golden Wax' has large leaves, 3-6in (7.5-15cm) long, which when young are a beautiful yellow and

gradually turn yellow-green as they age. It produces terminal panicles of white flowers, about 6in (15cm) long, during late summer. Another good form is *L.l.* 'Excelsum superbum', which has large green leaves mottled and margined rich yellow and creamy white. It bears the same large white flower panicles.

Cultivation and Propagation All the above privets will grow about 6ft (180cm) high, if left untrimmed. They will grow in any type of soil and in either sun or shade. Plant in either autumn or spring. For floral work you will need to grow specimen shrubs. Any necessary shaping can be undertaken when material is removed for use.

Propagation is by hardwood cuttings secured in autumn and rooted in a nursery bed in the open ground.
Uses *Ligustrum* is considered to be the arrangers' stand-by foliage. The leaves clothe the stem in a uniform manner from the tip to the main stem. The plain green and variegated types have a slightly glossy surface. As the stems are long and regular in shape, they are ideal for creating an outline, mainly in traditional and formal styles.
Conditioning Stand the stems in water, removing any leaves that are likely to be submerged, for up to 2 hours.
Preserving The foliage will preserve in glycerine, the dark green form usually does best. Select the leaves when they are mature and place them in the solution. I tend to cut more than I need as the success rate is dubious.

Mahonia

Central and North America, Asia
Evergreen
Berberidaceae

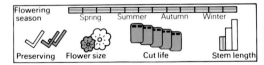

This small genus of delightful shrubs provides all kinds of colour interest, with their glossy, fragant flowers and attractive berries. They are early-flowering, providing a good source of pale colour for the winter garden.

Mahonia aquifolium (Oregon grape) is a very hardy subject from western North America. It is a shrub of suckering habit, height 2-3ft (60-90cm). Its pinnate leaves some 6-12in (15-30cm) long are composed of between five and nine holly-like, spiny, glossy green leaflets. Their colour varies with the season: in late autumn and throughout the winter older leaves turn

Mahonia aquifolium

purple or bronzy green, and some have splashes of bright red on the upper surfaces. In spring they revert to dark green, in stark contrast to the emerging reddish-yellow new shoots. Terminal clusters of yellow flowers begin to appear during early spring, but the main flush of flowers is usually in late spring. These are followed later in the year by blue-black berries which often stay on the shrub right through the winter.

The species is parent to a number of hybrids. One of the best is 'Charity', a shrub of strong, erect habit and handsome appearance, height 6ft (180cm). It has fine pinnate foliage of glossy green, with leaves 18in (45cm) long or more. Terminal spikes of deep yellow, fragrant flowers are carried from midwinter to early spring. 'Atropurpurea' is a form specially attractive in winter, when the leaves turn red-purple.

M. bealii is native to China and is a very hardy plant, height 6ft (180cm). It has large leathery, glossy green leaves, which are yellowish-green on the lower surfaces. The leaves are pinnate, 12-18in (30-45cm) long, and individual leaflets overlap each other to a certain extent. The short, erect, light yellow flower spikes, 3-5in (7.5-12.5cm) long, appear from winter to spring and are followed later by small bluish-black berries.

M. japonica has dark green, glossy leaves composed of many spiny leaflets. Its pale yellow racemes of flowers are produced from winter to spring and are sweetly scented. It grows up to 10ft (300cm) high.

Cultivation and Propagation Mahonias will grow on a wide range of soils and do well even on chalk. They are fond of a partially shaded place either beneath trees or near buildings, providing there is some moisture about their roots. Planting of new shrubs should take place either in autumn or spring. There is no need for annual pruning, but any that proves necessary should be undertaken in the early spring, when new growth is about to commence.

Propagation can be achieved by seeds which are sown in the spring. It is necessary to collect the berries in the autumn and stratify these in sand until the time comes for sowing. Another satisfactory method of propagation is by rooted suckers removed in the early spring or by division of roots at that time. One can also take half-ripe cuttings of shoots of the current year's growth, during late summer, and insert these in sandy soil in a closed and shaded frame.

Uses This plant has so many admirable qualities. The arrangement of the leaf and stem formation is unique. In large designs a rosette of reasonable proportions can be used as the focal area. The herring bone formation of the leaves is a fascinating shape to include in a foliage arrangement.

Conditioning They are quite tough and will condition without problem. Stand the stem in water, the leaves may be partly submerged.

Preserving Amongst the most reliable of the preserving foliages. Whole stems can be cut and stood in glycerine as well as individual sprays. The process should take up to 2 weeks. The colour will vary a little, but in general it will be medium brown.

Parrotia

Northern Iran and Caucasus
Deciduous
Hamamelidaceae

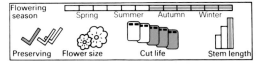

Parrotia persica – autumn foliage

*P*arrotia persica is a tree much loved for the fine autumn colouring of its large beech-like leaves. These change from their customary dark green to become brilliant crimson and gold before leaf-fall. This is undoubtedly one of the finest trees for autumn hues, but is also interesting for its flowers, which consist of tufts of small red stamens appearing on the bare branches during winter. Another attactive colour feature of this tree is the grey, flaking bark.

This is a strong-growing tree which, if not pruned, attains a height of 24ft (720cm) or more. However, with some regular pruning and shaping annually it can be maintained as a large shrub of broadly spreading habit.

Cultivation and Propagation *Parrotia* likes a moist yet well-drained soil and, for best autumn colour, a sunny situation. Light soils will need a generous application of well rotted garden compost or peat to improve their moisture-holding capacity, when preparing the ground. Planting may be undertaken at any time during the dormant season.

Propagation can be achieved either by layering of branches in the spring or by seeds sown in a sandy compost in spring and placed in a garden frame.

Uses Noted for its autumn foliage in tints of amber, crimson and gold. The stems grow to varying lengths and can be used throughout the design. They may be used with fresh autumn flowers and leaves, but I favour its use as a highlight arranged with preserved foliage and berries. As you will only be using the foliage in the autumn it will be fully matured.
Conditioning A short drink of water will be sufficient to condition it.
Preserving As with most striking autumn foliages, leaves that are interesting colour combinations should be pressed for use in collages.

Pernettya

Prickly Heath
Southern Hemisphere in New Zealand, Australia, Tasmania, the Falkland Islands and South America
Evergreen
Ericaceae

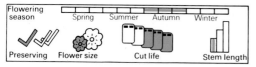

*P*ernettya mucronata is the species of main interest, a plant native to Chile and southern Argentina. This is a very hardy ground cover shrub with pointed oval, spiny, glossy dark green leaves. During early

Pernettya mucronata

summer it displays small heath-like flowers and these are followed in the autumn by the finest display of berries any shrub could produce. The berries on individual shrubs may be white, various shades of pink, lilac, purple or crimson. It is a good idea to plant a pernettya where it can be readily seen from the house, as the berries persist into winter unaffected by harsh weather and provide continuing colour interest while many other plants have gone into dormancy.

To ensure a mass display of berries, in most instances it is necessary to grow male and female plants together. A reliable nursery or garden centre should be able to advise on partnering the plants.

The following cultivars can be recommended for the colour and quality of their berries: 'Bell's Seedling', large, dark red berries (this is a self-fertile form); 'Cherry Ripe', bright cherry red berries; 'Davis's Hybrids', a selection of berried forms which have large berries and mixed colours; 'Lilian', pink berries; 'Snow White', white berries speckled pink; 'White Pearl', large, brilliantly white berries.

Cultivation and Propagation *Pernettya* requires a cool moist lime-free soil, preferably in a sunny place, but will succeed in a lightly shaded situation. It likes soils of a peaty nature and where necessary peat should be added to the soil when preparing the ground for planting. Where one is faced with a limey soil *Pernettya* can be grown in large tubs filled with lime-free compost. Always purchase pot-grown stock so as not to disturb the roots when transplanting. Planting is best undertaken during autumn or spring. No regular pruning will be necessary. If growth is getting out of hand, some light pruning may be undertaken in the early spring when new growth is about to commence.

Propagation of the species can be achieved by seed which is sown during early spring, in seed-trays or seed-pans containing a peaty compost. The seeds are then placed in a closed garden frame. The named cultivars listed here may be propagated by layering them into specially prepared peaty soil, in the spring, or by half-ripe cuttings secured in late summer and inserted in a closed and shaded garden frame containing a compost consisting of equal parts, by bulk, of peat and sand.

Uses The autumn berries of the *Pernettya* will console the passing of summer and its glorious bounty. This is an ideal subject to arrange with preserved foliages and flowers that linger past their flowering time. As the berries persist almost into the winter it is a subject to arrange with holly in a traditional manner.

Conditioning It needs only a slight amount of time to condition, and the berries rarely fall.

Preserving It is a generous shrub with its berries, which compensates for the inability to preserve them. Summer foliage may be preserved in glycerine but this will reduce the supply of an interesting fresh piece of material.

Philadelphus coronarius 'Aureus'

Philadelphus

Mock Orange
Widely distributed in the Northern Hemisphere
Deciduous
Philadelphaceae

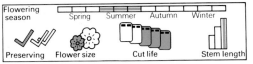

All the shrubs described here are quite hardy and bear fragrant flowers which appear during midsummer. Philadelphus hybrids range in height from 3ft (90cm) to 10ft (300cm), with forms suitable for all types of gardens and with flowers that may be single, semi-double or double. The following is a selection representative of the full range.

Philadelphus 'Beauclerk' is a shrub of curving habit, height 6ft (180cm). It bears single white, very fragrant flowers about 2in (5cm) across. The bases of the petals are flushed rosy pink.

P. 'Belle Etoile' is of a semi-arching, compact habit, height 5ft (150cm), and its single white flowers have fringed petals that are flushed maroon at the base. The flowers are 2in (5cm) across and are highly fragrant.

P. coronarius is a species thought to originate in central and south-eastern Europe. This is a vigorous shrub of spreading, rounded habit, height 10ft (300cm). The creamy white, strongly fragrant flowers appear in

Philadelphus coronarius 'Sybille'

Philadelphus 'Virginal'

midsummer. It has two forms with good coloured foliage: *P.c.* 'Aureus' has rich yellow leaves, becoming yellow-green as they age; *P.c.* 'Variegatus' has green leaves with creamy white margins. Both the species and its cultivars are quite adaptable to being grown on dry soils.

P. 'Manteau d'Hermine' is a very dwarf hybrid of dense habit which produces creamy white, fully double flowers with a rich vanilla fragrance, height 3ft (90cm).

P. 'Sybille' is a delightful shrub with arching branches, height 4-5ft (120-150cm). Its small, squarish white flowers are strongly fragrant; the flower petals are fringed and flushed purple at the bases.

P. 'Virginale' is a strong-growing shrub of erect habit, height 10ft (300cm). It bears great clusters of large, double or semi-double, brilliant white, fragrant flowers, individual blooms being up to 2in (5cm) across.

Cultivation and Propagation *Philadelphus* will grow quite happily on a wide range of garden soils, but the lighter ones should be given a dressing of peat, to improve their moisture-holding capacity, when preparing the ground. It can be grown in either a sunny or slightly shaded situation. Planting should be undertaken during the dormant season. *Philadelphus* should be pruned immediately after flowering. Remove the older branches which have flowered and show no signs of producing vigorous new shoots. It is also a good idea, with old shrubs, to remove one or more of the old thick main branches right down to ground level, which stimulates new growth.

Propagation is by either half-ripe cuttings taken in late summer and inserted in a heated propagation case with the bottom heat set at 68°F (20°C) or by hardwood cuttings taken in the autumn and inserted in the open ground.
Uses Choice of variety will be a difficult decision for those planting a *Philadelphus* for the first time. It has so many attributes, in both the flowers and the foliage. Long arching sprays of creamy, white flowers enhance the outline of a full massed design of similar coloured flowers. *P. c.* 'Aureus' is one of the most outstanding foliages — in the spring it is a bright golden yellow, becoming green/yellow in the summer. It will add distinction to any design of spring or early summer flowers.
Conditioning Immature foliage can be difficult, but not impossible, to condition. Cut the stem in the morning and float it in a dish of water for about 1 hour, then stand it in deep water for a further 2 to 3 hours. It is important that this foliage does not come into direct contact with any heat source, when conditioned or arranged. If the stem wilts, dip the lower ½in (1.25cm) of recut stem in boiling water for 10 seconds and return it to the conditioning dish. Mature foliage and flowering stems will not

require such drastic action, a deep drink of water will be sufficient.
Preserving Individual blooms can be pressed; double flowers, to retain their form, should be dried in desiccant.

Phormium

New Zealand Plax
New Zealand
Evergreen
Lilaceae

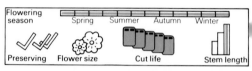

Phormium tenax 'Purpureum'

Although herbaceous in appearance, phormiums have semi-woody rootstocks, hence their description as sub-shrubs. *Phormium tenax* has stiff, erect, sword-shaped leaves, blue-green in colour. Individual leaves are 4-7ft (120-210cm) long and about 4-5in (10-12.5cm) wide. Established plants produce bronzy red flowers on tall spikes during late summer and autumn.

P.t. 'Bronze Baby' has coppery red leaves that droop gracefully at the tips, height 2ft (60cm): *P.t.* 'Purpureum' has bronze-purple foliage, height 4-7ft (120-210cm); *P.t.* 'Variegatum' has leaves striped in green and creamy white, height 6ft (180cm).

Cultivation and Propagation These plants like a moist soil and will even succeed on boggy ground in either full sun or slight shade. Light soils should be given a good dressing of garden compost or peat to increase their moisture-holding capacity, prior to planting. Planting

hould be in autumn or spring. Protect the
rowns of the plants in cold winter weather.
 Propagation is by seed sown during spring in
peat-based compost, in a greenhouse or
arden frame, or by division of the roots in late
pring.
Jses *Phormium tenax* is a sculptural foliage. The
road sword-like leaves are beyond compare
or establishing the height of a design. It is at
ome in the hands of a modern arranger as well
s a traditionalist. This leaf may be used as it
rows in vertical design or rolled and pinned to
reate a modern design of geometric patterns.
Conditioning It needs very little conditioning,
hough it has no objections to standing in water
or up to two days.
Preserving The leaves may be pressed under
he carpet between sheets of newspaper. I have
ad some success at preserving it in glycerine,
hough the edges of the leaf tend to discolour
pefore the process is complete. However, a
ittle judicious snip with a pair of sharp scissors
will correct this annoying fault.

Pittosporum

Australasia
Evergreen
Pittosporaceae

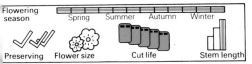

Pittosporum tenuifolium 'Silver Queen'

Pittosporum tenuifolium **is a species from
New Zealand which has attractive wavy-
edged, oblong leaves on fine black stems. The
cultivar** *P.t.* **'Silver Queen' is a particularly
desirable form, having silver-grey variegated
foliage and black twigs. Small dark purple,**

**fragrant flowers appear in late spring, but are
not of significance. The shrub is slow-
growing, eventual height 10ft (300cm).**

Cultivation and Propagation Plant in a warm
sheltered part of the garden in a well drained
fairly light soil during autumn or spring. No
regular pruning is necessary. Any shaping or
removal of damaged branches should be
undertaken during spring.
 Propagation is by half-ripe cuttings 3in
(7.5cm) long taken with a heel in summer and
inserted in a heated propagating case.
Uses The leaves of the *Pittosporum* are produced
in light rosettes and are an invaluable supply of
delicate form and colour to lighten the centre of
a massed arrangement of flowers and foliages.
They should be allowed to mature so that the
leaf colour is at its most intense before use.
Conditioning *Pittosporum* conditions without
any problem. Simply stand in water for
2 hours.
Preserving Any leaves that display a
particularly fine colour variegation should be
pressed for use in collage work. More
substantial branches can be preserved in
glycerine. Sadly the variegation is lost but the
resultant dark brown colour has its own
fascination.

Prunus

Cherry
Japan and China
Deciduous
Rosaceae

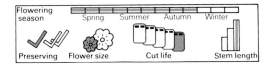

There are numerous cultivars of the
ornamental cherries that provide bright,
fresh blossom and foliage colour interest.
Although cherry blossom is a classic flower of
spring, flowering times vary, the autumn
cherry continuing to bloom through winter if
the weather is mild. The following are particularly fine examples, all quite easy to grow.
 Prunus serrulata **'Tai Haku' (great white
cherry) is a vigorous tree, height 21ft (630cm),
which displays pure white single flowers in
pendulous clusters in spring. The young
leaves are red-bronze, becoming green as they
open out. In autumn the foliage takes on
attractive yellow and orange tints.**
 P.s. **'Ukon' is an equally vigorous form of
similar height; its young coppery brown
foliage makes a fine backcloth for the semi-
double, pale greenish-yellow flowers in late**

Prunus serrulata 'Tai Haku'

Prunus yedoensis

spring. Leaves turn red-brown in autumn.

P. subhirtella 'Autumnalis' (autumn cherry) is a delightful small tree with red tints in its autumn leaves. Once these have fallen, semi-double white flowers appear along the bare, twiggy branches, and may be borne spasmodically through winter. With the onset of severe winter weather flowering ceases, but as soon as conditions improve, further flowers emerge.

P.s. 'Autumnalis Rosea' is less reliable for winter flowering but often produces semi-double deep pink flowers in autumn, with the main flush of blooms appearing during late spring. Both these cultivars attain a height of 15-18ft (450-540cm).

P. yedoensis (Yoshino cherry) originates from Japan and is an outstanding early flowering, graceful tree. During spring, the arching branches are smothered in masses of

slightly fragrant flowers, which are at first pale pink, later fading to white. Its foliage also has some attractive autumn tints, height 15-21ft (450-630cm).

Cultivation and Propagation These trees will grow quite happily on any ordinary, well-drained garden soil containing some lime, in an open sunny situation. Planting may take place at any time during the dormant season. Little pruning is necessary, but you can remove any unwanted branches immediately flowering ceases.

Propagation is a task for the experts.

Uses This very large family offers an exciting choice of spring blossom. It is generally used in lavish quantities in large arrangements and pedestals. Special forms like *P. s.* 'Ukon' are at their best seen in small arrangements, baskets or low dishes with mixed spring flowers.

Conditioning The buds can be opened if they are conditioned in warm water. This process can take up to a week to complete, then they can be arranged. They do not require any special pre-treatment, a deep drink of water is sufficient.

Preserving The leaves are of no importance to preserve. The only way to capture the flowers is by pressing or desiccant drying.

Pyracantha

Firethorn
China, Southern Europe and Asia Minor
Evergreen
Rosaceae

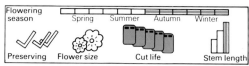

Pyracantha is a well-known spiny, hardy shrub which provides a brilliant display in the late autumn and winter, with bunches of colourful berries produced in considerable quantities. All varieties listed here have broadly lance-shaped, shiny dark green leaves, varying in length according to species from about 1-3in (2.5-7.5cm), some finely toothed. All these shrubs display masses of tiny white flowers during early summer.

Pyracantha angustifolia is of rather stiff, spreading, bushy habit and vigorous growth, height 10-12ft (300-360cm). It bears orange-yellow berries which in some years remain on the branches until spring.

P. coccinea is the parent of a couple of very desirable cultivars. P.c. 'Mohave' is of vigorous bushy habit and produces a fine crop of orange-red berries. *P.c.* 'Red Column' is a stiff, erect shrub and bears large blood red erries, height 10ft (300cm).

P. rogersiana is a small-leaved species of igorous spreading habit, bearing red-orange erries. *P.r.* 'Flava' is a cultivar with attractive ellow berries, height 12ft (360cm).

P. 'Soleil d'Or' is of less vigorous growth nd more spreading habit and is a useful ubject as a ground cover shrub, height 5ft 150cm). It bears a heavy crop of orange-yellow erries.

P. 'Watereri' is a shrub of compact habit vhich has a fine display of scarlet berries, in ome years retained until the spring.

Cultivation and Propagation *Pyracantha* will hrive in a wide range of soils including limey ones, either in a sunny or partially shaded ituation. Purchase pot-grown plants and plant luring autumn and spring. It makes a particularly good climber to train up a house

Pyracantha coccinea 'Mohave'

Pyracantha 'Soleil d'Or'

wall or a large spreading shrub in the open. When grown on walls or fences there will be the need for some pruning in the early spring each year, to reduce some of the longest shoots of the previous year's growth. Light pruning in this way will do no real harm, but one is removing shoots which would have been producing flowers and berries in due course. The same is true of shrubs growing naturally in the open ground.

Propagation is either by half-ripe cuttings taken in late summer, inserted under a closed and shaded garden frame, or by hardwood cuttings taken in the autumn and inserted in a closed garden frame.

Uses This is another shrub that is generous with its autumn fruits. The berries are carried in clusters on a medium to long stem and can be used throughout a formal arrangement of autumn flowers and preserved foliages. Clusters arranged in a modern container are most effective.

Conditioning Stand the cut stems in deep water for 2 hours to condition them.

Preserving Though you are robbing yourself of good autumn material, the foliage will preserve in glycerine. Do this in the summer when the leaves have matured. The colour changes to a dark olive green.

Rhododendron including Azalea

Asia and North America and Europe
Evergreen and Deciduous
Ericaeceae

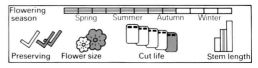

This is a vast genus encompassing many hybrid forms. Azaleas were formerly categorized separately but are now classified under Rhododendron. All of these shrubs provide a lavish display of flowers: the smaller forms can be planted in formal beds or featured individually and azaleas make very vivid container plants; the larger Rhododendron species and hybrids develop a very fine woody, naturalized effect in spacious gardens. They are rather particular as to conditions, however, requiring moisture-retentive but well drained, lime-free soil.

HARDY EVERGREEN SPECIES
Rhododendron ferrugineum is a species native to central Europe which bears clusters of rosy red flowers appearing in midsummer. It is a

small shrub of compact habit, height 3-4ft (90-120cm).

R. hirsutum, also from central Europe, is of similar height and habit and bears clusters of pink flowers in midsummer.

R. hippophaeoides is a fine evergreen shrub of erect habit, of Chinese origin, which has clusters of lavender-blue flowers during late spring, height 5ft (150cm).

R. yakushimanum is a native of Japan which forms a shrub of erect, compact, rounded habit, height 4ft (120cm). Its clusters of flowers in early summer are first pink, then turning to white.

HARDY EVERGREEN HYBRIDS

R. 'Britannia' is a slow-growing shrub of rounded, compact habit with clusters of glowing crimson flowers in early summer, height 4ft (120cm).

R. 'Vulcan' is of more vigorous growth and has clusters of bright red flowers during early summer, height 5ft (150cm).

R. 'Jacksoniii' is a particularly tough hybrid rhododendron built for survival in even the most unsuitable conditions. This is a shrub of rounded habit and compact growth which produces its clusters of maroon-marked rose pink flowers early in the spring, height 5ft (150cm).

R. 'Pink Pearl' is a vigorous shrub which bears large clusters of bright pink flowers, later fading to soft pink, in early summer, height 7-10ft (210-300cm).

R. 'Rosamundii' is slow-growing and displays its clusters of pale pink flowers in spring, height 4ft (120cm).

R. 'Cunningham's White' is a strong-growing shrub which produces lax clusters of white flowers, with pale yellow eyes, in late spring, height 6ft (180cm).

R. 'Unique' is a small shrub of rounded, compact habit which bears clusters of creamy white flowers with crimson speckles during late spring, height 5ft (150cm).

R. 'White Cloud' is a shrub of robust habit with large clusters of pure white flowers in early summer, height 7-10ft (210-300cm).

R. 'Butterfly' is a compact shrub bearing clusters of butterfly shaped, primrose yellow flowers, speckled deep red, during late spring, height 5ft (150cm).

R. 'Souvenir of W.C. Slocock' is robust and bears clusters of pale yellow flowers during early summer, height 7-10ft (210-300cm).

R. 'Yellow Hammer' is a shrub of slender, erect habit which bears tubular, bright yellow flowers in pairs, both terminally and along the branches, during spring and, in some years, again in autumn, height 5ft (150cm).

AZALEA – DECIDUOUS HYBRIDS

While these tend to be smaller than rhododendrons many attain a height of 4-6ft (120-180cm) while some can reach 8ft (240cm). All flower in early summer. The following selection represents some of the many hybrids available, in the following categories:

Ghent hybrids (GH), 5-8ft (150-240cm); Knaphill and Ebury hybrids (KN), 5-6ft (150-180cm); Mollis hybrids (M), 4-6ft (120-180cm); Occidentale hybrids (O), 6-8ft (180-240cm). They are listed in the following colour groups: red/orange; yellow/orange; pink; white.

'Koster's Brilliant Red' (M), glowing orange-red; 'Royal Command' (KN), vermilion red; 'Satan' (KN), geranium red; 'Floradora' (M), orange flushed apricot, spotted with dark crimson; 'Gibraltar' (KN), deep orange (with good autumn foliage tints); 'Dr Ossthoek' (M), deep orange-red.

'Golden Sunset' (KN) deep yellow with orange blotch; 'Narcissiflora' (GH), fragrant creamy yellow, double flowers (good autumn foliage tints); 'Sunbeam' (M), vivid yellow flushed apricot with orange blotch.

'Berryrose' (KN), rose pink with yellow blotch; 'Coronation Lady' (KN), salmon-pink with orange blotch; 'Norma' (GH), fragrant rose pink, double flowers; 'Strawberry Ice' (KN), light pink flushed deeper pink with orange blotch.

'Daviesii' (GH), fragrant white flowers (yellow when first open), with yellow blotch; 'Silver Slipper' (KN), fragrant white flowers flushed pink with orange blotch; 'Whitethroat' (KN), brilliant white, double flowers.

AZALEA – EVERGREEN HYBRIDS

These are of low spreading habit and attain a height of 2-4ft (60-120cm). Their flowering period is early summer, unless otherwise stated. While they are commonly referred to as Japanese azaleas, this is not entirely correct, for both in the USA and Europe a good deal of hybridization work has been undertaken resulting in many new introductions. The selection here comes from the following categories:

Gable hybrids (G), originated in the USA; Glenn Dale hybrids (GD), USA; Kaempferi hybrids (KF), Holland; Kurume hybrids (K), Japan; Vuyk hybrids (V), Holland; Wada hybrids (W), Japan.

'Blue Danube' (V), bluish-violet; 'Johann Sebastian Bach' (V), deep purple; 'Addy Wery' (K), bright scarlet; 'Hatsugiri' (K), bright crimson-purple; 'Sakata Red' (K), orange-red; 'Aladdin' (K), salmon-orange; 'Bungonishiki' (W), semi-double, reddish-orange flowers; 'Blaauw's Pink' (K), salmon-pink flowers in late spring; 'Esmeralda' (K), pale pink; 'Rosebud' (G), double silvery pink flowers; 'Willy' (KF), soft pink; 'Driven Snow' (GD), brilliant white; 'Martha Hitchcock' (GD), white margined with magenta; 'Palestrina' (V), ivory white with a faint hint of green.

Rhododendron hippophaeoides

Azalea 'Palestrina'

Rhododendron yakushimanum

Azalea 'Gibraltar'

Rhododendron 'Jacksonii'

Azalea 'Dr Ossthoek'

Cultivation and Propagation Rhododendrons and azaleas can be grown on any reasonably fertile lime-free soil, providing it is moisture retentive and at the same time well drained. Dry sandy soils will need generous amounts of peat incorporated in them. An annual mulching of sandy soils is also necessary both to help preserve soil moisture during the summer months and to add to the soil's humus content. On chalky soils, you may either build a raised bed or grow rhododendrons and azaleas in tubs, to avoid this problem.

Always purchase container-grown evergreen rhododendrons and azaleas where available, as in this way they can be planted out with the very least root disturbance. Plant out in autumn or spring. They can be planted from containers quite successfully even in early summer, if they are planted beneath the shade of trees and they are watered frequently. Deciduous azaleas may be planted at any time during the dormant season. No regular pruning required. Simply remove the old flower heads with your fingers. If a large branch needs removing, do this in spring as new growth commences. Stems may need thinning as they get old and overcrowded.

Propagation may be achieved from seed sown in a greenhouse in the spring, by grafting onto rootstocks, in the open garden during December/January, or by layering during midsummer.

Uses The soil in my garden will not allow me to grow this magnificent shrub, which is disappointing as it is the finest of materials for arranging. Unless you are lucky enough to grow copious numbers, use the flowers where they are seen to best advantage, possibly as a focal unit or as a single branch arranged on pins in a low dish.

Conditioning Cut the stem as the flowers are opening, lightly crush the end and place in warm water for about 4 hours. The water can be allowed to cool over this period.

Preserving Individual leaves may be floated in a dish of glycerine to preserve them. They will darken to a rich greeny brown. Single flowers may be pressed, but if dried in desiccant they will retain their bell shape.

Ribes

Flowering currant
North America
Deciduous and Evergreen
Grossulariaceae

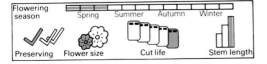

R̲ibes sanguineum is a deciduous shrub of robust, bushy habit, height 6-8ft (180-240cm). It has attractive fresh green foliage and during late spring produces drooping racemes of rosy red flowers.

R. sanguineum has several notable cultivars: 'King Edward VII' with brilliant crimson flowers; 'Pulborough Scarlet', very deep red flowers. *R.s.* 'Brocklebankii' has pale pink flowers and delightful golden yellow leaves but is less vigorous, attaining a height of 3-4ft (90-120cm).

R. speciosum, a spiny-stemmed semi-evergreen species from California, is a little less hardy. This shrub bears pendulous clusters of bright red, tiny fuchsia-like flowers in late spring.

Cultivation and Propagation *Ribes* will thrive in any ordinary soil in either a sunny or partially

Ribes sanguineum

Ribes sanguineum

haded place. Planting may occur at any time during the dormant season. No regular pruning is required. The removal of an old branch should take place immediately after flowering ceases, in the spring.

Propagation is by hardwood cuttings inserted in the open ground in the late autumn.

Uses The true value of the flowering currant is in its long stem of fresh young foliage and tassels of pink to red flowers. This is very useful for getting flower colour to the extremities of an arrangement at a time of the year when there is an abundance of short-stemmed flowers. It is more suited to formal arrangements, though the variety 'Brocklebankii' looks extremely pretty cascading from the sides of a basket.

Conditioning The flowers can be induced to open by standing the stems in warm water. Providing the foliage does not come into contact with the water, they can be left for several days.

Preserving Unfortunately it is one of those foliages that will not preserve on the stem. I recommend that you concentrate on the blossom, preserving the clusters of tiny flowers in desiccant. Once they have dried attach them with the aid of a little quick-drying glue to a small branch of *Corylus* 'Contorta' that has been mounted onto a base. The effect is oriental.

Rubus

Brambles
Widely distributed
Evergreen and Deciduous
Rosaceae

Rubus tridel

Rubus cockburnianus

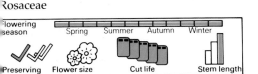

*R***ubus cockburnianus** (whitewashed bramble) develops long, arching, spiny stems covered strangely with white wax. These look particularly striking during the winter, especially if planted in front of an evergreen hedge. It is a deciduous shrub growing to 8ft (240cm) high. The pinnate leaves, up to 8in (20cm) long, are of fern-like appearance and have green upper surfaces and white undersides. Small purple flowers, of no significance, appear in summer and are followed by black fruits.

R. tricolor is an attractive evergreen species of low, trailing habit, height 1ft (30cm), which makes good ground cover. The spineless stems are covered with brownish bristles and clothed in shiny dark green, heart-shaped leaves up to 4in (10cm) long, covered with whitish felt on the lower surfaces. White flowers appear in summer, and these are followed by bright red fruits.

R. tridel 'Benenden' is a deciduous cultivar with long arching, spineless stems. It has green leaves, 3-5in (7.5-12.5cm) long with three to five lobes, and in late spring bears masses of fragrant white flowers. This tolerant shrub may be grown in full sun or partial shade, height 8ft (240cm).

R. ulmifolius is a European native species with semi-evergreen leaves that have whitish, felty undersides. It is the parent of the cultivar *R.u.* 'Bellidiflorus', a shrub of rapid growth bearing rose pink double flowers during late summer, height 8ft (240cm).

Cultivation and Propagation All the above species and cultivars thrive in any ordinary garden soil. Plant in either full sun or partial shade during the dormant season. Pruning

Rubus tridel

Salix hastata

Salix lanata

technique depends upon whether one is dealing with the flowering forms or those grown for their attractive stems. The ones grown for their flowers are pruned to remove some of the older wood in the late autumn. The ones with the attractive stems have all the old growth removed down to ground level in the spring, when the new shoots are about 10in (25cm) high.

Propagation is by layering of the stems where the tips touch the ground and calls for no special attention, as it occurs quite naturally.
Uses *Tricolor* will quickly spread to give you lots of cutting sprays for outlining traditional arrangements. For the modernists *cockburnianus* is an indispensable material. In the winter bundles of the ghostly white stems can be arranged in a tall container, possibly using preserved rosettes of *Choisya ternata* to establish a textural contrast at intervals.
Conditioning They need little in the way of preparation for conditioning. A deep drink of water for 2 hours will be sufficient.
Preserving The leaves generally do not preserve well, though the small flowers will dry in desiccant.

Salix

Willow
Northern Hemisphere
Deciduous
Salicacae

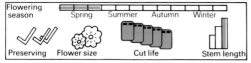

Flowering season	Spring	Summer	Autumn	Winter
Preserving	Flower size		Cut life	Stem length

This is a range of shrubs and trees of interest for the soft foliage colours and small furry catkins. *Salix lanata*, a native of Europe and Asia, is commonly referred to as the 'woolly willow'. It forms a low shrub some 2-3ft (60-90cm) high, of spreading habit. It bears broadly oval, silvery green, downy leaves on stiff, erect stems which display attractive woolly catkins in spring.

S. hastata makes a rounded shrub about 5ft (150cm) in height. It has a very fine form in *S.h.* 'Wehrhahnii', which has large leaves with dull green upper surfaces and grey-green undersides. In spring it bears masses of silvery grey catkins, which later turn yellow.

S. matsudana is a tree native to China and Korea and it provides the very interesting form *S.m.* 'Tortuosa' (contorted willow). As the name indicates, the most fascinating characteristic of the tree is the strangely contorted branches and twigs, which have strong sculptural quality after leaf-fall. During he growing season it bears long, narrow, pointed green leaves with grey-green lower surfaces, and the spring catkins are silvery in colour. It is a large tree, eventually 30-40ft (900-1200cm) high.

Cultivation and Propagation *Salix* will flourish in any fertile moisture-retentive soil in a sunny situation. Plant during the dormant season. No regular pruning is required. Trim back unwanted branches when dormant.

Propagation is by hardwood cuttings secured in the late autumn and inserted in the open ground.

Uses A much admired tree or bush for its fluffy catkins produced in the spring. The long whip-like branches are clothed in golden mounds, ideal material for including in a basket or a formal arrangement of *Forsythia* and other spring flowers. The branches of *S. m.* 'Tortuosa' are well known to the arranger. They appear in all styles of arranging from modern to period arrangements. Usually only one branch is necessary, but it is wise to inspect it carefully and remove any crowded twigs that will detract from the completed design.

Conditioning Even the young foliage conditions easily; a short drink of water is all that is needed.

Preserving An attempt should be made to preserve the catkins. Cut the stems before the pollen has matured. Stand them in glycerine solution after removing the leaves. The process will take up to a week.

Senecio

Widely distributed
Evergreen
Compositae

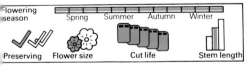

Shrubby species of Senecio contribute useful grey tints to the range of garden colour. *Senecio laxifolius* has blunt oval, slightly undulating green-grey leaves with a grey-white down, especially on the lower surfaces. In summer it displays terminal clusters of yellow daisy-like flowers. It has a spreading, lax habit, height 4ft (120cm).

S. monroi is similar in character but the leaves are smaller and the shrub forms a more compact shape, 3-5ft (90-150cm) high. It also bears yellow daisy-like flowers in summer.

Cultivation and Propagation Plant in the winter in any ordinary well-drained soil in sun

Senecio laxifolius

or light shade. They do well in coastal districts. Any pruning should be done in spring.

Take half-ripe cuttings in autumn and insert in sandy soil in a coldframe.

Uses This particular genus produces a cluster of yellow flowers which should be removed so that the food supply is directed to producing stronger and more luxuriant foliage. The leaves are quite striking, being grey/green on the surface and light silvery grey underneath. The arching stems are an invaluable outline for arrangements of soft pink or blue flowers. Used in small numbers they add an unusual note to an all-foliage design.

Conditioning Immature growths will benefit from having the end of the stems burned for 10 seconds before conditioning them in water. The ends of branches of old wood should be lightly crushed before conditioning.

Preserving *Senecio* will not preserve by air drying or by glycerine. The individual leaves of *S. monroi* are, however, worth pressing.

Skimmia

Eastern Asia
Evergreen
Rutaceae

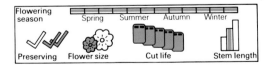

Skimmia is a shrub of slow growth and bushy habit. The one most commonly seen growing in gardens is *Skimmia japonica*, which attains a height of 3ft (90cm) and more or less equal spread. It has glossy green, aromatic, pointed oval leaves. Tiny dull white flowers appear in spring which have a

Skimmia japonica

fragrance like that of lily-of-the-valley. Flowers of male plants have the strongest fragrance, but it is female plants that produce attractive clusters of bright red fruits, provided both male and female are grown together. The fruits colour up in autumn and remain in excellent condition through winter.

There is a more vigorous clonal cultivar, *S.j.* 'Fortunei', with female flowers that produce fruits in large clusters, even when the plant is grown as a solitary specimen.

Cultivation and Propagation *Skimmia* can be grown quite successfully on a wide range of soils including chalky ones. Choose a partially shaded place. Planting should be undertaken either in autumn or spring. No regular pruning is necessary. It is simply a matter of shortening straggly growth from time to time and this can be done when removing material for display.

Propagation may be from seeds sown in a garden frame in spring, by half-ripe cuttings secured in late summer and inserted in a closed and shaded garden frame, or by hardwood cuttings secured in the late autumn and inserted in a closed garden frame.

Uses *Skimmia* is a foliage which will link the centre of the design with the extreme points. This type of foliage is generally referred to as intermediate foliage. The rosettes of leaves are usually placed to emphasize the focal area, or if they are in an all-foliage arrangement, as the focal point.

Conditioning *Skimmia* is extremely accommodating and stands well with very little conditioning. About 1 hour in water is all it requires. The flowers that appear in the centre of the rosette are quite dainty and are a useful addition in a design of late May and early June flowers. In the autumn, the berries appear, to be used with other garden fruits and preserved materials.

Spiraea

Northern temperate regions
Deciduous
Rosaceae

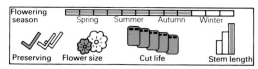

Spiraea bumalda 'Anthony Waterer'

*S*piraea × *arguta* (the bridal wreath) is a fine hybrid form which flowers during late spring. Its stems have a delightful arching habit and are clothed in small lance-shaped, bright green leaves, height 5-6ft (150-180cm). During flowering time the stems are smothered in masses of tiny white flowers.

S. bumalda 'Anthony Waterer' is another very attractive hybrid form which flowers from summer to autumn. It carries large terminal clusters of tiny, bright crimson flowers on shoots produced during the current year. This is a dwarf shrub with thin twiggy branches which attains a height of about 32in (80cm) and similar spread. The foliage consists of dark green, pointed leaves, some variegated cream and pink.

Cultivation and Propagation Both cultivars will thrive in any ordinary garden soil either in full sun or partial shade. Planting should be undertaken during the dormant season. Prune *S.* 'Arguta' immediately the flowers fade. Prune *S. b.* 'Anthony Waterer' in the dormant period.

Propagation is by half-ripe cuttings in late summer in a closed and shaded garden or by hardwood cuttings in the open ground in the late autumn. *S. b.* 'Anthony Waterer' can also be propagated by division of the roots during the dormant period.

Uses The 'Bridal Wreath' provides long arching sprays of white blossom that are most attractive in arrangements of blossom and spring flowers. The foliage of 'Anthony Waterer' is quite brilliant in the spring — glowing orange.

Conditioning 'Arguta' will condition easily, if the stems are stood in water for about 2 hours. Woody stems should be lightly crushed. 'Anthony Waterer' needs to be floated in water for 1 hour, then given a deep drink for a further 2 hours.

Preserving The flowers of 'Arguta' can be separated and preserved in desiccant. It is an invaluable flower for miniature arrangements and dried flower work.

Stephanandra

Asia
Deciduous
Rosaceae

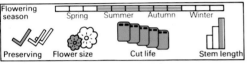

Stephanandra incisa

This is a near relative of Spiraea. It has insignificant flowers but is valued for its beautiful autumn foliage colours.

Stephanandra incisa is a small shrub of dense habit native to Japan and Korea, height 2½ft (75cm). It has arching, twiggy branches clothed in crinkled, heart-shaped, lobed and toothed, green leaves that turn yellow in autumn. Panicles of small, dull, greenish-white flowers appear in midsummer.

S. tanakae, also native to Japan, has arching twiggy branches and the same general leaf shape as *S. incisa*. However, it is an altogether larger shrub, height 6ft (180cm), with larger

leaves noted for their bright yellow and orange autumn tints.

Cultivation and Propagation Both these species can be grown successfully on any moist soil providing that they are planted in shade. Plant during the dormant season. Pruning consists of cutting all the old growth down to soil level during the dormant season to induce the production of vigorous new growth from the base in the spring.

Propagation is by hardwood cuttings secured in the late autumn and inserted in the open ground. *S. incisa* may also be propagated by the division of its roots in spring.

Uses Though the flowers can be considered dull, the plant should not be overlooked as it is a fine foliage for using as outline material, in all sizes of arrangements. The form and texture will harmonize and contrast with leaves that are growing at the same time and with foliages that have been preserved.

Conditioning Cut the foliage when the leaves are developed and stand them in deep water for 2 hours.

Preserving Sadly, this foliage does not accept liquid preservatives, but the leaves may be pressed to use in dried pictures or collages.

Syringa

Lilac
North Eastern Asia and Eastern Europe
Deciduous
Oleaceae

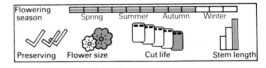

Syringa vulgaris 'Madame Lemoine'

Syringa vulgaris 'Sensation'

These fresh-leaved, large shrubs are commonly grown for both the attractive colours and notable fragrance of their blossoms. Lilacs vary in shape and height, and can be kept compact by regular pruning.

Syringa meyeri is a form introduced from China which is of rounded, bushy habit, height 5-6ft (150-180cm). During late spring it produces panicles of lilac-mauve flowers and usually carries a second flush of flowers in autumn.

S. microphylla also comes from China and is represented by *S.m.* 'Superba', a shrub of slender habit which bears panicles of fragrant, rosy pink flowers during early summer, with a second flush of flowers in autumn, height 5ft (150cm).

S. velutina, syn. *S. palibiniana*, native to Korea, is a more vigorous species of rounded, dense habit, which bears numerous panicles of fragrant lavender-pink flowers during early summer, height 8-10ft (240-300cm).

S. vulgaris is of eastern European origin and is the parent of numerous named cultivars of vigorous growth, bearing panicles of fragrant flowers in late spring and early summer. All of these cultivars grow to about 7-10ft (210-300cm) in height.

'Belle de Nancy', lilac-pink, double flowers, early; 'Charles Joly', dark purplish-red flowers, late; 'Katherine Havemeyer', strongly fragrant, purple-lavender, double flowers, mid-season; 'Maud Notcutt', pure white single flowers, mid-season; 'Madame Lemoine', pure white double flowers, mid-season; 'Michel Buchner', pale rosy lilac, double flowers of considerable fragrance, mid-season; 'Mrs Edward Harding', dark crimson-purple, semi-double flowers, mid-season; 'Primrose', primrose yellow single flowers, mid-season; 'Sensation', single purple-red flowers edged with white, mid-season; 'Souvenir de Louis Spaeth', deep wine red, single flowers, mid-season.

Cultivation and Propagation *Syringa* will grow on a wide range of soils, including chalky clay. They prerer a sunny situation. Pruning is an annual task. Stage one is the removal of all of the old panicles of flowers, immediately flowering ceases. At this time one should also assess the amount of young shoots which are being produced. If there are a lot they should be thinned out so as to concentrate the energies of the shrub. If an old shrub has just a few tall thick old stems and little in the way of new growth near to ground level, severe pruning is necessary in the early spring when new growth is about to commence. This consist of reducing the existing stems to within 2ft (60cm) of the ground and sacrificing that year's flowering.

The *Syringa* species can be propagated quite successfully from seed which is sown in the spring and placed in a closed garden frame. The named cultivars are increased by cuttings taken in midsummer. These are young shoots which have a heel or piece of the older stem attached to them at their base. These are inserted in sandy soil in a warm garden frame or in a heated propagation case in a greenhouse. It is also possible to propagate named cultivars from half-ripe cuttings secured in late summer and inserted in a closed and shaded garden frame.

Uses The range of colours available is considerable. Choose a cultivar that will associate with the colour scheme of your home and with the other materials that develop in the garden. It is a large blossom, though it can be trimmed to fit quite small designs. It looks at its finest when used in considerable amounts in a pedestal arrangement. The flowers develop at the end of the stem, so trim off any foliage that is likely to reduce the supply of moisture.

Conditioning Stand the cut and lightly crushed stem in water for at least 2 hours.

Preserving The head is large and will not accept glycerine. The leaves are uninteresting and will only take up valuable space if pressed.

Thuja

China, Japan and North America
Evergreen, cone-bearing
Cupressaceae

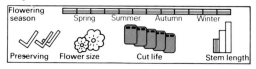

1 hour in the conditioning container.
Preserving The foliage will press successfully or small pieces may be preserved in desiccant.

Viburnum

Widely distributed throughout the Northern Hemisphere
Evergreen and Deciduous
Caprifoliceae

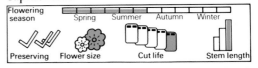

Thuja plicata 'Zebrina'

These well-shaped conifers contribute striking foliage colours to the garden display. *Thuja occidentalis* is the parent of numerous cultivars including *T.o.* 'Rheingold', a slow-growing subject with compact, conical growth which eventually makes a large shrub of 10ft (300cm) or more in height. Its beauty lies in its deep golden foliage, which remains very fine through all seasons of the year, although in the depth of winter it turns coppery gold.

T. plicata is the parent of *T.p.* 'Zebrina', a variegated form with delightful green and cream foliage. This is more rapid-growing, and makes a fine featured plant, for instance, planted in a lawn. It is erect and conical in habit, in time attaining a height of 24ft (720cm) or more.

Cultivation and Propagation *Thuja* thrives on a wide range of soils providing they are suitably drained. The golden and variegated forms should be planted in a sunny place, otherwise their foliage will not colour up properly. The various green forms will not suffer if they are planted in partial shade. Planting is best undertaken either in autumn or spring. No pruning is necessary except to cut out any reverted shoots as soon as they are detected.

Propagation is by cuttings of half-ripe shoots secured during late summer and inserted in a closed and shaded garden frame.

Uses *Thuja* is used as filler material. It is more delicate than the average evergreen foliage that decorators tend to rely upon. 'Zebrina' is a particularly fine form to grow, as the variegation will add substance to the design without darkening the effect.

Conditioning It is extremely easy to condition, in fact in an emergency it can be used straight from the tree, though it should have at least

Viburnum opulus 'Sterile'

Viburnum × *bodnantense* is a deciduous hybrid which has a number of selected forms, and one of the best of these is 'Deben'. This is a sturdy, branching shrub, height 10ft (300cm), which in spring bears clusters of strongly fragrant, pink-budded white flowers that appear from autumn to spring interrupted only by severe wintry weather.

V. opulus (guilder rose) is a deciduous species native to Europe, North Africa and western Asia. It is the parent of a number of cultivars, one of the best of which is *V.o.* 'Sterile' (snowball tree). This is of robust, spreading habit, height 8ft (240cm), and bears globose clusters of creamy white flowers up to 3in (75cm) across, during midsummer. It is clothed in bright green, lobed and toothed leaves, which develop interesting autumn tints.

Viburnum plicatum (Japanese snowball) is a deciduous shrub native to both Japan and China and it is of dense, spreading habit, height 8ft (240cm). During midsummer it produces large ball-shaped white flowers along its branches, each individual bloom

Viburnum rhytidophyllum

3-5cm (7.5-12cm) across. *V.p.* 'Mariesii' is a cultivar with horizontal branches and a great profusion of flowers which make the plant look as if it is covered in snow.

V. rhytidophyllum is a vigorous evergreen species of stiff, erect habit, height 10ft (300cm), which is native to China. It produces prominently ribbed and wrinkled, dark green leaves with white, downy lower surfaces, and these are 4-9in (10-22.5cm) long. Terminal flower heads appear in autumn but do not open until early summer, when they display their clusters of buff-tinted white flowers, up to 8in (20cm) across. These are followed by oval berries which are at first red but gradually turn black.

Cultivation and Propagation Plant *Viburnum* in a fertile soil amply supplied with humus. Choose a sunny place. Plant the deciduous ones any time during the dormant season but the evergreen species *V. rhytidophyllum* should be planted in autumn or spring. No regular pruning is necessary.

New shrubs may be propagated from seed but it takes many many months for them to germinate. Fortunately both species and cultivars may be propagated from half-ripe cuttings secured in late summer and inserted under a closed and shaded garden frame.
Uses I consider this one of the finest all-round shrubs for the flower arranger. It produces an ample supply of flowers and berries and some startling foliage in the autumn. Generally it is used in more formal designs. Some of the larger growing varieties are more suitable for pedestal arrangement. More discerning species like X *bodnantense* should be used in small numbers with other specialities from the spring garden in an arrangement where each flower can be seen clearly.
Conditioning Conditioning the flowering

branch can be difficult; a considerable number of leaves will need to be removed to allow the maximum amount of water to reach the flowers. This is particularly so with *V. opulus* 'Sterile'.
Preserving Unfortunately I have not been successful at preserving the foliage of *Viburnum,* but some of the leaves that have turned colour during the autumn are worth pressing.

Vinca

Central and Southern Europe, North Africa and Western Asia
Evergreen
Apocynaceae

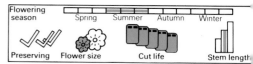

Vinca major

Vinca major (greater periwinkle) is a hardy species indigenous to central and southern Europe. This is a trailing shrub of vigorous growth, height 8-10in (20-25cm) and spread up to 4ft (120cm). It has shiny, bright green, ovate leaves 2-3in (5-7.5cm) long, and displays bright blue flowers on short stalks during early summer. There are two good variegated cultivars. *V.m.* 'Maculata' is splashed with rich yellow on the leaf centres, most pronounced in the younger leaves; *V.m.* 'Variegata' has leaves attractively splashed and margined with creamy white. Both of these have similar

owers to those of the parent plant and grow
o about the same height.

Cultivation and Propagation This ground-
cover shrub will flourish on any well-drained
soil in either a sunny or shady place, and it is
very useful for planting on banks and in other
difficult places where little else will grow.
However, the variegated forms do not colour
their leaves fully in deep shade. Planting
should be undertaken in autumn or spring.
Pruning consists of light trimming with shears
in the early spring just before new growth
commences.

Propagation can be by division of the roots in
the early spring or by cuttings taken in late
summer and rooted in a closed and shaded
garden frame.

Uses For arranging I would strongly
recommend *Vinca major*. If it is possible to grow
it in a position where the foliage cascades
without interruption so much the better. The
stems will be easier to pick and less likely to
come under attack from pests than its
counterpart grown in a border. The stems hang
down gracefully and are an ideal subject to use
as an outline for crescent or curving shapes. It
is a wonderful foil in a small design of foliage
where specially selected leaves have been
chosen for their variegation.

Conditioning Mature stems are easier to
condition. Simply stand them in a small
container of water for about 2 hours.

Preserving The flowers will press or dry in
desiccant. Sadly the foliage proves
unsuccessful.

Weigela

Asia
Deciduous
Caprifoliaceae

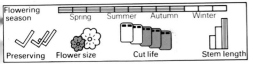

T he original Weigela species are now
greatly outnumbered by the many hybrids
which have been introduced.

Weigela florida 'Variegata', a hybrid of a
species native to China and Japan, is a
charming, free-flowering shrub of more
compact habit than its parent, height 5ft
(150cm). It has pointed, elliptical, green leaves
which are variegated creamy white on the
margins. The clusters of pale pink, slightly
fragrant flowers are borne terminally on
lateral shoots on the arching stems in early
summer.

W. 'Looymansii Aurea' is a hybrid noted for

Weigela florida 'Variegata'

its bright yellow leaves, height 6ft (180cm).
This looks particularly attractive when its
arching branches are displaying their
numerous clusters of pale pink flowers. After
the main flush of flowers, which appears in
early summer, it is quite common for this plant
to produce a second, lighter flush during
autumn.

Cultivation and Propagation Plant in a moist
fertile soil containing some humus in a partially
shady place. Planting may take place at any
time during the dormant season. Shorten all
the old flowering lateral shoots immediately
flowering ceases, as this will stimulate the
production of new shoots which will flower the
following year. When faced with an old *Weigela*
with numbers of thick old branches, one should
remove some of these to stimulate the
production of new, more floriferous branches.

Propagation is by half-ripe cuttings secured
in late summer and rooted in a sandy soil in a
closed and shaded garden frame, or by
hardwood cuttings secured in the late autumn
and inserted in the open ground.

Uses This is a shrub that will provide both early
blossom and useful foliage for later on in the
season. The flowers are borne along the stems
which generally arch in a flowing manner. The
colour is in the pink to red range and will
associate well with tulips and other spring to
summer flowers. They are flowers to use in
traditional styles. After the flowering season is
over new growth is produced. This should be
left until late summer before it is used. Cut the
foliage stem as long as possible, the bush will
benefit from severe pruning.

Conditioning Stand the stems in deep water to
condition for 3 hours.

Preserving The foliage will not preserve,
though individual flowers can be removed and
dried in desiccant.

COLOUR FINDER

In the Plant Directory flowering plants are listed in the colour sections according to a dominant or specially selected flower colour, but the entry also describes, where appropriate, recommended species and cultivars of other colours. For example, Verbascum appears in the yellow section but also has very attractive white and pink forms. This listing enables you to identify entries where alternative colours are described, and also gives access to individual colours among the range for each plant listed in the Directory under Assorted Colours. For example, Aster is in the red/pink/purple/blue colour range, while Zinnia has red, pink, white and yellow forms.

The flower colours of flowering shrubs are also listed here, and interesting foliage colours described in the entries on shrubs.

YELLOW
Alstroemeria 106; Antirrhinum 109; Aquilegia 109; Centaurea 112; Cheiranthus 113; Chrysanthemum 114; Dahlia 120; Dianthus 63; Digitalis 122; Eremurus 122; Euphorbia 92; Gaillardia 48; Gazania 49; Geum 54; Helichrysum 126; Iris 127; Kniphofia 50; Lilium 131; Limonium 133; Lupinus 134; Paeonia 57; Papaver 136; Primula 138; Ranunculus 139; Rosa 140; Tagetes 51; Thalictrum 78; Zinnia 144.

Flowering shrubs:
Cornus 154; Cytisus 156; Enkianthus 159; Forsythia 164; Hamamelis 166; Mahonia 170; Rhododendron and Azalea 177; Senecio 183; Syringa 185.

ORANGE
Clarkia 62; Cheiranthus 113; Chrysanthemum 114; Coreopsis 35; Cosmos 119; Dahlia 120; Eremurus 122; Geum 54; Gladiolus 123; Godetia 125; Helenium 36;

Helichrysum 126; Lilium 131; Lupinus 134; Narcissus 39; Papaver 136; Phlox 137, Ranunculus 139; Rudbeckia 41; Trollius 44; Tulipa 142.

Flowering shrubs:
Buddleia 149; Cytisus 156; Rhododendron and Azalea 177.

RED
Achillea 34; Anemone 107; Antirrhinum 109; Aquilegia 109; Armeria 61; Aster 110; Astrantia 98; Centaurea 112; Cheiranthus 113; Chrysanthemum 114; Clarkia 62; Coreopsis 35; Cosmos 119; Crocosmia 47; Dahlia 120; Dianthus 63; Dicentra 65; Gaillardia 48; Gazania 49; Gladiolus 123; Godetia 125; Helenium 36; Helichrysum 126; Helipterum 67; Iberis 103; Lathyrus 130; Lilium 131; Lupinus 134; Lychnis 68; Lythrum 76; Matthiola 135; Nicotiana 136; Papaver 136; Phlox 137; Pyrethrum 71; Primula 138; Ranunculus 139; Rosa 140; Scabiosa 89; Tulipa 142; Veronica 90; Zinnia 144.

Flowering shrubs:
Camellia 151; Cytisus 156; Escallonia 160; Hamamelis 166; Hydrangea 168; Rhododendron and Azalea 177; Ribes 180; Spiraea 184; Syringa 185.

PINK
Acanthus 97; Alstroemeria 106; Anemone 107; Antirrhinum 109; Aquilegia 109; Aster 110; Astilbe 53; Astrantia 98; Callistephus chinensis 112; Campanula 81; Centaurea 112; Chrysanthemum 114; Cosmos 119; Dahlia 120; Delphinium 83; Digitalis 122; Eremurus 122; Gladiolus 123; Godetia 125; Gypsophila 100; Helichrysum 126; Heuchera 55; Iberis 103; Incarvillea 56; Iris 127; Lathyrus 130; Lilium 131; Limonium 133; Lupinus 134; Lythrum 76; Matthiola 135; Monarda 57; Nicotiana 136; Nigella 88; Paeonia

57; Papaver 136; Penstemon 59;
Phlox 137; Primula 138; Ranunculus
139; Rosa 140; Scabiosa 89; Tulipa
142; Verbascum 45; Veronica 90,
Zinnia 144.

Flowering shrubs:
Ballota 148; Camellia 151; Cotinus
155; Cytisus 156; Deutzia 157;
Escallonia 160; Hydrangea 168;
Prunus 175; Rhododendron and
Azalea 177; Ribes 180; Rubus 181;
Syringa 185; Weigela 189.

PURPLE
Acanthus 97; Allium 105; Anemone
107; Aquilegia 109; Aster 110; Astilbe
53; Bergenia 62; Callistephus
chinensis 112; Centaurea 112; Clarkia
62; Dahlia 120; Delphinium 83;
Dianthus 63; Digitalis 122; Gladiolus
123; Helleborus 101; Iris 127;
Lathyrus 130; Lilium 131; Limonium
133; Lupinus 134; Lunaria 104;
Lychnis 68; Matthiola 135; Monarda
57; Nicotiana 136; Nigella 88;
Penstemon 59; Phlox 137;
Physostegia 70; Primula 138; Rosa
140; Rudbeckia 41; Scabiosa 89;
Senecio 72; Tulipa 142;
Xeranthemum 73.

Flowering shrubs:
Buddleia 149; Rhododendron and
Azalea 177; Syringa 185.

BLUE
Allium 105; Anemone 107; Aquilegia
109; Aster 110; Centaurea 112;
Erigeron 66; Gladiolus 123; Iris 127;
Lathyrus 130; Limonium 133;
Lupinus 134; Penstemon 59; Primula
138; Salvia 77.

Flowering shrubs:
Hydrangea 168; Vinca 188.

GREEN
Allium 105; Amaranthus 53;
Gladiolus 123; Helleborus 101;
Nicotiana 136.

WHITE
Achillea 34; Aconitum 79;
Agapanthus 79; Allium 105;
Anemone 107; Antirrhinum 109;
Aquilegia 109; Armeria 61; Aster 110;
Callistephus chinensis 112; Camassia
80; Campanula 81; Centaurea 112;
Chrysanthemum 114; Clarkia 62;
Dahlia 120; Delphinium 83; Dianthus
63; Dicentra 65; Digitalis 122;
Eremurus 122; Gladiolus 123;
Godetia 125; Helichrysum 126;
Helipterum 67; Heuchera 55; Hosta
74; Iris 127; Kniphofia 50; Lathyrus
130; Lavatera 68; Liatris 75,
Limonium 133; Lupinus 134; Lychnis
68; Matthiola 135; Monarda 57;
Molucella 94; Narcissus 39; Nicotiana
136; Ornamental grasses 95; Paeonia
57; Papaver 136; Phlox 137;
Physostegia 70; Platycodon 88;
Primula 138; Pyrethrum 71;
Ranunculus 139; Rosa 140; Saxifraga
71; Scabiosa 89; Senecio 72;
Thalictrum 78; Tulipa 142; Vaccaria
73; Verbascum 45; Xeranthemum 73;
Zinnia 144.

Flowering shrubs:
Buddleia 149; Camellia 151; Choisya
153; Cornus 154; Cytisus 156;
Deutzia 157; Fatsia 163; Hydrangea
168; Philadelphus 173; Prunus 175;
Pyracantha 176; Rubus 181;
Spiraea 184; Stephanandra 185;
Viburnum 187.

COLOURED FOLIAGES
Yellow/cream variegation: Buxus 150;
Eleagnus 158; Euonymus 161; Fagus
163; Griselinia 165; Hedera 167;
Ilex 169; Weigela 189.
Purple/red foliage: Acer 146; Berberis
148; Corylus 155; Cotinus 155;
Phormium 174.
Grey foliage: Artemisia 146; Ballota
148; Chamaecyparis 152; Eucalyptus
160; Salix 182; Senecio 183.

INDEX